W9-COR-279

10 Things to Consider in Setting Your Child's Allowance

1. *When to start (or stop) an allowance.* Usually, begin an allowance when your child starts school. Stop paying an allowance when your child begins to earn his or her own money or moves out of your home.

2. *The child's age.* The younger the child, the smaller the amount of the allowance; the older the child, the bigger the allowance.

3. *What the allowance is supposed to cover.* If you provide money for almost all your child's needs, then the allowance can be smaller than if you expect your child to pay for certain things. As kids get older and become responsible for paying for more things, the allowance may have to be adjusted accordingly.

4. *Your family income.* You can give only what you can afford. Be as generous as you think appropriate. If you can't afford to give what you think the allowance should be, explain why.

5. *Allowance given to other children in the family.* What you give your other kids, or what you gave them at a particular age, becomes common knowledge in the family. Usually, you want to give a bigger allowance to older kids, with the understanding to younger kids that they'll get there someday.

6. *Where you live.* It's true that your neighborhood affects the allowance you might consider paying. In more affluent neighborhoods, kids usually get more than in less affluent ones.

7. *Conditions for the allowance.* You may want to put strings on the allowance, such as performing certain chores around the home. Where these chores really add up, you might give more allowance than if there are no conditions to the receipt.

8. *Enforcing conditions.* If the allowance is conditioned on performance of certain jobs, decide up front what happens in the case of nonperformance. You may cut back on the amount, suspend it for a time, or leave the allowance intact and exact punishment in some other way.

9. *How often to pay the allowance.* You can pay once a week, once a month, or at any other interval. For younger kids, once a week is advisable because they can't manage their money for longer periods. Older kids may be able to budget for a monthly allowance.

10. *Control over the allowance.* You can give the money and let your child use it in any way he or she wants. Or, you can exert influence over its use. While you can't (or shouldn't) control its use completely, you can provide guidance on how to make the most of the money.

alpha
books

tear here

10 Rules for Your Child to Follow in Spending Money Wisely

1. *Set priorities.* Your child should know whether he's paying for necessary things before using an allowance on nonessentials. Otherwise, he's come up short for the things he needs.

2. *Set goals.* If your child wants to get a toy or other item, determine when it's realistic to get it. Some items may be short-term goals, others long-term goals.

3. *Put savings first.* Your child should spend only what's left over after money has been set aside for savings. This savings should be used for long-term goals.

4. *Make a budget.* Doing this will guide spending so that money will stretch to meet anticipated expenses.

5. Know spending limits. If you don't want your child to spend too much on presents for the family or for a friend's birthday, you can set or suggest dollar limits.

6. *Make a shopping list.* This ensures that what's needed remains the target of a shopping trip and that money isn't spent on impulse purchases.

7. *Become a bargain hunter.* Look for sales and discounts to stretch spendable dollars, but recognize when "bargains" aren't really good buys (for example, when things aren't needed).

8. *Learn to recognize value.* The price of an item doesn't necessarily reflect its quality. Ask whether your child is getting the most for her money. How well is a product built?

9. *Don't overspend.* Don't get into the habit of using tomorrow's allowance on today's purchase. An occasional advance may be warranted for a very good reason. By planning ahead for purchases and setting some of the allowance aside, however, the money will be there when needed.

10. *Save receipts.* This habit is worth developing. It allows your child to get refunds or exchanges for unwanted goods. And when he starts charging his purchases on a credit card, it's the only way to check that charges on the monthly bill are correct.

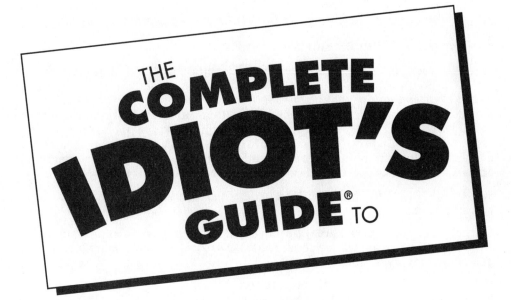

THE COMPLETE IDIOT'S GUIDE® TO

Raising Money-Smart Kids

by Barbara Weltman

alpha books

A Division of Macmillan General Reference
A Pearson Education Macmillan Company
1633 Broadway, New York, NY 10019-6785

To my husband, Malcolm Katt, for his help and support.

Copyright © 1999 by Barbara Weltman

Macmillan Publishing books may be purchased for business or sales promotional use. For information, please write: Special Markets Department, Macmillan Publishing USA, 1633 Broadway, New York, NY 10019.

International Standard Book Number: 0-02-863381-4
Library of Congress Catalog Card Number: 99-64464

02 01 00 99   4 3 2 1

Interpretation of the printing code: the rightmost number of the first series of numbers is the year of the book's printing; the rightmost number of the second series of numbers is the number of the book's printing. For example, a printing code of 99–1 shows that the first printing occurred in 1999.

Printed in the United States of America

Alpha Development Team

Publisher
Kathy Nebenhaus

Editorial Director
Gary M. Krebs

Managing Editor
Bob Shuman

Marketing Brand Manager
Felice Primeau

Acquisitions Editors
Jessica Faust
Michelle Reed

Development Editors
Phil Kitchel
Amy Zavatto

Assistant Editor
Georgette Blau

Production Team

Development Editor
Matthew X. Kiernan

Production Editor
Jenaffer Brandt

Copy Editor
Krista Hansing

Cover Designer
Mike Freeland

Photo Editor
Richard H. Fox

Illustrator
Brian MacMoyer

Designer
Scott Cook and Amy Adams of DesignLab

Indexer
Tim Tate

Layout/Proofreading
Angela Calvert
Mary Hunt

Contents at a Glance

Contents

Foreword

How young is old enough to start instilling smart money habits in your child? To lay the foundation for a financially secure future, it's almost impossible for parents to start too soon. Research shows that by the time most children start kindergarten, their beliefs, values, expectations, and motivations regarding money are well established. So they're *already* learning something about personal finance at a very young age chiefly by observing how Mom and Dad and everyone else they know in the world manage their money. The challenge for us parents is to make sure our kids are learning the right stuff.

The early signs are not exactly encouraging. Study after study shows that kids today are woefully lacking in personal finance skills and basic knowledge of how the economy works. One survey, for instance, found that the vast majority of kids don't know that paying by credit card is a form of borrowing, nor do they realize that banks charge their customers interest when they take out a loan. Many pre-schoolers think the way to get more money is to go to a machine—the ATM, that is—and don't have a clue that you have to put your own money in first to be able to take money out later. As for kids' consumer smarts, well, it's pretty hard for a child to learn to be discerning when they're being bombarded with an estimated 20,000 to 40,000 advertisements a year.

Yet to prosper in the new millennium, our children will need to be smarter about managing money than any previous generation. That's because the financial rules have changed dramatically in the years since we were kids. When we were young, you couldn't get a credit card unless you had a steady job; you expected that your job would last for life; you didn't have to manage your own retirement funds; and you didn't have to sift through all the complex savings instruments that are now available to do so. It's a whole different world now, as any parent who's ever been downsized, run up a few credit card bills, or been bewildered by the choices on a 401(k) account, knows all too well.

Fortunately for parents, there is now a wonderful guide to help us help our children learn what they need to know about money. In *The Complete Idiot's Guide to Raising Money-Smart Kids*, Barbara Weltman provides you with the essential information you'll need to get your child started on the right financial path. In the pages that follow, you'll find dozens of simple but effective strategies, along with valuable resources, that you can use to teach your children to be wise about money—to live within their means; make smart decisions about how they spend, save, and invest; earn as much as their potential allows; and take control of their financial lives rather than letting their finances control them. From piggybanks to mutual funds, from lemonade stands to paying for college, *The Complete Idiot's Guide to Raising Money-Smart Kids* shows us the ropes in clear language that makes even the most sophisticated concepts easy to understand. It's for Mom and Dad, as well as for their sons and daughters.

One thing's for sure: The consequences of *not* teaching your kids about money are clear and they are stark. If children don't learn at home, they're going to learn by the school of hard knocks. And we all know that is a very costly, very time-consuming, and very painful way to learn.

The time to start the lessons is now, by reading Barbara Weltman's invaluable guide and putting her advice to immediate good use with your kids. In the process, I suspect, you just may find yourself becoming a whole lot wiser about managing your own finances as well.

—Diane Harris

Diane Harris, a contributing editor to Parenting *magazine and author of its "Money Matters" column, has been a personal-finance journalist for twenty years. A former senior editor at* Money *and* Working Woman *magazines, Ms. Harris often appears on television as an expert on financial matters, with recent guest spots on the* Today *show,* Live! With Regis and Kathie Lee, *and* Good Morning America. *She is also co-author, with businesswoman Georgette Mosbacher, of a personal finance book for women called* It Takes Money, Honey: A Get-Smart Guide to Total Financial Freedom. *Ms. Harris has two young children, both of whom, she is happy to report, are well on their way to becoming money-smart kids and eventually, she hopes, financially responsible and successful adults as well.*

Introduction

Why is money like sex? Because many parents let their children learn about it in the streets rather than explaining things in the home. Unfortunately, the results are not good. According to an *NBC Nightly News* report, a quarter of a million young people declare bankruptcy before they're 25. They don't know the first thing about money. They take on too much debt and can't get out from under it. But it doesn't have to be this way.

Parents are comfortable helping their kids learn to ride a bike and swim, to master reading and the multiplication table, and even to understand the birth of a sibling or the death of a pet. Parents can and should certainly become comfortable with the topic of money. After all, money is just a basic fact of life—it's an integral part of daily living for people of all ages.

Unlike current events, algebra, or chemistry, money matters for the most part aren't taught in schools. A first-grade class may have a unit on identifying coins; a senior high school class may learn about inflation. But few classrooms are being used to explain the big stuff, such as why too much debt can ruin a person's financial life, or the little stuff, such as balancing a checkbook. If kids don't learn about budgeting, saving, investing, and other money concepts from parents, then they may not learn enough to avoid financial problems.

Kids see money in operation all the time, through trips to the supermarket, the ballpark, and the mall. But *seeing* money change hands doesn't give kids any real sense of what money is all about. And cash is no longer king. Paying by plastic may appear deceptively easy to kids who don't see the monthly credit card bill when it comes in. Kids are constantly bombarded with advertising designed to entice them to spend their (or your) money. Yelling at kids to turn off the lights when leaving a room because you don't own the electric company has very little meaning to a 10-year-old. Preaching about the virtues of saving money to a teenager also may fall on deaf ears if kids haven't learned this lesson already.

That's the challenge for you: to give your children an idea of what money is, what it takes to get and keep it, and how to be responsible about it.

How to Use This Book

If you're like me, you don't plan to support your kids for the rest of their lives. You want them to get an early start on learning about money so that they'll become responsible adults. I've raised three kids who are now off in college, and I'm pretty confident that they've mastered many of the things I've included in this book, such as how to be responsible about using credit cards, how to save for things they need in the future, how to handle their money from working, and more. Soon they'll be on their own financially, so I feel like I've done my job.

This book will guide you step-by-step in mapping out a game plan for teaching your kids about money. The information in this book will help you explain basic concepts and more complex ideas to put your kids on a sound financial footing. Some portions of the book are geared to younger kids; others relate to teenagers and older kids.

Of course, some of the ideas in this book are my opinion about how things should be. You don't have to share my position, but I hope you'll think about it before you try to influence your child.

I've also tried to provide you with resources for finding out more about various money-related topics. Many of these resources are found on the Internet. If you don't have a computer in your home, your child may be able to use one at school to track down information (or you may be able to use one at your local library). In some cases, telephone numbers of key resources have also been provided.

This book contains seven separate parts. Each part covers a different aspect of money, including ways to get it and ways to part with it wisely.

Part 1, "A Dollar Is Not Just Nickels and Dimes," gives you an idea about what money skills your child should have at a particular age. It helps you assess your own values about money and what you hope to pass on to your children. It explores ideas about money you may take for granted but that you'll need to more fully understand if you're going to explain things to your kids. You'll also find out what family money matters you should share with your children and at what age to do so. This part also discusses various ways in which you can teach your values and ideas about money to your kids through the use of games, activities, and other methods.

Part 2, "Money Concepts Made Easy," gives you the information you need to explain what money is all about. In today's world, important aspects of money, such as inflation and taxes, also need to be shared with your children. In addition, this section explains some practical things, such as tipping.

Part 3, "Money Makers for Kids," covers ways in which kids acquire money. This includes the weekly allowance you may decide to give, as well as money the child can earn through a job or even a business. It also includes money the child receives as gifts or awards, such as birthday money or contest winnings.

Part 4, "Big (and Little) Spenders," helps you decide what spending responsibilities you can shift to your child as he gets older. It also guides you on how to explain making choices and budgeting. Finally, this part tells how kids should be encourages to share their wealth with others by gifts and donations.

Part 5, "Rainy Day Precautions," explains the importance of saving money. Helping your child to set goals now will serve him for a lifetime. You'll also learn some ways in which a child can achieve savings objectives. You'll even see why it's never too early to start retirement savings and how you can help.

Part 6, "Investing Made Easy," takes the lessons of savings one step further. You'll see how starting early can produce big returns for your little investors. You'll learn about ways for kids to invest, from stocks to mutual funds, and you'll find out about online trading and other ways your child can use a computer to learn about investing. Finally, you'll see how collecting Barbie dolls, baseball cards, and other objects can be both fun and profitable.

Part 7, "**To Be or Not to Be a Borrower**," helps you explain what debt is all about. Learning the lesson now can mean staying out of financial trouble in the future. You'll help your child understand whether to borrow from you or sisters and brothers, and what buying on credit really means. You'll also get ideas for finding student loans to help pay for college. Finally, you'll get to test your child's money savvy so you can be confident of his ability to move out on his own.

Road Signs

As you travel through the pages of this book, you'll see special bits of information signified by little pictures to guide you. They'll give you a little extra help in navigating your way through the numerous and varied concepts you're trying to convey to your kids.

Watch Your Step

These warnings caution you about things you should avoid if you want to help your kids stay out of money trouble.

Piggybank on It

This is extra information that you can use—a phone number, a Web site, or a tip—that can help you do something better or easier.

Money ABCs

These are words and expressions on money matters that may be new or confusing to your kids.

Financial Building Blocks

This larger box is a catchall: It gives you interesting facts and figures on money and money matters.

Special Thanks to the Technical Reviewer

The Complete Idiot's Guide to Raising Money-Smart Kids was reviewed by an expert who double-checked the accuracy of what you'll learn here, to help us ensure that this book gives you everything you need to know about raising money-smart kids. Special thanks are extended to David Beach.

Acknowledgments

I want to thank my husband, Malcolm Katt, for reviewing the chapters on investments. The suggestions he made, in light of his nearly 30 years on Wall Street, helped me to clarify many investment concepts throughout this book. I also want to thank my friend, Bruce Glickman, CPA, who supplied some important numbers. And finally, I'm grateful to my editor, Matthew X. Kiernan, who helped to round out the rough corners and bring this book into focus.

Part 1

A Dollar Is Not Just Nickels and Dimes

It seems a universally accepted fact that money habits are learned young and last a lifetime. This means that parents can have a profound effect on their children's financial lives.

But the subject of money isn't easy, for a number of reasons. First, you bring to it your own baggage—attitudes, feelings, and knowledge (or lack of it). Second, the subject is more or less taboo to talk about. Third, the concepts are numerous and difficult to grasp at any age.

Despite these reasons that may make money a touchy subject, you, as a parent, may want to get beyond all that to help your child in this area.

In this part of the book, you'll learn about the three main ways in which you can influence your child when it comes to money: attitudes, perspective, and skills. You'll find out what your child should know about money in each stage of childhood. You'll learn to identify your own money values and decide what you want to pass along to your child. You'll learn to open up about the topic of money with your child so that he gains a proper perspective about it. And you'll find out how you can best teach money concepts and ideas to you child, no matter what the age.

Money (and How It's Handled) Matters

It's often repeated that money can't buy happiness. And, yes, plenty of millionaires are miserable. But the lack of money or the inability to handle it well can certainly cause just as much unhappiness. For example, money issues are a leading cause of marital troubles and divorce. So, to avoid problems throughout life, a child needs to learn about money—and the earlier your child starts to learn, the better. And who better to teach financial responsibility than you, the parent?

In this chapter you'll learn about your role in educating your child about money. You'll see what money skills or concepts your child should master, depending on his age. You'll learn about how to help your child, who's already a consumer, become a wise shopper. Finally, you'll get an idea about changing rules for money and the latest ways to educate your child on money matters.

Setting the Stage

If you earn a living or manage a household, you deal with money every day. You pay bills and, hopefully, save for the future.

You always want the best for your child, and when it comes to money, you probably want certain things to happen. You want your child to grow up to become a responsible adult, one who is self-supporting and in control of her finances. But before your child has moved out of your house, you want her to accomplish these goals:

➤ Become responsible about handling money

➤ Learn the work ethic: getting a job and doing it well

➤ Start to handle credit wisely, without taking on too much debt or failing to repay it

➤ See the importance of saving money for the future and becoming a saver

➤ Become a savvy investor, putting savings to good use

For the most part, these things don't happen automatically. A child isn't born with a natural instinct to select a mutual fund or make a budget. Money matters have to be taught, and you're in a position to do it.

Financial Building Blocks

Schools don't teach young kids about saving, budgeting, investing, and other important money concepts they need to know. A few schools may give instruction in these concepts, but not until they're seniors in high school. Thus, it's generally up to a parent to teach issues about money.

Laying the Groundwork

Handling money is a skill that is learned, and the habits learned when a child is young will last for a lifetime. You certainly want your child to develop good habits that will serve him well.

You can take an active role in teaching your child about money. You can talk about and explain money concepts you want him to know. Alternatively, you can take a passive role, teaching by example. In this case, you let your child observe you in action, whether shopping at the supermarket or making deposits at the bank. Or, you can combine the two and be proactive as well as passive. Whichever style you adopt, you're probably going to have the greatest influence on him.

As your child gets older, other influences will start to take effect. What you say and do will be only one piece of information he processes. The media—TV, movies, ads, rock music—continually bombard him with messages. What his friends do and say will matter a great deal as he starts to become more independent from you.

So, the sooner you get started on being his money guru, the greater your influence will be.

Setting the Rules

A teacher in a classroom usually tells the students the rules of the class. Kids learn that they must ask permission to leave the room, that they must raise their hand and be recognized before they can speak, and that they must remain quiet during certain times.

Like the teacher in the classroom, it helps if you have rules to follow when it comes to teaching about money. However, these rules are for you, not your child, to follow. You set them up by making a conscious decision to behave in a certain way. Of course, it may not always be easy to follow all the rules. And, in some cases, rules are made to be broken. But by thinking about the way you'd like to act when you're conveying money messages, you'll have some guidelines to follow.

Here are some dos and don'ts you may want to follow.

➤ *Do set a good example.* You need to get your own financial house in order before you can be a role model for your child. If you have bill collectors calling your home night and day, your child will figure out in no time that something's wrong with what you're doing.

➤ *Don't assume that your child knows a particular money concept.* I know one child who thought that "interest" meant that she had to be very concerned about (literally, show an interest in) her savings account.

➤ *Do let your child make mistakes.* You can help him understand why he made them and how to avoid them in the future, but the real-life lesson learned from the mistakes—painful as they might be—will be harder to forget.

➤ *Don't use money to control your kid.* Money shouldn't be used as a reward or a punishment. Doing this will only teach your child to gauge your response to her actions rather than learn about how money works.

➤ *Do praise your child for good decisions she makes about money.* If she decides to get an after-school job to earn some extra cash, your hearty approval will reinforce her positive action.

Piggybank on It

Think about how your parents taught (or failed to teach) you about money. Then decide how you'll act with your child. If you don't make a choice, you'll probably act in much the same way as your parents did.

➤ *Don't interfere with your child's money decisions.* If he has saved up to buy a toy that your gut tells you he'll lose interest in very quickly, don't talk him out of the purchase. Let him use his money as he wants, as long as falls within the parameters you've set together (for example, he shouldn't use his lunch money for this purpose).

➤ *Do increase your child's money responsibilities as he gets older.* This will give him wider experience with money matters.

➤ *Don't hesitate to get expert advice.* You aren't necessarily an expert on all money matters, so you may want to turn to an expert for help in a particular area. For example, if your child has received a sizable check as a birthday present and wants to invest it, talk with a stockbroker or financial consultant about what may be the best vehicle for your child.

➤ *Do help your child achieve her objectives.* If she wants to save for a particular game, guide her in how much she'll need to set aside each week or month, and tell her how long it will take her to reach her goal.

➤ *Don't have unrealistic expectations for your child's money education.* While you can set goals you'd like your child to achieve (as explained in the following section), don't be too disappointed or punish your child for failure. As with any learning experience, it's always two steps forward and one step back.

Your Goals for Your Child

You're probably no stranger to setting goals. You may have had the goal of graduating from college or buying a home. Maybe you've achieved your goals; maybe you're still working on them.

Piggybank on It

If your child has mastered the goals for his age category, don't be shy about tackling tougher money concepts. You'd be surprised at how delighted he will be that you think him capable of learning more.

You may not have thought about teaching money matters to your kids in terms of goals, but it helps to do so. Setting goals helps you measure your (and your child's) progress.

Set goals that you want to see your child achieve. The goals you now decide on depend in part on the age of your child and what she already knows. You can always adjust your personal goals as you go along.

Experts differ on what they believe to be minimum achievements for a particular age. One expert suggested that a child's money education should start as soon as he's old enough not to eat the money. Another expert favored savings plans for preschoolers.

You, of course, can set any goals you want. Here are some you might consider as *minimum* achievements for a child's age. When your child completes an age category, test his money knowledge to make sure that he has mastered the goals you've set.

➤ *Ask him questions.* See whether his answers show that he has achieved the different goals.

➤ *Watch her in action.* Doing is even more powerful than saying. Put her to the test to see if she succeeds.

Goals for Kids Age 6 to 10

Kids starting elementary school are outgrowing the myths of early childhood—the tooth fairy, the Easter bunny, and even Santa Claus. It's time to start learning the realities of money.

If your kid falls in this age category (essentially elementary school age), you want to be sure that she masters certain basic money concepts:

➤ *Identifying money.* Make sure that she knows the difference between a nickel and quarter.

➤ *Making change.* Make sure that she knows how to present enough money to cover a purchase and to count her change.

➤ *Being responsible for money.* If she loses the dollar that was in her pocket, she has to know that it's her loss (you won't replace it). This will teach her to be more careful in carrying money.

➤ *Understanding that things cost money.* From the candy she eyes at the supermarket checkout counter to the premium movie channels on TV, she must know that nothing comes free.

➤ *Handling an allowance.* Make sure that she learns to live with the allowance she's given and to meet any expectations for it that you might set. For example, this may include a modest savings plan to pay for things she wants.

Goals for Kids Age 11 to 13

As your child gets older (essentially middle school age), his responsibilities when it comes to money should increase. Your expectations of his money skills should also increase at this point.

Watch Your Step

Lucky enough to have a precocious child? She may be years ahead in reading and math but still lack the fundamentals about money. Just because she's smart, don't assume that your child knows a thing about money.

Here are some things you might expect of your child at this age:

➤ *Setting up a savings plan.* As your child ages, he's better able to set goals that are more far-reaching. For example, he might want to save for a summer experience—a day at Great Adventure or Six Flags.

➤ *Setting up a savings account.* The old piggy bank may have been okay in elementary school, but once his savings grows, it's time to bank it in a commercial institution.

➤ *Giving to charity.* Even if it's only a little money, it's about time to learn about giving to worthy causes.

➤ *Shopping wisely.* Children this age may spend time at the mall on their own; they need to know about shopping for value.

Goals for Youths Age 14 to 18

By this age (essentially high school age), your child already has one foot out the door. You want her to have a firm grasp of certain money essentials because it may be only a matter of a few years—or even months—before she's away from your watchful eye.

Here are some things that should be mastered by a youth in this age group:

➤ *Saving for college.* College is an investment worth making—and for this age group, it's just around the corner.

➤ *Getting a job.* Nothing teaches about the value of a dollar as fast as working for it.

➤ *Learning about investments.* Your child may not yet have the bucks to buy a Treasury bill or 100 shares of Microsoft, but it's important that she understand at this age how these investments differ and what investing in general can do for her.

➤ *Understanding what a budget is all about.* Money isn't infinite (unless you've been supplying it without restriction), so she should know how to make a budget and allocate the money she has to spend among the things she needs.

Financial Building Blocks

Kids are painfully ignorant about debt. According to a 1997 *Consumer Reports* study, 40 percent of teenagers didn't understand that banks charge interest on the loans they make. Many teens don't even realize that credit cards are a form of borrowing.

➤ *Learning about credit cards and other debt.* Whether your child is ready for her own credit card is not the criterion for teaching about debt and how to handle it. It's never too early to learn the perils of having too much debt and how that can happen.

➤ *Understanding about the different kinds of taxes.* If your child already had a job, she knows that Social Security and Medicare taxes are withheld from her paycheck. When shopping in most states, she has paid sales taxes on things she has bought. And if she earns enough or has investments, she'll pay income taxes as well.

Kids Are Consumers

Whatever your child's age, you can bet she is a consumer. Clothes, food, games, restaurants, and even vacation spots are all pitched at kids every day. And kids bite. They want the latest toy, the newest cereal, or the most fashionable pair of jeans. They've been educated (or brainwashed) through commercials and promotions to want these things.

Financial Building Blocks

Even though they may be spending your dollars, kids between the ages of 4 and 12 influence more than $180 billion of purchases a year (according to recent statistics in *Consumer Reports*). Teenagers have an even greater impact on spending. These are numbers too great to be ignored.

Given how much money is at stake, it pays to make sure that your child knows what she's doing when it comes to spending money. It's your job as a parent to set limits and explain what advertising means.

Just Say No

Kids are taught in school to say no to drugs. But it's up to you to teach them to say no to sales pitches directed at them.

The first aspect to saying no is teaching your child that he can't always have everything he wants. It's up to you to say no first. Saying no to a request for this candy bar or that toy may sound negative at first, but it's really a positive thing because it teaches your child some important concepts:

Piggybank on It

A little discomfort on your part while you set limits will serve you well in the long run. You may be nagged and pleaded with now, but once the lesson is learned that what you say goes, you'll avoid whining, tantrums, and demands when you say no.

➤ *Delayed gratification.* Wanting something immediately is not always possible—or even desirable. If he really wants something, he may get it in the long run, but he'll have to wait. Having to wait after a certain period of time may actually help him to enjoy that item even more.

➤ *Respect for someone else.* Your word matters. What you say goes. Learning to listen to you when you say no will also help your child listen to you about other things.

Raising Sales-Resistant Kids

Your child can't help it: He's constantly bombarded with ads and promotions for products and services. Advertisers know that kids are easy targets, susceptible to sales pitches geared toward them.

Financial Building Blocks

Believe it or not, according to a 1997 *Consumer Reports,* 34 percent of teenagers didn't realize that you can't judge how good a product is by how much it's advertised. Kids see ads and assume that what's in them is fact.

Your child needs to learn that it's not always in his best interest to buy what the ads tell him he needs. Teaching your child how to be sales-resistant is discussed in more detail in Chapter 6, "Economics 101."

It's a Brave New Money World

Aldous Huxley predicted test-tube babies, mind-altering drugs, and other scientific marvels in his *Brave New World.* Many of his predictions have already come true. But he didn't include the changes that have taken place in the world when it comes to money matters.

The world is a different place today than it was just a decade ago (let alone when Huxley was writing in 1932). Things we might have taken for granted previously are no longer the rule. In the not-too-distant past, a kid grew up and chose a career path or took a job at adulthood. He stayed there for his working years and, if lucky, lived to see retirement. A company pension and Social Security ensured his financial well-being until his death. Even if he was lucky enough to live to retirement, he didn't expect to have many years in that status.

Today, things are radically different, and these changes have an effect on money matters. For example, kids start to plan early for their futures. Many begin thinking about college and careers before they've even entered high school. And there's good reason for doing so:

➤ *College costs can be staggering.* Planning to meet the high cost of college is beginning increasingly earlier.

➤ *The jobscape is changing.* Manufacturing jobs are disappearing, and new Information Age jobs are being created every day.

➤ *People don't stay at one job for their entire working career.* Instead, they can expect to have multiple jobs and even multiple careers during the course of their life.

➤ *Retirement years can last as long as one's working years.* It takes money to live in retirement and meet the high cost of health care that can accompany advancing age.

➤ *Company pensions and Social Security cannot always provide a secure retirement income.* Personal savings for many becomes the primary source of retirement income.

It's time to realize that your kids are up against new realities when it comes to money. With that comes new ways to learn about money.

Planning for the Future Now

The changing realities of demographics, technology, and the workplace all affect money. Your child must learn about money within the context of these new realities. You probably didn't learn these concepts as a child; most likely, you learned them as an adult. But your child needs to recognize the new money facts of life. Here are just some new facts of life that require new thinking about money matters.

Financial Building Blocks

According to the U.S. Census Bureau, a person born at the start of the last millennium had a life expectancy of only about 46 years. Today that life expectancy has nearly doubled. A child born today can expect to live to 79 (even older for women, while slightly less for men). A division of the National Institutes of Health projects life expectancy to increase by the year 2040 to 86 for men and 91.5 for women.

➤ *Life expectancy means that kids must take a longer view of life than ever before.* They must recognize that their working years may go on for half a century. In that time, they may have several different careers. They'll need to think about things such as expensive long-term care and other concepts that we parents never did at their age.

➤ *Taxes have a bigger impact on financial decisions.* Taxes today influence the type of investments that people make, such as deciding when to buy and sell. They also affect the type of retirement savings vehicle people use (for example, a tax-advantaged plan such as a company 401(k) plan or a personal IRA). Kids may expect to earn more money than we do, but they'll also pay more of it into Social Security and Medicare. When I started working full-time back in 1970, the top amount that any worker paid into the system was less than $300 a year. Today, high-earners pay more than $5,000, and there's no ceiling on annual contributions for Medicare.

➤ *Insurance is something that a person really can't (or shouldn't) live without today.* Decisions about taking or switching jobs are greatly influenced by the availability of health care. People know that through middle age, there's a greater likelihood today of becoming disabled than dying, and they want to protect their livelihood in such an event. People today also have a greater need to protect themselves from lawsuits and must insure against many different types of possible liabilities.

➤ *Computer technology is part of the work and investment landscape.* It's essential to be computer-literate Because computers are used on or in connection with just about every job today—even many artists and musicians wouldn't be without them. Computers also allow people to make and monitor their investments online.

Using Technology to Learn About Money

Computer technology isn't only for the workplace or making investments: It's also a great learning tool.

Kids may not know what they should about money, but the opportunity to learn is right there at their fingertips. The advent of the Internet means that kids sitting at home, in school, or in their public library can tap into resources that let them get a jump on their financial education:

➤ They can learn all about money.

➤ They can start up businesses of their own online.

➤ They can make investments online.

Throughout this book, the chapters list addresses of Web sites for various money-related topics. There's also a compilation of listings in Appendix B.

The Least You Need to Know

➤ Wanting your child to become a responsible adult requires you to educate her about money matters.

➤ You must take the lead in educating your child about money because the schools don't do it.

➤ Set age-appropriate goals for your child to achieve in understanding and handling money.

➤ Teach your child that there are limits when it comes to buying things.

➤ Teach your child to become sales-resistant.

➤ The Internet provides a new way for kids to learn about money matters.

The Morality of Money

Money isn't good or evil; it's just an integral part of everyday life. It's what you do with that money that determines whether it goes to good or bad use.

Approaches to money—both making it and handling it—are governed by your values. The storekeeper who places a premium on honesty won't cheat a customer; the con artist who believes in "Do unto others *before* they do it to you" can be expected to rip off his own brother. Understanding your values is key to instilling values in your child.

In this chapter, you'll confront your own thoughts, feelings, and values about money. After all, you can't decide what you want to pass on to your child unless you know your own mind first. You'll also get some concrete ideas on the values and concepts you want to instill in your child when it comes to money.

You and Your Money

The word *money* for you probably triggers both a practical and an emotional response. First, you may think about what you earn, the bills you have to pay, or what you'd like to buy in the future. This is your practical side.

You also may experience some emotional reaction to the word *money*. You may feel overwhelmed or need to feel in control. You may feel comfortable, or even cavalier.

Whatever you may be thinking or feeling about money can very well influence how your child views—and ultimately handles—money. A fall 1998 survey on Teens and Money by USA Weekend showed that 77 percent of those between the ages of 12 and 18 learned a lot about money matters from their parents.

Financial Building Blocks

According to a 1997 poll published in *USA Today*, adults say they learned money habits from their parents at an early age. Key habits included these:

Budgeting money	77 percent
Donating to charity	80 percent
Shopping wisely	85 percent

Your Head and Your Money

As a parent, you face the demands of paying the rent or the mortgage, the doctor bills, the grocery store totals, and the cable TV bill every month. You probably also are planning for future expenditures, such as a new roof, a vacation, or your child's college education. You do this whether you like it or not, whether you feel comfortable or distressed. It's just your responsibility, and you try your best to handle it.

You map out how you're going to get the money you need, decide what you must or would like to spend it on, and how much you can save for the future. Again, being practical dictates your actions here.

Obviously, practicality is important because it allows you to deal with your money responsibilities every day.

Your Heart and Your Money

Practicality is only one side of the coin, though. You also have an emotional side that affects how you handle your practical side. For example, if you're comfortable with money (which doesn't mean that you're financially fixed—only that you're at ease with money concepts), you probably pay your bills on time and don't get into over-spending trouble. But if you're intimidated by money, you may be reluctant to face your money chores or may spend without regard to the consequences. You also might delay making investment decisions.

Ask yourself these questions:

➤ Are you a spender or a saver?

➤ Do you buy, buy, buy, whether you need the thing—or even whether you can afford it?

➤ Do you hold onto a penny just to feel good about having it in your pocket, even though you deny yourself the things you logically know you can afford?

Obviously, it's ideal to fall somewhere in the middle of these two extremes of spend-thrift and miser, spending only what's needed within your budget while also saving enough for future needs. In reality, however, most of us tend to fall on one side of the fence or the other.

You see, your emotional side colors what you do with respect to money—whether you meet your responsibilities or let them slide, and whether you spend your money wisely or horde it like Ebenezer Scrooge. Your child also has an emotional side and may already be a spender or a saver.

Watch Your Step

Some people have an unhealthy love of money. They've failed to heed the biblical caution that "The love of money is the root of all evil" (I Timothy 6:10, New Revised Standard Version).

Value Lessons

Values work as your guidelines in life. They stand like tall oaks in a forest, fixed and strong. You don't always live up to the values you treasure, but that doesn't mean that those values need to change. For example, you may highly value honesty, but you'd never tell your child that his performance in the school play was terrible.

You have your own set of values—what you learned as a child from your parents and what decisions you've made as an adult. However, you aren't the only one that teaches your child values. He also gleans values from what he is taught in school; what he watches on TV, sees in the movies, and listens to on the radio and on CDs; and what he sees demonstrated by his friends and their families.

Your challenge is to sort out your own values and recognize the values transmitted by outside influences. By doing this, you can take affirmative steps to enforce—and re-enforce—the values you want

Money ABCs

The word **value** has two meanings when it comes to money. First, values are your acts, customs, and ways of dealing with things—including money. Value also refers to the worth of an item in terms of money. Both concepts will be discussed throughout this book.

your child to adopt. After all, values aren't inherited like your brown hair or your artistic abilities; values need to be taught.

Your Values

Before you try to instill values in your child, you'd better be clear on exactly what those values are. If you hold to one set of values but want your child to adopt a different set, it probably won't work. Your actions in following your own values will undermine your efforts.

But how do you know what your values are? Have you ever thought about them? Have you ever put them in words? This following little quiz might help clarify the issues. Don't worry—there are no failing grades or scoring system. Just be honest with your answers. The function of this quiz is simply to open your eyes to exactly what you value in relation to money matters.

Money Values Quiz

1. When a sales clerk gives you too much change, you:
   a. Pocket the change.
   b. Point out the error and return the excess.
   c. Donate the excess to charity.

2. When a neighbor gets a new car, you:
   a. Think it should have been you who deserved it rather than your neighbor.
   b. Think it's great that your neighbor was able to buy it, and wish her well.
   c. Don't give it a second thought.

3. When you read about young kids shoplifting comic books, you think:
   a. It's only child's play, and they'll grow out of it.
   b. It's terrible, and they should be punished.
   c. It's too bad they got caught.

4. The state lottery is up to $25 million, so you:
   a. Withdraw money from your savings account to buy tickets to increase your odds of winning.
   b. Spend the same $1 you do every week for fun.
   c. Don't do anything because you need your money for other things.

5. Your credit card bill has a balance that you can't pay in full, so you:
   a. Continue to shop and don't give the bill a second thought.
   b. You charge only absolute necessities until you've paid off your bill.
   c. You charge up a storm because there's still a way to go on your credit limit.

---

6. A portion of your town is damaged in a storm. Fortunately, your house is okay, so you:

    a. Are glad you've been spared, and that's that.

    b. Donate your time and money to helping your neighbors.

    c. Increase your homeowners insurance.

7. When you were young, you broke a neighbor's window and had to pay for the repair. When your child asks you about it, you:

    a. Deny it.

    b. Acknowledge it and encourage your child to learn from your mistakes.

    c. Minimize the event, saying it was a long time ago.

8. You want a big-screen TV (who doesn't?) so you:

    a. Buy it on credit and worry about how you'll pay for it later.

    b. Save up for it.

    c. Use the money you'd been saving for your child's college fund to buy the TV.

Values are defined by certain concepts you stand behind. Unfortunately, some people's values are viewed as negative by most other people.

Here's a list of words for values—positive and negative—associated with money. Ask yourself which words you stand behind and want your children to follow:

Charitable	Selfish
Frugal	Wasteful
Generous	Miserly
Hard-working	Lazy
Honest	Dishonest
Independent	Controlling
Resourceful	Unimaginative
Responsible	Irresponsible
Satisfied	Envious, jealous

Watch Your Step

Talk about your values with your spouse. If you and your spouse have markedly different views when it comes to values, you need to arrive at some common ground so that you don't transmit mixed messages to your child.

Children who won't share their toys in kindergarten or who cheat on their sixth-grade math quiz are displaying negative values (selfishness and dishonesty). A teenager who takes out the garbage regularly without being reminded, or the middle-schooler who brings to the school office the backpack left in the lunchroom are displaying positive values (responsibility and honesty). Values aren't only used in how your kid behaves in school or at home, though; they play a key role in how your child deals with money now and for the rest of her life.

Outside Influences

Some groups, such as the Amish and Hasidic Jews, limit the contact their children have with the outside world. For the most part, they don't own TVs, read local newspapers, or send their children to public schools. Their children learn only the values of their well-defined culture.

Most Americans, however, allow their children to be exposed to all kinds of influences. Some of these turn out to be good; others are bad. By recognizing that these other influences can support or undermine your efforts, you'll be able to handle the situation. Here are just some of the ways your child is exposed to values in the outside world:

➤ *School.* Children enter school at the age of 5, or even younger. The teacher becomes an important figure in your child's life, and what "teacher says" is often quoted by your child as a fact. Sometimes this may contradict your own statements (you'll repeatedly hear "but teacher says…" from your child). In the best of all possible worlds, the things your child learns in school will reinforce what you're trying to teach in your home. However, be on the lookout for concepts that are in opposition to where you stand. This will allow you to tell your child why you believe your position is the one she should follow.

➤ *Peers.* When your child is young, the influence of friends is modest. As he or she gets older, however, peer pressure becomes a very strong influence. Hopefully, you will have already instilled values—as well as the ability to resist negative peer pressure—by the time such pressure is brought to bear.

➤ *Religious institutions.* Many families have strong ties with their church or other religious group. Values are one of the key teachings of religion, and, presumably, your personal values are in sync with those of your religion.

➤ *Your extended family.* Older brothers and sisters, aunts and uncles, grandparents, and other members of your extended family can have a big influence on your child's values. Seeing an aunt

Money ABCs

Peer pressure is the ability of your child's contemporaries to influence your child's behavior. This starts in preschool and continues through the teen years. This pressure can be both positive or negative, but it can't be ignored. It's a powerful influence on your child because it enhances self-esteem.

lavish gifts on the family or a grandfather who never parts with a dime will certainly leave an impression on your child. These outside influences must be acknowledged, but you're the first line of defense: Your child hears it from you first.

➤ *Pop culture.* Subtle as well as direct messages are transmitted each day to your child by television programs, music on the radio, computer games, and Hollywood movies. These messages can have a great influence on the values your child adopts.

While outside influences can't be ignored, the good news is that strong parental influence is greater than any outside influence, especially until the teenage years. Be aware of the influence that you have, while staying on guard to any influence that may undermine your messages.

Deciding on Values

Now that you've examined your own attitudes and values toward money, you may want to think about the things you want your child to understand. Take a look at these old adages: Some have weathered the years because they continue to be true, and others may be tomorrow's classics.

➤ *Money can't buy happiness.* Explain that having money doesn't solve a person's problems. You need only look at those well-paid athletes and movie stars who are in the headlines for taking drugs, getting divorced, parenting illegitimate children, and having trouble with the law to see that this adage holds true.

➤ *Self-worth isn't (or shouldn't be) measured in dollars and cents.* Explain that money can bring security and creature comforts, but it doesn't mean that the person who has the money is valued in that way. Again, drug lords and Mafia dons have plenty of money but certainly aren't regarded as upstanding citizens by those who know what they do. A person is defined by what he does and how he acts, not by his wealth.

➤ *Keeping up with the Joneses is impossible.* It's fruitless to compare your financial situation to your neighbor's. This kind of jealousy makes you continually dissatisfied with what you have. No matter how much money you acquire, there's always a wealthier Jones out there. The constant complaint of many children is that so-and-so has this toy or this item of clothing, and they want it, too. Is this any different from keeping up with the Joneses?

➤ *Money, like manure, only does good when you spread it around and encourage small things to grow.* Spoken by Dolly Levi in *The Matchmaker*, this phrase should serve as a reminder that saving money in a mattress doesn't accomplish anything but feed a miser's soul. On the other hand, using money to pay for an education, to start a business, or to donate to charity are certainly worthwhile endeavors—and all good reasons for having money.

➤ *Getting a car from a parent at 16 isn't a constitutional right.* Many people are under the impression that things are coming to them and that they're entitled. This notion has been nurtured by the proliferation of various government programs that hand out money for all sorts of things, such as cash for *not* growing corn. After the programs are in place, they seem to become a right—life, liberty, the pursuit of happiness, and Social Security benefits, for example. We tend to lose sight of the fact that benefits are provided as long as the law allows it, but there's no absolute requirement (other than perhaps political necessity) for doing so. This entitlement attitude applies to children who see friends getting all sorts of things and who then assume that everyone should have it, that they're entitled to it.

➤ *A fool and his money are soon parted.* This wise old English proverb stresses the importance of smart money management. Acting impetuously can cost a person dearly. The earlier your child learns the value of making a budget, saving money, resisting impulse buying, and investing with care, the less likely he is to act the fool and lose his money.

Piggybank on It

You don't have to go it alone when it comes to fixing values. You can find help on what your values mean to your child in various books, such as *Dr. Spock's Baby and Child Care.* You'll find a listing of other helpful books in Appendix C.

Honing Your Parenting Skills

Being a parent isn't easy. Once your child is born, you're a parent for life. Unfortunately, learning how to be a parent isn't part of the normal school curriculum. As the movie *Parenthood* pointed out, you don't need a license to become a parent. Most people just wing it, more or less parenting in much the same way as their parents did.

However, in today's Information Age, it's easy to get guidance on parenting issues, including how to instill values in your child. You can find parent training programs, such as Parent Effectiveness Training, Systematic Training for Effective Parenting, and Confident Parenting. (Many times you can find out about programs in your area through your child's school.) You also can track down books on just about any aspect of parenting, or search the numerous Web sites for related information. Check out the following sites for ideas on general parenting skills:

Piggybank on It

One book you might want to start with is *The Complete Idiot's Guide to a Well-Behaved Child* (listed in Appendix C).

➤ www.ciccparenting.org

➤ www.kidscampaigns.org

➤ www.tnpc.com

➤ www.positiveparenting.com

➤ www.familyeducation.com

➤ www.connectedfamily.com

➤ www.parentsoup.com

Whether you feel that you need outside guidance on your parenting skills is up to you. The point to remember is that the parenting skills you use to teach your child about how to stay safe from strangers, how to get along with playmates, and what rules apply in your home are the same skills you'll use to teach your child about money.

The Least You Need to Know

➤ You should recognize that you view money not only practically, but also emotionally.

➤ Your child's values toward money are colored by many different influences, with you being the strongest influence of all.

➤ Understand your values toward money so that you can transmit them to your child.

➤ Use your parenting skills to teach values to your child.

THANKS MOM.

TOP SECRET

Chapter 3

Sharing Your Family Money Secrets

In This Chapter

➤ Why you don't tell your kids your money secrets

➤ What you and your child can gain from sharing money secrets

➤ Going about the business of explaining family money matters

Certain things are considered out of bounds for conversation in polite society: religion, politics, and, of course, money. But it's not only in social gatherings that money talk is taboo. Many families never talk about it, even with each other. This lack of discourse means that your child may miss the opportunity to learn about money or may develop misconceptions about it.

In this chapter, you'll see why the subject of money is often a big family secret. You'll learn why it's important to share information, and you'll learn what information to share with your child, and at what age.

Keeping Money Skeletons in Your Family Closet

In most families, two things are almost never discussed: sex and money. Sex as a topic of conversation may be out of bounds largely because parents are too embarrassed to explain things, Or, perhaps they plan to talk about it when children are older—of course, they often find that when the children reach that older age, there's little they want to hear from their parents or that think they don't know already.

But the family's money may not be discussed for several reasons that may differ substantially from those associated with discussions on sex. Assuming that you agree that it's important to talk about money (the reasons why are discussed later in this chapter), then you should see what's preventing you from talking about your family's money matters so that you can get on with things.

What's Blocking You?

If you're not already talking about money with your children, examine the reasons for that. Ask yourself the following questions:

➤ "It's none of their business." Do you think that children should *not* be in on the family's money situation? And that only grown-ups should know what's going on? Why do you feel this way?

➤ "I'm trying to protect them from painful realities." Do you believe that you're able to shield your children from the unhappy truths about your money situation? And do you really think you should?

➤ I'm afraid they'll tell the neighbors my business." Do you lack confidence in your child's ability to keep a confidence? How do you think your child will feel if he finds out that you don't trust his ability to keep a secret?

➤ My parents never talked about money with me." Do you believe that despite your parent's silence you turned out okay when it comes to money? We tend to parent our children in much the same way as our parents did us.

➤ "I'm ashamed of my bank account." Do you feel that you're not doing as well financially as you should and want to keep this information private? You may be living above your means, putting up a good front and trying not to let the truth be told.

➤ "I don't want my child to make large financial demands." Are you afraid that if he knows you can afford it, he'll ask for the moon? Isn't your fear really concern about your ability to set limits and say no?

Watch Your Step

Even if you don't talk about money, your kids will learn about it from you anyway, from your behavior and attitudes. You might as well discuss things that will help your kids become responsible about handling money.

Maybe you have other reasons besides those listed here for not talking about your family's money situation. Whatever your reasons, it's time to recognize that certain money information needs to be shared. Understanding why you're not already doing this will help you move on.

Financial Building Blocks

You can't protect your kids from having money concerns. According to a fall 1998 "Teens and Money" survey of kids in grades 6-12 conducted by *USA Weekend,* more than half of all kids worry about their family's finances (with 12 percent who worry a lot).

Benefits of Sharing Information

Sharing family money matters doesn't mean confessing to your children where every nickel goes. It means giving information that is age-appropriate.

However sound you may think the reasons are for *not* talking about your money with your child, many compelling reasons exist for opening up on the subject:

➤ *Avoiding family friction.* If your children understand what the family can afford, you can eliminate the constant tension that results from trying to keep up with the wealthier Joneses down the street.

➤ *Providing a sense of security.* The old saying that knowledge is power applies to an understanding of family money matters. The unknown can be very scary. When a child knows the score—even if it's bad—she can usually live with it.

➤ *Getting kids involved in money solutions.* If you lose a job or have financial setbacks, it might be helpful for your teenager to know about it. This just might serve as motivation for him to get a part-time job, or family discussions could result in cutbacks on allowances or other child-related spending.

➤ *Setting a good example.* As a parent, you're in a unique position to influence not only the next generation, but also generations to come. How you behave with your child will influence how she acts with her own children.

Airing Out the Family's Money Secrets

So you've made the decision to be more open about money matters with your child. Good for you! Whether or not you're entirely comfortable with this decision, you need to decide exactly *what* information you're going to share—and when. You don't have to share everything, and what you do share is dictated in part by the age of your child.

You'll want to consider two general areas when sharing information:

➤ The family's daily finances

➤ When a family crisis arises

Piggybank on It

Consider having family conferences at Sunday dinner, or whenever else it's convenient. Usually these meetings are used to air grievances or discuss problems of family members. In any case, make sure that the topic of money is on the agenda.

Piggybank on It

As children get older, they also can be party to the budget. For example, a teenager can be given a clothing allowance for a season (for example, when starting school) or some other period. Then, it's up to him to decide when and how much to spend on a pair of jeans or new sneakers.

After you see the kinds of information to be shared, you'll get some idea of when you should share it.

Daily Finances

Growing up, I heard my father routinely say, "Turn off the lights when you leave a room; I don't own the electric company." The message from my parent was clear: We didn't have money to waste. I, in turn, complained to my children each month that the phone bill was more than $100. It wasn't until after my daughter started to work that she understood what a $100 phone bill really meant—before that, I could have said the bill was more than $1,000 or more than $10, and these numbers wouldn't have meant anything to her other than the fact that her mother was angry.

The point of these stories is simple: If children are aware of family finances, they can better understand how to behave. This will cut out the need to nag and can make your children more responsible.

What information should be shared? Does your child have to know your annual salary, the dollar amount of the monthly mortgage payment, or the size of the family savings account? The answer is probably no—the numbers are meaningless because there's nothing to compare them to. You child doesn't know what his friend's parents earn or what their mortgage payments are.

What your child does need to know is where the family stands financially. This means telling a child certain things:

➤ *Who makes money decisions in the family.* Usually, parents work things out together and present a united front to children. But the days of "ask your mother" or "wait until your father gets home" are still common enough. Money decisions may still be made by the parent who earns more.

➤ *How money-related decisions are made.* Children want things *now*, but parents know they need to save for things later. There's always a tension between spending and saving.

➤ *The family is on a budget.* Children need to understand that in most households, money isn't an unlimited commodity. There's only so much to go around, so decisions need to be made on how to allocate the money that's available.

If your family is like most, money doesn't flow like the mighty Mississippi that can run forever. It's more like rainwater collected in a pail that can be ladled out as needed. Explain that if a cupful is taken for one thing, it's not there for something else.

Sticking to a budget means that there has to be give and take in deciding how the family's money will be spent. Some families are more willing than others to make sacrifices to accommodate a child's wants—just ask the parents of our Olympic hopefuls what they had to do without so that their children could pay for the costs of training.

Crises

Very few families can claim to see their children grow to maturity without experiencing some family crisis along the way. With the divorce rate in the United States at about 50 percent, the dissolution of the family is by far the most common crisis that many children experience.

Divorce brings many financial changes to the family. It may mean that the mother has to work full-time, that there's less money in the child's household, and that money may be a serious issue between parents.

Children of divorced parents *shouldn't* be in on the details of child support payments: That's something between the parents, and wrangling about it usually results from the parents' broken relationship. This information should have nothing to do with the children; bringing them in on the issue only forces them to take sides and makes them feel conflicted about doing so.

With any family crisis, there's usually an important aspect of money involved in the events. Consider the following crises (besides divorce) that can happen in any family, and think about how each one can impact the family's finances (positively or negatively):

➤ *Unemployment of a parent.* The family may be put on a bare-bones budget. Unemployment compensation may cover necessities, but extras are now out of the question. The other parent may go to work. Roles within the family may be upset, with the former breadwinner acting now as the bread baker.

➤ *Bankruptcy.* Personal bankruptcies are in record numbers today. Some of this may be because of poor money management, such as overcharging on credit cards that can't be repaid. But some bankruptcies result from forces beyond one's control, perhaps if a fire or other natural disaster wipes out a business, or if a lawsuit against the family results in a staggering judgment. While the bankruptcy laws are designed to allow a person to keep certain things—a home and furnishings, a car, and a wedding ring—other assets are used to pay the debt and give the debtor a fresh start. Bankruptcy isn't the time for taking vacations or making frivolous purchases.

➤ *Job relocation.* A relocation can mean the family has more (or less) money to spend, depending on the new town or city. For example, if the family moves from a small town in the Midwest to New York City, the sticker shock of a family meal at McDonalds may be astounding. The family may have to spend more on housing and, as a result, have less to spend on entertainment and other extras.

➤ *Remarriage.* As with a job relocation, a remarriage may be positive or negative, from a financial point of view. The nature of the situation depends on the new spouse and whether new children are coming into the family. When children from two families come together in a remarriage, issues arise over how much money there is to spend and how each set of children has been raised so far to regard money.

➤ *Serious illness of a family member.* The emotional cost of a serious illness is paramount, but the financial cost cannot be denied. Even with medical insurance, a serious illness brings financial consequences, especially if the one who's sick is the parent who used to be the main provider.

➤ *Death of a parent.* As with a serious illness, the emotional price of death can't be minimized. Unfortunately, there may be a financial price on it as well. Some parents may carry adequate insurance to support the family and even provide for a college education for the children. Others may leave *some* assets to help, but the other parent may have to work, incur child-care expenses, and struggle along. Still others may not leave *anything* to help the family.

What children need to know in a crisis is that it's not their fault and that you're taking care of things. When they're little, they want their routine to continue unabated. If they've been getting dance lessons, they want to know that the lessons can continue. You, in turn, should keep this in mind when deciding what you're going to spend money on during the crisis period.

As children get older, you can bring them into the inner circle of money matters during the crisis. For example, you might tell a child that her college savings is safe and will be there for her when she needs it. Or, you might have to say that the savings will have to be used now to support the family and that payment for college will have to be worked out later.

The prospect of death is particularly scary for children. They fear not only losing their parents, but also ending up an orphan like Oliver Twist begging for more food. It

Watch Your Step

Don't let your child's chronological age dictate what you tell him. Tailor your remarks with his intellectual age in mind as well. Some 10-year-olds are as savvy as other 16-year-olds.

may be reassuring for children to be told that if you die, they'll be taken care of, both personally (with a guardian you've named in your will) and financially (with life insurance and other property).

Information for Your Child's Age

The time you share certain financial information and the way you do it depends on your child's age. Obviously, a 6-year-old won't understand the technicalities of bankruptcy, but he can grasp the concept that things are tight and that he can't have an expensive birthday party.

You may want to follow some guidelines in sharing family money information with your kids:

➤ *Elementary school age.* For daily finances, tell them about limits on family spending in general. Explain that the family is on a budget (if it has one). Children should know some specific things that they can understand, such as whether your home is owned or rented, and whether you're saving for certain anticipated expenses that means doing without for now. Let them contribute ideas to a family wish list. In a crisis, share the fact that a crisis will impact the family's money. Tell them whether it's temporary or whether it requires re-engineering the family's finances.

➤ *Middle school age.* It's time to get more specific about money. Children can—or should—understand at this age what things cost. Let them listen in on discussions about money. Encourage them to ask questions about anything they don't understand. In a crisis, children of this age also can handle more details. For example, in a divorce, they can understand why you need to move to a smaller home and why everyone must get along with less.

➤ *High school age.* At this age, you can't keep things from them any longer (they probably already know the money score at home). Depending upon your situation, you might want to show your children your monthly budget, explain how much you spend for items such as groceries, and whether you're committed to saving for your retirement. You may want to involve them in your budgeting process, taking their input into account. Be sure to tell them where you keep important papers that may be needed in a crisis. As a minimum, they should know about your will, records of financial accounts (banks, brokerage accounts, mutual funds, and so on), and the names and numbers of financial and other advisers (your accountant, attorney, life insurance agent, stockbroker, and others).

The Least You Need to Know

➤ A parent's personal hang-ups may keep him from talking about the family's money matters with his child.

➤ Sharing family money matters can help avoid family friction and provide a sense of security for children.

➤ Sharing information about daily finances doesn't mean accounting to children about the family's every dime.

➤ Talking to children about money during a family crisis can alleviate some of the anxiety that they're already feeling.

➤ What you tell your children about family finances depends on their age.

Chapter 4

Teaching About Money

In This Chapter

➤ Gearing up for teaching

➤ Setting yourself up as an example

➤ Talking about money

➤ Using the wide world as a learning tool

➤ Playing games

You may not be a licensed school teacher, but you're probably the best instructor your child could have when it comes to money. Whether you earn a lot or a little, whether you're good at managing money or not, and whether you know a lot or a little about money and investments, you can help your child get started on the road to financial well-being.

You can use many different techniques to convey information and attitudes about money. Even without trying, your child will pick up things from you just by what you say and do. Of course, there are also more structured ways to teach you child about money.

In this chapter, you'll learn about different ways you can convey ideas and concepts about money to your child. You'll see how you can teach by example, and you'll learn that how just talking about money can be a great teaching tool. You'll also see how just about every place you go and everything you do can serve as a learning experience on money. Finally, you'll find out about games that your child can play to learn about money at any age. First and foremost, however, you'll find out what general areas you should be directing your efforts toward.

Money Concepts You Should Convey

The topic of money is a big one. Where do you start? How do you go about teaching it?

Specific topics are discussed in each chapter in this book. For the most part, though, all money education is focused on certain general topics:

➤ *Earning money.* This means putting in personal time and effort to receive payment.

➤ *Saving money.* This means setting aside money today so that it will be there in the future.

➤ *Spending money.* This means using money that's been earned or saved to pay for things.

➤ *Borrowing money.* This means using money that will have to be repaid in the future at more than what was originally received.

According to some child experts, a parent can start explaining about earning money, saving money, and spending money as soon as children can speak. Kids probably can't understand what borrowing is about until they're in elementary school and can appreciate what interest on borrowing really means.

Monkey Sees and Hears—and Monkey Does

By now, it's not news to you that your child picks up on just about everything you do and say. You're the main example of how to act. Whether consciously or unconsciously, your child will mimic your behavior.

Financial Building Blocks

According to a nationwide survey of high school students sponsored by Jump$tart Coalition for Personal Financial Literacy, almost 60 percent of the kids surveyed said that they learned about managing their money "at home from my family." This compares with only 11 percent who said that they learned about money management at school.

When it comes to learning about money, how you act with it and what you say about it is perhaps the most influential thing you can do to instruct your child. This means that you should be sensitive to what you say and do about money matters; you're in a unique position to have a positive (or negative) influence on your child's ability to handle money.

Your actions and words about money should be consistent. If you say one thing but do another, your child will see through this hypocrisy very quickly. On the other hand, consistency will reinforce all your efforts; what you say will support what you do, and vice versa.

Setting an Example

Children are smarter than you think. It won't take your teenager long to know you're in financial trouble if the bill collectors are calling every day and you've instructed him to say you're not in.

Setting a good example isn't dependent on how much money you earn or how much you have in the bank: It's about instilling the values and attitudes you hold about money (these are discussed in Chapter 1, "Money [and How It's Handled] Matters"; and Chapter 2, "The Morality of Money"). You could be living on a tight budget and might show your child a thing or two about responsibility.

Watch Your Step

Financial words can be very confusing because one word can have two or more very different meanings. For example, kids are always talking about bonding with each other— they probably don't have the vaguest idea that "bond" also refers to a debt instrument. And an "instrument" isn't only something you play to make music; it's also a financial obligation that makes money. Don't assume that your child understands the money-meaning of a word.

Talk Isn't Cheap

When I was in elementary school, I used to ride my bike to the candy store down the block to get my father a copy of the *World Telegram Sun,* an afternoon newspaper that had the closing stock market prices. (The New York Stock Exchange closed at 3:30 in the afternoon until 1974, when the closing bell was changed to 4 P.M.). When he'd come home from work, we'd sit down to dinner as a family. Between courses, my father would thumb through the paper and casually tell my mother as she was serving dinner various stock prices, noting what was up and what was down for the day. The alphabet soup of ITT, RCA, and IBM didn't mean a lot to me at the time, but looking back, I confess that I did learn a lot about investing just by sitting at the dinner table. My dad was no tycoon, but his talk about the market helped me learn the terminology—stocks, bonds, splits, dividends, and more—just by being there.

Today, it's no longer the norm that families sit down to dinner together each night. Hectic schedules lead many families to eat on the run, one by one. Children lose out on the opportunity to pick up valuable information in an offhanded way. Still, there are many opportunities for talk:

➤ *Family meals.* With a little extra effort, the family may be able to dine together on some nights during the week. There's always the opportunity for a weekend meal together, too, even if it's Sunday brunch.

35

➤ *In the car.* Suburban moms and dads say they're always in the car—I used to think I spent more time carpooling each day than sleeping. This may sound like a negative thing, but you certainly can turn it into a positive. Usually your kids are in the back seats, so they're captive audiences for conversation. Even when kids get older and are driving on their own, parents still spend a good deal of time in a car with their children, driving to doctors appointments, soccer games, and school events. There's plenty of time for talk.

➤ *Leisure activities.* Parents often socialize with their children through sports or other leisure activities. A round of miniature golf or an afternoon of fishing can provide opportunities for conversation.

All the World's a Stage

Shakespeare said it, and he was right. You don't have to sit in a classroom to learn. My kids learned more about the Civil War by visiting the Gettysburg battlefield than by studying it in a textbook. Likewise, your child can learn more about money from being out in the world than trying to learn about it from a book.

Here are just some of the ways your child can learn about money by being out in the world:

Financial Building Blocks

Taking a trip to New York City with your kids? Consider walking around the Financial District in the Wall Street area. On weekdays, you can take in free tours of the New York Stock Exchange and the Federal Reserve Building (call 212-720-6130 for reservations). Seeing the Federal Reserve's subterranean vault of gold bullion is an eye-popper for all ages!

➤ *Shopping at the supermarket.* If your child is old enough to read, he's old enough to read food labels. This is the first step in learning to comparison-shop. If a 12-ounce box of Rice Krispies costs $3.49 and a 15-ounce box of Cheerios costs $3.69, which is more expensive? (In many cases, the store will provide the cost per ounce on a label on the shelf, but you should be able to figure this as well.) In this example, the Rice Krispies costs a lot more than the Cheerios (a little more than 29¢ an ounce, versus less than 25¢ an ounce for the Cheerios). Another money skill that can be practiced at the supermarket is tendering money and making change. If the bill is $77.85, let your child fish in your wallet for the bills and coins to be tendered as payment. Having exact change is only the most elementary way to tender money, so teach your child how to present *more* cash than required and how to count change.

➤ *Shopping at the mall.* As kids get older, they can start to see more of how things work by observing at the mall. Sale signs for 25 percent off teach about discounts. The addition of sales tax on clothing shows that the final price of an item isn't what's on the price tag. A little explanation on your part about discounts and sales taxes can add a lot to your child's money vocabulary.

➤ *Listening to the radio or television.* Financial news is always a hot topic. On news radio, there's a stock market update every few minutes. And there's always talk about interest rates, oil prices, Federal Reserve actions, trade deficits, job layoffs, and housing starts. These concepts all have a big impact on our daily lives, including how secure jobs are and how much certain things cost. Most of this information just goes right over your kids' heads. But when topics such as these come on the air, it might help to explain them to your kids (unless they've learned them in school and can explain them to you!). Once they know what the lingo means, they'll start to pay more attention to future broadcasts.

Games Kids Can Play

Games aren't only about winning and losing: They're an important way we all learn certain concepts and strategies. When it comes to kids and money, games can be especially useful because they teach money ideas appropriate to certain age levels in a fun way.

Financial Building Blocks

Computer games are more popular than board games. Sales figures tell the story: Sales of board games currently amount to only a quarter of the sales for computer and video games. The old-fashioned board game can't compete for the attention of most children, who now gravitate toward computer and video games. The main reason, say kids, is the excitement generated by electronic formats.

Obviously, math skills are an important aspect of understanding money ideas, so games that enhance math skills are certainly worth consideration. But math skills aren't the only component to understanding money ideas. Becoming comfortable with economic terminology and ideas is another key aspect of learning about money matters.

37

Piggybank on It

Playing board games not only lets your child enjoy the game and the company (with you or friends playing along), but it also presents an opportunity for you to discuss concepts that may arise from the game. For example, if you're playing Monopoly with your child, you can explain the difference between owning and renting something.

Board Games

Before there were computers and video games, children used to pass rainy days playing board games with friends, siblings, or parents. Today, computer and video games compete for your child's attention. Still, when they're not alone, a board game can be a great way to play and socialize at the same time, especially if you're involved playing it.

Not many board games can be used to teach money concepts, but here's a listing of some to consider. The age range is provided by the game manufacturer, but if you think your 7-year-old is up to playing Easy Money, go for it.

You can check out other money-related games and toys—and even buy them online—by visiting the Web site www.etoys.com.

Game	What It's About	Age Range
Cool Cash Bingo	Adding coins and making change	6–8
Easy Money	Spending money	9–adult
The Game of Life	Using money words and ideas	8–adult
Junior Monopoly	Buying amusement park attractions	5–9
Monopoly	Buying property, and building houses and hotels	7–adult
Payday	Getting from one payday to another	7–adult
Pit*	Understanding stock market concepts	Unknown
Presto Change-O	Earning and spending while re-balancing accounts	Unknown

This old game is expected to be reintroduced by Parker Brothers some time soon. It can still be found at garage sales and in thrift shops.

Computer and Video Games

Electronic games offer children an unbelievable range of activities. Most games, however, are combat-oriented. Touring the aisles of Babbages, CompUSA, KayBees, and other stores that stock computer and video games will quickly show you that it's not easy to find educational material for sale, let alone money-related educational material. A number of games enhance math skills, but these games don't teach money ideas. Still, some money-related games are available.

Here's a listing of computer games that can be used to teach money skills. You can find out about these and other games—including what they do and what they cost—at www.BrainPlay.com.

Game	About It	Age Range
Brain Bytes: Money Math	Counting money, making change	5–8
Math for the Real World	Solving math and money problems	10–14
Mighty Math Kindergarten, First and Second Grades	Learning math and basic money skills	5–8
Money Town	Learning money math, recognizing coins, making change, and spending and saving money	5–9

The good news is that you don't need to go out and buy any games: You can find them all on the Internet. While the games are usually free, you need to pay an online service, such as America Online (AOL) or some other service provider, to access the Internet.

Here's a list of some online games that can be used to learn about finance and develop money skills. For many online games, there's no winner—you just play to have fun and learn.

Piggybank on It

A big plus to most online games is that they can be played alone. Your child can use them even when there's no one else to play with.

Game	About It	Age Range
www.irs.gov/taxi/	Figuring after-tax earnings from summer jobs	16 and up
www.kidsbank.com	Teaching about money and how banks work	6–12
www.mainXchange.com	Trading virtual dollars on real publicly traded companies	12–20
www.moneyopolis.com	Solving problems of earning, spending, and saving money	12–14
www.ustreas.gov/kids/trez.html	Following Trez, an alley cat and Treasury resident, and coloring him in different activities	6 and under

The Web site of the Bureau of Engraving and Printing is developing a game called Count the Cash that will help kids learn whose face is on the different bills (keep checking the B.E.P. Kids' Page at www.moneyfactory.com/index.htm).

Other online stock market investing games are featured in Chapter 22, "Online Options for Kids."

Other Games

Games aren't limited to a board and game pieces or a computer, however. Word games can be played while driving a car, and quiz shows can be played by watching television. Unfortunately, most of these games aren't money-oriented; most test general knowledge and word skills.

One game stands out for covering money-related issues, though. *The Price is Right*, a show that has been on the air for decades, challenges contestants to determine what things cost. Viewers, like your kids, also can learn a thing or two about pricing from watching this game show.

You might even want to make up your own games for your child. Try games that might be done at quiet times, such as when your child is sick in bed or is tired after a busy day. These games also come in handy on trips in a plane, train, or bus (or a car, if you're not the driver) to make the time seem to pass quickly.

➤ *For elementary school kids.* Test their money IQ by asking them to name who appears on coins and bills currently in circulation. Don't know yourself? Here are the answers:

Denomination	Famous Person
Penny	Abraham Lincoln
Nickel	Thomas Jefferson
Dime	Franklin D. Roosevelt
Quarter	George Washington
Half-dollar coin	John F. Kennedy
$1 coin	Susan B. Anthony (Sacajawea starting in 2000)
$1 bill	George Washington
$2 bill	Thomas Jefferson
$5 bill	Abraham Lincoln
$10 bill	Alexander Hamilton
$20 bill	Andrew Jackson
$50 bill	Ulysses S. Grant
$100 bill	Benjamin Franklin
$500 bill	William McKinley

Denomination	Famous Person
$1,000 dollar bill	Grover Cleveland
$5,000 dollar bill	James Madison
$10,000 dollar bill	Salmon P. Chase

➤ *For middle-schoolers.* Ask them how many words they know that mean "money." Some answers (a surprising number of which relate to food) might include these: bills, bread, bucks, C-note, cabbage, cash, change, coins, currency, dinero, dough, fins, five-spot, gelt, greenback, moola, potatoes, sawbuck, two-bits.

➤ *For kids of any age.* You can make up anagrams from financial terms. Simple anagrams, involving only a few letters, are best for elementary school kids. The more difficult ones with a greater number of letters in the word are geared to older children. Here are some anagrams to get you started—don't let your child peek at the answers before she gives up.

Anagram	Solution
Enyep	Penny
Hasc	Cash
Satex	Taxes
Yemon	Money
Triced	Credit
Enyocom	Economy
Gogtream	Mortgage
Flitanion	Inflation

The Least You Need to Know

➤ Parents have the greatest influence on their kids when it comes to handling money.

➤ Talking about money ideas in your daily routine can present important information in a casual way.

➤ Seeing how money works in action is a more effective learning tool than reading about it from books.

➤ Computer and board games can be used to teach kids about money in a fun way.

Part 2
Money Concepts
Made Easy

When children think of money, they picture the coins they use to buy bubble gum and plastic toys from vending machines at the supermarket. To grown-ups, money refers to all means used to pay for things, including checks and credit cards. Understanding the big picture of money is the first step for children to learn about finances.

Money is a complex subject, so learning about it generally means introducing concepts at different ages, with more difficult ideas explained as children get older. For example, a 6-year old may grasp the idea of paper money and credit cards, but an older child is more likely to understand inflation (something even some grown-ups may have difficulty with).

In this part of the book, you move from the basic to the more complex principals of money. Using the techniques you've seen in the earlier chapters, you'll begin to help your children get a handle on the fundamental ideas of money they'll use for the rest of their lives. The chapters in this part are organized from the most simple ideas intended for the youngest children, to the more complex ideas meant for teens and up.

Chapter 5

What's Money?

In This Chapter

➤ Learning to identify money and make change

➤ Keeping a checkbook

➤ Paying with plastic

Children come into contact with money at a very early age. They're given coins to handle from the time they're old enough not to swallow them—and they usually use their coins in vending machines to get candy and gum.

But coins are only the tip of the money iceberg. As children get a little older, it's time to introduce them to the broader picture of money.

In this chapter, you'll discover what money concepts should be explained to children starting at a young age. You'll also find out how you can reinforce the learning experience with hands-on activities for them.

Intro to Money

As song writers Buddy DeSylva, Lew Brown, and Ray Henderson once said, the best things in life may be free—but most things cost money. Buying toys and candy, going to the movies, and renting video tapes all cost money. While our ancestors may have bartered for much of what they needed, trading a chicken for a doctor's house call or a basket of eggs for a bolt of calico, today we use hard cash.

Grown-ups know that the tiny dime is more valuable than the larger nickel and penny, but to children, this may be hard to understand. The very first step in learning about money and finance, therefore, is understanding what money is all about.

Financial Building Blocks

One of the best ways for kids to learn about money is to see how it's made. Take a free tour at the U.S. Mints in Philadelphia and Denver (there are no tours at the mints in San Francisco and West Point, NY). Or, consider touring the Federal Bureau of Engraving and Printing in Washington, D.C. Free tours are also given on Saturdays at the Main Treasury Building, the third-oldest federally occupied building in Washington (after the White House and the Capitol).

Money ABCs

Money is any medium of exchange that can be used to pay for goods and services and to measure the value of things. **Currency** is a term for a country's money in circulation—that is, coins and bills.

Piggybank on It

Coin collecting is certainly a great hobby for kids to get into. This hobby not only teaches about money, but it can prove financially rewarding as well (for more information, see Chapter 23, "Joys and Rewards of Collecting").

The two main skills that children need to know when it comes to money—and the earlier, the better—is being able to identify money and being able to tender money and make change. They probably won't learn these skills in school, either because the primary focus in most schools is math, not money. One expert suggested that kids can start to learn about money as soon as they're old enough to know not to put it in their mouth—you know your child better than anyone, so you know when you can start. Certainly, by the end of the first few grades in elementary school your child should have mastered counting money and making change. If your child is older or can already do these tasks, you can skip this section and move on to the section on using checks.

Identifying Money

Money comes in different shapes and sizes—it comes in metal and in paper. Different units of money have different values that can be used to pay for different things. Size doesn't count—it's the denomination of the money that matters. Adults take these simple facts for granted, yet they're precisely the things that prove problematic for children.

The important concept to convey to your child is that money is based on the dollar. Coins are merely fractions of that unit; bills are multiples of that unit. One hundred pennies, or one-cent coins, make up a dollar; Twenty nickels, or five-cent coins, make up a dollar; and so on.

Financial Building Blocks

Coins in circulation today are the Lincoln penny, the Jefferson nickel, the FDR dime, the Washington quarter, and the Kennedy half-dollar. The Susan B. Anthony dollar coin is still in circulation; starting in 2000, the Sacajawea dollar coin will start to circulate.

Bills in circulation today include the $1, $2, $5, $10, $20, $50, and $100 bills. Distribution of bills in denominations of $500, $1,000, $5,000, and even $10,000 ceased back in 1969.

Understanding that money is based on the dollar unit allows you to explain about equivalents: that 10 pennies will buy the same as one dime; that four quarters will buy the same as a dollar bill. Ask your child to think of how many combinations of coins might equal 25¢ (for example, three nickels and one dime). The answer: 14 combinations (which includes simply using one quarter). You can repeat this game with other amounts, such as 50¢ or a dollar.

Ever wonder what "E Pluribus Unum" means? Are your kids stumped by the mint marks on coins? You can find the answer to these and other questions on coins at the Department of the Treasury's Learning Vault (www.ustreas.gov/opc/opc033.html). Find answers to questions on paper currency at www.ustreas.gov/opc/opc0034.html.

Making Change

The word *change* refers to the loose coins you have in your pocket. It also means the difference between what something costs and the money that's been tendered to pay for it. Every adult has had the experience of facing a teenage cashier who can't make change. Like teenagers who can't tell time because of digital watches, they can't make change because of today's cash registers that tell them what the change should be. In effect, these cashiers never learned the simple task of making change. If you don't want your child to be that teenager, it's up to you to make sure that the idea of making change doesn't become a lost art. Making change can be easily mastered once your child is familiar with the different coins and bills, and can count in multiples of these pieces of money.

Piggybank on It

No matter what your age, it's always important to count the change you're given. Doing this is the same as having made the change yourself (you have to check the change-maker's math). It's also a good practice to announce the amount of money you're tendering (for example, "here's $20") so that the change-maker won't short you on the change.

As with tying shoes, there are different ways to accomplish the same thing. The easiest technique for making change is counting forward from the amount spent to the amount tendered. For example, if an item cost 68¢ and the amount tendered is three quarters, or 75¢, then count forward with coins from the 68¢ cost, as follows: 69, 70 (with a penny each), and 75 (with a nickel). In other words, the change should be 7¢ (two pennies and one nickel).

An alternative technique is the subtraction method. Here, subtract the cost of the item from the amount tendered. Repeating the earlier example, subtract 68¢ from 75¢, which is 7¢. Then count out the coins to equal 7¢ (two pennies and one nickel).

Using Checks

After a child understands about coins and bills, it's time to explore other ways to pay for things. As an adult, you know that cash isn't necessarily king, as the saying goes. It's not a good idea to send cash through the mail or to carry a lot of cash when shopping, so other methods of payments should be used. One method is to pay by personal check.

A check isn't only a mark that's made when an assignment has been handed in or a task completed—it's also a piece of paper that represents money. A personal check works like cash. As you know, you give it to someone to whom you owe money. That person can turn your check into cash or use it just like money. A check is like a promise to the person you're giving it to that the amount you've written on the check is backed up by money in a checking account.

A checking account is a type of bank account. Checking accounts aren't investment accounts because you generally don't earn any interest on the money you keep in the account. Depending on the type of checking account, you may have to keep a certain amount of money there (called your *balance*). The balance generally is figured on a monthly basis and is called a minimum monthly balance. That balance on average during the month can't dip below a set amount (such as $100 or $1,000). If it does, you'll be charged a fee.

Financial Building Blocks

Personal checks aren't the only checks around: Money orders can be used just like checks. A **money order** is a check that's bought from the post office or a commercial business (such as a supermarket or a check-cashing store) in the amount needed. (Money orders from the post office are called postal money orders.) In any case, there's a small fee for each money order.

A check is proof that you've paid for something. A check is readily accepted as payment by most places and should be used instead of cash when sending payment by mail.

Younger children don't have any need for a checking account. They should know what a checking account is and what it's used for, but they don't need one of their own. However, once a teenager starts to earn money or goes off to college, it may be helpful to have a checking account to pay school telephone bills and other expenses. When your child is in high school, it becomes necessary for her to learn how to write a check, keep tabs on the account, and balance the checkbook.

Writing a Check

If a child has never written a check before, it usually takes only a few minutes to explain how to do so. Just follow these steps while referring to the picture of a check that follows:

➤ Enter the date in the space provided at the top right of the check. It doesn't matter whether you write "January" or use the number "1" to signify that month.

➤ On the line that says "Pay to the Order of," you write the name of the person or company you owe. Your child doesn't have to write "Mr." or "Mrs."; just the person's name will do.

➤ At the end of the line for "Pay to the Order of," you enter the amount of the check in numerals. Be sure to put a decimal after the dollar amount. It's helpful to write the cents as a fraction as well, the numerator of which is the amount of the cents and the denominator of which is "xx."

➤ On the next line, write out in words the amount of dollars in the check and the word "and," and then enter in numbers the amount of cents. For example, write "Twenty-one and 13 cents." Again, use the "xx" under the cents amount.

➤ On the line in the lower-right corner, your child should sign (not print) his name as it appears on the account.

➤ On the line in the lower-left corner (sometimes labeled "Memo"), your child can—but doesn't have to—enter what the check was for. This serves as a reminder of why you made the payment. If the check is for payment on an account, your child can enter his customer or account number on this line.

Photo of a check.

Heather Smith
987 Main Street
Anyplace, CA 90000

$\frac{50-235}{219}$761

3334

_____ 19 _____

PAY TO THE
ORDER OF _____ | $

_____ DOLLARS

YOUR BANK
Anyplace, CA 90000

MEMO _____   _____ MP

⑆008745352⑆ ⑈0090235211⑈ 3334

BNY STYLE 62

Keeping Track of Things

Your teenager should want to know how much is in his account at any given time. This is important so that he doesn't go overboard and write a check for more money that he actually has. The only way to keep track is to record all his checking activities.

Watch Your Step

Be sure to subtract any fees and charges to the account. For example, there's generally a fee for printing your checks, and there may be monthly or per-check fees as well. To reduce fees and charges, college-age children may be eligible for special student accounts that generally have modest or no fees and no required minimum monthly balances.

When a check is cashed by the person he has given it to, the bank subtracts that amount from his account. A subtraction from the account is also called a *debit*.

The record of checking activities is made in a *check ledger*, called a *checkbook register*. To keep track of the account balance, enter into the check ledger the amount of money that's been put into the account to open it. This is called a *deposit* (it's also called a *credit*). Then, every time a check is written, enter information about the check—the date it was written, the check number, who it was written to, and the amount of the check. Subtract this amount from the balance. Every time money is added to the account, this amount is also added to the balance. As your child can see, the balance is constantly changing.

Balancing a Checkbook

Now that your teenager knows how to write checks, she'd better make sure that she reviews her checking account each month. Each month the bank sends a statement showing all checking account activity. Some people simply rely on the bank statement to verify what's in their account. Believe it or not, however, banks make mistakes (and so can your child when she enters in the check ledger deposits she has made or checks she has written). Mistakes and overcharges to the account or other problems can be corrected if she balances the checkbook each month and brings the error to the bank's attention.

It's essential to keep track of how much she's spending, however, so that she doesn't bounce a check. To do this, she must not only be accurate when entering amounts in you're the check ledger, but she also must balance the account each month.

Balancing a checkbook isn't hard to do; it just sounds difficult. Follow these five easy steps (and the figure that follows) to find the correct bank balance.

1. Have your teenager write down his closing balance. The closing balance can be found on the front of the bank statement.

2. Add any deposits he's made that did not yet appear on his statement (because he made them *after* the closing date of the statement).

3. Add the amounts he wrote down in steps 1 and 2.

4. Total up all checks that he has written but that have not yet cleared (because they aren't shown on his statement as having been cashed by the party to whom he wrote the check).

5. Subtract the amount in step 4 from the amount in step 3. This is your child's balance.

Money ABCs

Bouncing a check means that there isn't enough money in the account to cover the amount of the check. Bouncing a check is costly (banks levy bank charges), can hurt your child's credit rating (explained later in this chapter), and can even result in criminal charges if he knowingly writes a rubber check (one that will bounce).

Balancing a checkbook doesn't mean putting the checkbook on your head and try to keep it from falling off. Rather, it means reviewing all deposits and payments to make sure that they even out and that the bank (or you) didn't make any mistakes.

Steps	Amount
Step 1: Closing balance	$_____
Step 2: Add unreported deposits	+_____
Step 3: Total of steps 1 and 2	$_____
Step 4: Add uncleared checks	_____
Step 5: Subtract step 4 from step 3 to find the balance	$_____

If your child's numbers don't agree with the bank's numbers, he should double-check his figures. Make sure that he has subtracted any charges for ATM withdrawals or checking account fees, or that he has added any interest to which he's entitled. If, after double-checking the balance, he still think he's right, he should contact the bank and explain the discrepancy. If the bank is wrong, it will adjust the account. But don't expect adjustments if your child waits many months after the month in which the error arose. He should be sure to balance his checkbook each month to catch mistakes immediately.

Paying with Plastic

Checks aren't the only alternative to cash: there's also plastic cards. Two types of plastic cards can be used to pay for things:

➤ Credit cards

➤ Debit cards

While children are living at home, using plastic as a form of payment may not be essential. However, when they go away to college or move out, they'll probably need to have credit cards or other forms of plastic to pay for things. Teenagers can find general information written by college students about credit and debit cards at the Web site www.cohums.ohio-state.edu/english/People/Hogsette1.eng.htm).

Piggybank on It

Your can use a computer program, such as Quicken, to keep track of your child's finances. These programs can balance a checkbook automatically.

Credit Cards

If your kids watch television, they can't avoid seeing Jerry Seinfeld touting the benefits of using the American Express Card or John Lithgow pushes MasterCard. These are credit cards that can be used to pay for goods and services at businesses that accept them. Typically, stores display a picture in their front windows of the cards that can be used for payment there.

Money ABCs

Credit cards allow you to pay for things up to your credit limit (a fixed dollar amount that you are notified about when you receive your card). For example, you may have a $1,000 credit limit, allowing you to buy up to $1,000 in items with the card. Once you pay this amount back, you can again spend up to this limit.

Debit cards are tied to your bank account and allow you to spend up to the amount in your bank account. Your spending limit is determined by the amount in your bank account.

Different types of credit cards exist: bank cards (which are general credit cards—MasterCard, VISA, and Discover), general credit cards (issued by companies other than banks—American Express, Diners Club, and Carte Blanche), and proprietary cards (issued by stores for use only at certain stores—Macy's, Express, and The Limited).

Unless you decide to give them a duplicate of your credit card (you can ask for a second card from the issuer), your children can get their own credit cards by applying for one. They usually have to be at least 18 before they can get one.

As a person gets older, applying gets easier because applications are sent to consumers frequently (it seems like almost daily). College kids are bound to receive a number of offers for credit cards. The credit card company determines whether a person is a good credit risk because it expects that the credit card holder will repay whatever is charged on the card. If your child is approved for the card, she then can spend up to her credit limit.

Financial Building Blocks

According to statistics from the Phoenix Home Life Insurance Co., about 60 percent of all college students have credit cards. Unfortunately, only 20 percent know what the term "buying on credit" means. This lack of understanding about the use of credit cards leads to big financial trouble.

When she applies for her first credit card, she may be turned down even though she never has failed to pay a bill before. The reason: She has little or no credit history. However, she may be able to convince the company to issue her a card—even with a low starting credit line—if she takes the initiative. When sending in the application, include a brief letter explaining that although she has no credit history, she'll be a good credit risk for the company because she understands her obligation to make timely payments and that the company should give her a try. This strategy has worked for several people I know.

Watch Your Step

It's not a good idea for you to give your child unlimited use of your card or to co-sign for a separate card for your child. If your child is irresponsible about debt, it could ruin your credit history.

Two types of bank credit cards exist: unsecured and secured. Unsecured cards are issued on the basis of your good credit. Secured cards require you to deposit a set amount, such as $250, with the bank issuing your card. You then receive a credit line equal to the amount you have on deposit. Using a secured credit line is costly because you may earn little or no interest on your deposit. However, it's a good way to build up a favorable credit history.

Each billing cycle (typically every 28 or 30 days) your child will receive a bill. Check it carefully because mistakes can be made (for example, he may be charged for something he didn't buy). The bill contains a lot of information that he should know about: It shows all purchases for the month, a minimum required payment amount, and space for the payment he decides to make. If he didn't pay his bill from the prior month in full, the bill also will show the interest your child been charged.

The beauty of using a credit card is the convenience of not having to carry cash with you. A credit card also gives you an extra benefit: You get until your next bill to pay for an item. This is sometimes called a *float*.

How many credit cards should a person have? Even if he's given the cards by the credit card company without any effort on his part, it's generally not a good idea to have more than one or two cards. First, the cumulative credit lines can lull him into buying over his head and going into debt. Second, he'll have too many bills to keep track of. Third, credit cards can cost money just for owning them—many (but not all) charge an annual fee of $20 or more.

A credit card can behave like an ATM card (see an upcoming section in this chapter), allowing your child to receive cash if he has arranged with the credit card company to get a PIN number. Of course, the amount of cash he can withdraw cannot exceed his credit limit. Cash advances also come at a premium because interest starts to accrue immediately; there may be fees and higher interest rates for cash advances than for regular purchases.

Certain credit cards are called *rebate cards* because they entitle you to certain paybacks if you spend certain amounts (www.cardlearn.com/rebate.html). The most popular rebate card, now used by more than 42 million Americans, is Discover. This card gives you a cash rebate of 1 percent of your annual purchases. Some MasterCard and VISA cards give frequent flyer miles and other benefits.

Debit Cards

A debit card looks and feels like a credit card, and it can be used for payment of goods and services in just about any place that accepts bank credit cards. However, these types of cards are very different.

A debit card doesn't require your child to prove you're a good credit rating. It doesn't allow your child to buy on the float. A person can get a debit card because she has a bank balance in a checking or savings account. The debit card is then used in the exact same way as writing a check or making a personal withdrawal from that account. The amount of the payment is subtracted from your child's bank account usually within three days of the purchase.

Money ABCs

A **credit history** isn't a story written in a book—it's a record of a person's borrowing and payment habits over the course of time. Credit histories are maintained by credit reporting bureaus, which are commercial companies that supply this information to credit card companies, banks, and other lenders.

Watch Your Step

If your child doesn't pay his bill in full each month, he will rack up interest charges. Over time, he can wind up paying more in interest than he charged on the card. The lesson: Urge your child to spend only within his ability to pay. Stress the importance of paying the bill in full each month to avoid interest charges.

If your child is in college, she may already have a debit card and doesn't even know it. Her school may issue a student ID card that she can use to pay for items on campus, such as food, laundry, and soda machines (for example, at SUNY Albany, it's called the Podium Card). These student IDs often allow you to deposit funds for your child (usually up to $500), from which she can then draw on by using the card.

Even if your child is not in college, she may already be using a type of debit card. *Special purchase debit cards*, such as phone cards, allow a person to use as cash the amount that's put into the card. A $20 phone card, for instance, gives your child $20 worth of phone use.

ATM Cards

Another type of plastic card is becoming commonplace as well. If your child has a bank account, she can access the money *other* than by writing a check or making a withdrawal in person. She simply uses an automated teller machine (ATM for short) to withdraw money from her account. Withdrawals must be made in multiples of $20 (for example, $20, $40, or $100). ATMs can also be used to charge cash on a credit card.

To use an ATM machine, two things are required (besides money in the bank):

➤ An ATM card issued by the bank (there's no fee for issuing the card to your child)

➤ Your child's own personal identification number, called a PIN for short

ATMs are everywhere—in malls, in airports, and on just about every corner. They create a temptation to get at money on a whim, without regard to a budget. Stress to your teenager that she shouldn't be so casual about using ATMs, for these reasons:

➤ She can use up her money in a flash.

➤ She usually pays a fee each time she uses her ATM card. These fees can mount up to many dollars each month if she's not careful.

Money ABCs

A **personal identification number (PIN)** is a three- to five-digit code number that your child selects as her personal identifier to access her account through an automated teller machine.

Piggybank on It

Debit cards are safer to use than credit cards because your child can *never* spend more money than she has. Purchase will not be authorized in an amount that's more than what's in your child's checking account.

Watch Your Step

The only two people who should know your child's PIN number are your child and his banker (he probably won't tell even you). Tell him to memorize the number: He shouldn't put this number in his wallet because if it's stolen, the thief can gain access to the account.

A debit card can act as an ATM card, so a separate card to withdraw money from a checking account isn't needed.

The Least You Need to Know

➤ The U.S. money system is based on the dollar, with coins being fractions of that unit and bills being multiples of it.

➤ A checking account is important for college-age and older children to use when paying their bills, but high-schoolers should know what a checking account is and how to manage it.

➤ Balancing a checkbook will avoid bouncing a check for lack of funds and will make sure to catch banking or personal errors.

➤ Credit cards can be used to pay for things up to the holder's credit limit.

➤ Debit cards allow payments up to the funds in the account against which the cards are drawn.

➤ ATM cards can be used to access funds in checking accounts without having to cash a check.

Chapter 6

Economics 101

In This Chapter

➤ Getting a grip on the price of things

➤ Learning the difference between necessities and luxuries

➤ Looking at commercialism

➤ Tipping

As kids get older, they need to learn how the world works from a money point of view. After all, they're going to be out there soon enough making their own spending and investing decisions. These decisions can't be made wisely without understanding certain money ideas. Many of these money concepts are difficult to explain but are essential to becoming a financially responsible adult.

In this chapter, you'll learn about money ideas that adults take for granted but that should be explained to children. You'll see that understanding what things cost isn't an easy concept to grasp. You'll also see that finding out about things like inflation add a whole new dimension to the world of money. You'll see how and where commercialism works on your child and will learn what you can do to limit its effects. You'll also learn what kids should know about tipping.

What Things Cost

Kids have no idea what things cost. When they're very young, there's no difference to them between the cost of a candy bar and the cost of a video game. To take things one step further, there's no difference to them between a low-priced video game and a high-priced one. Price is meaningless to them.

Older kids may know what things cost, but they may have little idea about whether they're getting value for their money. They may know that a pair of sneakers costs $100, but are they worth the money?

That's why it's important to help your child understand what things cost and whether there's value in that cost. There are several ways you can do this.

➤ *Give your child an allowance.* Nothing teaches kids quicker about what things cost than by giving them their own money to spend. This decision-making freedom allows them to get the feel of prices. Allowances are discussed in Chapter 8, "Making Allowances."

➤ *Shop and talk.* When you're out shopping with your child, show him price tags. Point out when things are costly or not. In KayBees, I overheard a parent telling a young child that a particular game cost only $8. The parent said, "This is a good buy." Explain about discounts and sales.

➤ *Let your child read up on things. Zillions*, the *Consumer Reports* magazine for children, can help kids become smart consumers. This magazine helps them see through ad hype and make informed decisions.

➤ *Get schools to educate kids about commercialism and ad propaganda.* The Consumers Union, a nonprofit organization that publishes *Consumer Reports*, advocates making schools ad-free zones and taking other initiatives to education our children. You can learn about its position at www.consunion.org/other/captivekids.htm (explained in greater detail later in this chapter).

Money ABCs

You can tell your child that a **sale** is a mark-down of the price of an item. The sale price can be expressed as a dollar amount—the sweater that originally cost $40 is on sale for $34. Or, the sale could be expressed a percentage off the original price—20 percent off.

Necessities Versus Luxuries

As a parent, you know that the weekly grocery bills are necessities, while dinner out on a Saturday night can be classified as a luxury (even though you may feel like you *need* it). This distinction between what you can't go without and what is only icing on the cake is something that you've learned.

But your child may think that getting a new wardrobe every season is essential. This thinking isn't confined to your elementary school child, either: Your teenager may still harbor this belief. In her mind, getting the wardrobe may help her social standing with her peers, but you know that it isn't a necessity. Having a pair a shoes that fits and a warm winter coat are necessities.

Understanding this distinction while kids are young will help them make good decisions on how to spend their money when they're older.

Help your child to learn the difference between what he needs and what he might want or wish for by letting him make a list. In the first column, have him list the things he requires; in the next column, have him write down all the things he may desire. (Some hints on necessities in addition to rent, food, heat, and telephone include school, doctor's visits, medicines, and clothing.)

Necessities	Luxuries

As your child will see after completing the list, many things must be paid for first before the extras can be considered. You also should review his list and help him reassign certain items from necessity to luxury. Explain that no matter how important that video game may seem to him, it's not a necessity!

As children get older and can distinguish between necessities and luxuries, the next step is learning about value for one's money. This concept is explored in Chapter 13, "So Many Choices (So Little Money)."

Planning Purchases Versus Impulse Buying

It has been estimated that as much as 20 percent or more of our money is wasted because we make unplanned purchases without regard to the value of what we're buying or whether we really need it. Unless you show your children how to plan for purchases, they also will become impulse buyers and waste their money.

On your next shopping excursion with your child to the supermarket, the drug store, or the mall, make a shopping list. These are the things you've planned for.

Piggybank on It

Learning to make lists is a habit that can serve your child throughout his life. He'll get used to thinking ahead—not only about how he spends his money, but also about how he spends his time.

While shopping, check the list to make sure that you've bought what you planned to. You don't want to overlook anything, but at the same time, you want to avoid purchasing luxuries that you didn't intend to.

When you come home, check your packages. Compare what's in them to what was on your list. Were there things in your packages that you didn't planned for? If you went overboard this time, make sure that you're more careful on your next shopping excursion.

Your child can make her own shopping list for the things she needs to get (even if you're paying for the things on the list). Let her make a shopping list when you're out together looking for school supplies on opening school day, or when you're hunting for school clothes or Christmas presents.

Deconsumerizing Your Kids

Kids are big consumers, and corporate America knows it. That's why retailers target kids with more than 30,000 commercial messages each year. These ads aren't limited to the TV they see at home, the billboards along the road sides, or the print ads in magazines and newspapers, either: They're also presented in the classroom every day.

Financial Building Blocks

Kids' purchasing power is powerful. According to a report by Consumer Union on the commercial pressures of kids at school, elementary school children spend about $15 billion a year, most of it on toys and games, food and beverages, and clothing. These children also influence their parents' spending to the tune of $160 billion; teenagers spend $57 billion of their own money each year.

As parents, you may not even be aware of how great the commercial pressure is on your kids. When we were kids, ads aimed at kids generally were limited to cereal and toy commercials during Saturday morning cartoons. Today, the ads are everywhere. As a parent, you can't do too much to shield your child from being bombarded by advertising. But you can help her become more critical of what she sees and hears.

Most troubling for you and your child is the incursion of commercialism into the classroom. Corporations are now providing educational materials, programs, contests, and even product giveaways to be used in the classroom. It's no accident that Apple is trying to put computers in every classroom in America. It's not altruism that's motivating the company; it's the hope that using its product will develop brand loyalty in the children who continue to buy Apple Computers when they're older. This has several implications for kids:

➤ The materials come with a price tag: a logo, message, or other connection with a commercial enterprise. They're really just advertisements designed to heighten brand recognition. The companies give the materials to schools because they anticipate that the school children who use them will then buy these products later.

➤ The materials may be biased or contain incomplete information. They may favor the company that's distributing them, giving kids a one-sided or incomplete view of things.

Actions for Changing Your Schools

As a parent, you need to know what's going on in the classroom. While corporate educational materials help schools stay on budget and keep school taxes down, they also create some problems to watch for. How you address these problems in your community—making schools ad-free zones, adopting guidelines for materials, providing special education on commercial messages to help kids analyze ads—is up to you and your community.

You can do at least six things to limit the commercial indoctrination of your kids in the schools:

1. Check out your child's school for commercialism. Walk through the schools and observe where ads—subtle and not so subtle—are found. You can use a survey designed for this purpose that's available from the Center for Commercial-Free Public Education, at www.commercialfree.org/walk.html.

2. Understand where the commercialism is coming from. If your child's school uses Channel One, stay tuned. You may have just found your primary target.

Financial Building Blocks

Channel One is a so-called "educational channel" that's being broadcast in 40 percent of our country's middle and high schools. Although it does provide educational material, surveys show that the majority of air time is really a form of advertising directed at kids.

3. Find out what school policy is for corporate-sponsored materials. Ask at the school office, and also ask the head of the school board and the president of the PTA. A policy may already be in place that's just not being followed. If so, your job is to bring that failure to the attention of the powers that be.

Financial Building Blocks

Society of Consumer Affairs Professionals in Business (SOCAP) and IOCU guidelines call for requiring all educational material to meet minimum standards of accuracy, objectivity, completeness, non-commercialism, and other criteria. These guidelines can be found at www.consunion.org/other/captivekids/guidelines.htm.

4. Get the school board to ban advertising or corporate logos on instructional material, sports uniforms, and equipment. This isn't an overnight process, though. It requires persistence on your part to drum up support and create a willingness in the community to pick up the financial slack created by tossing out corporate support.

5. Raise community awareness of the problem. Write a letter to the editor when appropriate to make your position known. Talk at PTA meetings. Try to get the topic of commercialism scheduled as a PTA program to spread awareness of the problem.

Money ABCs

Marketing is a process by which people get what they want through creating and exchanging products and services with each other for value (money, products, or services).

Advertising, a part of marketing, is how a company tells the public what it has to sell.

Promotion, another part of marketing, is a way of stimulating an immediate sale.

6. Turn for help to organizations already fighting commercialism in the schools. They'll be able to suggest steps you can take, if you haven't already done so. These organizations include those listed here:

Center for the Analysis of Commercialism in Education (www.uwm.edu/Dept/CACE/)

The Center for Commercial-Free Public Education (www.commercialfree.org)

Consumers Union (www.consumersunion.org)

Corporate Watch (www.corpwatch.org)

Rethinking Schools (an educational journal) (www.rethinkingschools.org)

Actions for Countering Commercialism

Helping to change the school environment is one important thing you can do to limit the commercialism to which your child is subjected every day. After all, she's a captive audience in the classroom.

But whether or not the schools change, you as a parent can educate your child so that she'll be more savvy in evaluating ad messages and making consumer choices.

➤ Limit the time your child watches TV. This will cut the number of ads to which she's exposed.

➤ Tell your child about Madison Avenue. It's not just a street in New York City; it's a synonym for advertising and the place where many marketing ideas are developed and disseminated.

➤ Explain what marketing is all about. As the saying goes, forewarned is forearmed.

➤ Discuss the impact of ads on what you and your child want to buy. Another useful adage, "Don't believe everything you see," applies here. Ads are designed to suggest something—quality, status, or some other attribute we'd all like to have. Just because the ads suggests this, however, doesn't make it so.

Money ABCs

A **tip** is money given as an additional payment for services. It's also called a **gratuity**.

Tips on Tipping

When you take early elementary kids to Denny's, they may be confused about why you've left some money on the table after you've eaten. They may even be tempted to pick it up, thinking you've merely forgotten it. After all, they don't have the vaguest idea that the money is a tip and that you've purposely left it on the table.

Tipping is a part of the way things work—it's also good manners. But it's up to you to explain what tipping is and to teach your child when and how to tip.

When Your Child Should Tip

Tipping started as a way of rewarding good service. Tips were viewed as gifts to servants. Today, tips are a part of the way we pay for things. Different countries have different customs on tipping

Piggybank on It

Tipping isn't mandatory—your child won't be arrested if he doesn't leave a tip in a restaurant. In fact, he should know that he shouldn't tip (or that he should leave only a minimum amount) if he has received especially bad service. Sometimes places don't treat kids right because they think they won't tip. If your child gets this treatment, he shouldn't reward the servers for bad behavior.

Watch Your Step

It's not necessary to tip a waiter if a gratuity has already been added to the bill automatically (the menu should specify that there's a fixed gratuity). However, even if this is so, a tip is still good manners if the service was exceptional.

Piggybank on It

An easy trick for figuring the tip for a restaurant meal is using a multiple of the tax. For example, in New York City, where the tax is 8.25 percent, doubling the amount of the tax on the bill will give a tip of 16.5 percent (not much more than the usual 15 percent). Where tax is 5 percent or so, it can be tripled to find the tip.

(in China, for example, it's an insult to tip). Here, however, tips are *expected* in certain situations. It's helpful for your child to know when it's appropriate to tip so that as he gets older and goes out in the world without you, he'll know what to do.

Your child might run into some of these more common places that call for tipping:

➤ *Restaurants*. Tip the waiter or waitress on the basis of the bill.

➤ *Taxis*. Tip the driver on the basis of the fare.

➤ *Pizza or other food delivery*. Tip the driver on the basis of the cost of the food.

➤ *Coat check attendant*. No tip is required if there's a charge for checking a coat. Otherwise, the tip is usually a fixed amount (see the following section).

➤ *Parking garage and valet parking*. Tipping here works similar to tipping for the coat check attendant: If there's a charge for valet parking, no tipping is required. Otherwise, follow the instructions that follow.

How Much to Tip?

Knowing when to tip is only half the battle. Your child also needs to know how much to tip and how to figure that amount. Here's a little guide to what's usually expected in the way of tips. This serves as only a guideline, though: Great service can always be rewarded with a larger tip, while poor service may not be worth any tip at all.

Type of service	Amount of tip
Wait staff	15 percent of bill (before the addition of tax)
Taxi driver	15 percent of fare
Food delivery person	$2 for a bill of $10 or less $2.50 for a bill of $10–$20 $3 for a bill of $20–$30 $3.50 for a bill of $30–$40 At least 10 percent for bills more than $40
Coat check attendant	$1 to $2 per coat
Parking attendant	$1 to $2 per car

The Least You Need to Know

➤ Young kids need to learn what things cost; older kids need to learn about value.

➤ Necessities are things that kids must have; luxuries are just things they'd like or wish they could have.

➤ Learn to avoid impulse buying by making a shopping list.

➤ Kids are inundated with commercial messages, even at school.

➤ Tipping, though not mandatory, is a part of the way we pay for things.

Chapter 7

Going Beyond the Basics

> ### In This Chapter
>
> ➤ Learning about economic forces
>
> ➤ Paying sales taxes
>
> ➤ Paying employment taxes when children work
>
> ➤ Claiming exemption from income tax withholding on a job

When children are in elementary school, inflation, taxes, and other grown-up subjects lie beyond the students' abilities. However, once kids start working part-time, go shopping on their own, and get out in the world, these economic factors can affect their paycheck and what it cost them to buy things. At that time, they should start to learn about more sophisticated economic factors at work. After all, these factors have a direct impact on what they have to pay for things, whether jobs are available for them, and what they actually net from their earnings.

In this chapter, you'll see what economic forces to tell your child about as he matures. You'll also see how you can help your child understand about the different kinds of taxes he'll pay, if he's not already paying them.

What's Our Economy All About?

In school, children may learn that the United States has a capitalist economy. They also may learn about historic events such as the Great Depression, but until they take a course in economics in college or their senior year in high school, they don't usually learn a lot about how the economy operates.

You might be asking yourself why kids need to know this. Good question. Economics sounds like a dreary academic activity, but it's not just for textbooks. Knowing about economics helps children to understand how things work. Kids are dealing with economic factors every day, even if they don't know it. When you start filling them in on some important financial issues, you might be surprised at the outcomes:

➤ Things that may make no sense to kids begin to come into focus, such as why a toy with a sale tag of $10 costs $10.80 when sales tax is applied at the checkout line.

➤ News reports they read about or hear on such topics as inflation and the price of crude oil start to make sense. A teenager will be able to understand why filling up the gas tank in the family car can vary from week to week.

➤ Taxes, a subject children may hear about in the news or when you're at the dinner table, are confusing to everyone. But children may already be paying taxes—on things they buy or on wages they earn. You don't have to be a tax expert to share what the different taxes are all about and how they can impact your child.

Money ABCs

Inflation is an economic condition that results from an increase in the money supply. It causes the value of things to fall and the price of things to rise. At its most basic level, inflation boosts the cost of goods and services.

Inflation

Grandparents can remember that a nickel used to buy a subway ride, a movie ticket, a pay telephone call, or a hot dog. Tell this to your child today, and he'd probably laugh. So what makes the same nickel subway ride of yesterday cost $1.50 today? A part of the explanation is *inflation.*

Financial Building Blocks

Historically, inflation has averaged about 3 percent a year. In the past several years, we have been in a low inflation environment (less than 3 percent). This low inflation is expected to continue in the foreseeable future, but many still remember double-digit inflation in the 1970s and early 1980s.

Why should kids be concerned with inflation? It can directly affect their buying power. Let's say your child receives a $10 allowance. If inflation is just 3 percent, then after one year your child would need $10.30 to buy the same things that her $10 allowance had in the previous year. It's not that she'd have to present $10.30 for an item marked $10; rather, the price of that $10 item may be increased for inflation, showing a price tag of $10.30. Kids have seen the price of a movie ticket jump from $6 to $7.50, and this increase can be explained in part by inflation.

If your child is a teenager and has a job, understanding inflation will put any salary increases in perspective. He'll want his wages to increase more than the rate of inflation so that the increase isn't just keeping pace with inflation; he'll want to make sure he's getting a real raise.

Other Economic Forces

Plenty of other technical terminology is bantered about these days when it comes to the economy. News radio reports may talk about economic forces every 10 or 20 minutes. Here are just some of the more common things your child may be exposed to and may want to know more about.

➤ *Unemployment figures.* Each month, the news reports on how many people are out of work and looking for jobs. You also hear reports about corporate layoffs and job creations. Unemployment figures can help explain to a 10-year old why his mother is out of a job, like so many other people. It's also useful for a job-hunting teenager to know whether unemployment is high or low. When she's looking for a summer job, low unemployment numbers means that job openings are abundant. If the unemployment rate is high, however, she should anticipate a lengthier job search and may have to settle for lower wages. Today, despite corporate layoffs, the economy continues to experience job creation, translating into more job openings than ever.

➤ *Interest rates.* You can't listen to a news report without hearing talk about interest rates, whether they're up or down. Children aren't interested in these rates because they primarily help you, the parent, in instances such as getting a lower-rate mortgage on your home. But younger children should know about

Money ABCs

The Dow is shorthand for the Dow Jones Industrial Average (DJIA), a composite of the prices of 30 stocks. The Dow is an index used to measure whether the stock market as a whole is up or down. The Dow is the most well-known average because it includes big companies that everybody knows, such as IBM, GM, and Kodak. But many other averages are around as well.

interest rates because these rates affect how they save their money and what they can expect to earn. Older children with bank accounts of their own will see how changes in interest rates affect what they earn on their savings. Teenagers with credit cards also may feel the effects of changing interest rates if they're paying finance charges on unpaid credit card balances.

➤ *The Dow.* As with interest rates, daily reports on where the Dow is at can't be avoided. Again, knowing about this benchmark can spark your child's interest in investing in the stock market. Middle school- and high school-age kids might play at investments by tracking real stocks without putting in any real money. Some may even become interested in becoming actual investors (as explained in Chapter 20, "Wall Street Tycoons Aren't Just Born…They're [Self] Made"; Chapter 21, "Mutual Funds Just for Kids"; and Chapter 22, "Online Options for Kids").

Money ABCs

Taxes are payments made to government. Income taxes are payments made on income you receive; such payments go to Washington toward the cost of running the country, or you may pay state income taxes to help cover these types of costs in your state. Sales taxes are payments charged on items you purchase; sales taxes go to state and local government. Other types of taxes include real estate taxes paid by homeowners, estate taxes paid when people die and leave a certain amount of assets, and luxury taxes on expensive goods.

Taxes Can Be Taxing

Taxes may be a constant topic of conversation among adults, but kids don't think about taxes at all. In fact, kids may not even know what taxes are. Yet children may already be taxpayers, even if they've never worked. They may have received gifts—when they were born, on their birthday, or at other events—that were invested for them. These gifts may have produced enough income to require a tax return to be filed on their behalf. You, as the parent, would have filed returns for your child and probably would have paid any taxes that were owed. But even if your child is not already paying taxes of some sort, she certainly will soon enough.

It's important for kids to understand not only what taxes are, but also when they should be taken into account.

Sales Taxes on Things Your Child Buys

Sales tax is a great opportunity for you to introduce your child to the concept of taxes. Sales tax is tangible and shows up in amounts that even in an elementary school child can grasp. It's also the tax that your child is bound to come in contact with first.

Suppose she wants to buy a 50¢ candy bar. Presenting 50¢ in a state that imposes a sales tax won't be enough to buy that candy bar. For example, if sales tax is 6 percent, then the cost of that candy bar isn't really 50¢; it's 53¢.

Perhaps you live in Alaska, Delaware, Montana, New Hampshire, or Oregon (or Alberta, Northwest Territories, or the Yukon) and you don't have any sales tax. It's still important to raise the topic. If you're driving with your child from your home in Oregon on U.S. 101 to California, for example, your child will pay sales tax on any candy bar she buys in California.

Explain that sales tax is a percentage of the cost of an item. The rate of tax is fixed by law, and it may apply to some items or services and not to others. For instance, medicines may be exempt from sales tax, while toiletries are not. In addition, different sales tax rates may apply to different items (for example, there may be a special rate on utility use and car purchases). Your child may also want to know what the sales tax is used for. As with other taxes, sales tax is a way for state government to raise money it needs to run—to pay government officials, to support schools, to provide assistance to the poor, to run prisons, and more.

In some states, there may be two parts to the sales tax: the state tax and the local (county or city) tax. The two parts are combined and just one total rate is imposed on a sale. What's the sales tax rate where you live? Let your child look at the following chart to see how widely rates can range, depending on where a person lives.

State	Rate*
Alabama	11 percent
Alaska	7 percent
Arizona	8.8 percent
Arkansas	6–8.625 percent
California	8.5 percent
Colorado	9 percent
Connecticut	6 percent
District of Columbia	5.75 percent
Florida	7.5 percent
Georgia	7 percent
Hawaii	4 percent
Idaho	7 percent
Illinois	9 percent
Indiana	5 percent
Iowa	7 percent
Kansas	7.9 percent
Kentucky	6 percent
Louisiana	10.75 percent
Maine	5.5 percent
Maryland	5 percent
Massachusetts	5 percent

continues

continued

State	Rate*
Michigan	6 percent
Minnesota	7.5 percent
Mississippi	7.25 percent
Missouri	8.225 percent
Nebraska	6 percent
Nevada	9.25 percent
New Jersey	6 percent
New Mexico	7.438 percent
New York	8.25 percent
North Carolina	6 percent
North Dakota	7 percent
Ohio	7 percent
Oklahoma	10 percent
Pennsylvania	7 percent
Rhode Island	7 percent
South Carolina	6 percent
South Dakota	6 percent
Tennessee	8.75 percent
Texas	8.25 percent
Utah	7.75 percent
Vermont	5 percent
Virginia	4.5 percent
Washington	8.5 percent
West Virginia	6 percent
Wisconsin	6 percent
Wyoming	6 percent

*This is the maximum rate within the state. The rate in your area may be lower if your county imposes less than the top rate within your state.

In Canada, there's a provincial sales tax in most of the provinces. There's also a federal Goods and Services Tax, called the GST, that's 7 percent throughout Canada. GST is similar to a value-added tax (a tax not adopted in the United States), which is an indirect sales tax added at each stage of production or distribution.

Province	Rate of PST*
British Columbia	7 percent
Manitoba	7 percent
New Brunswick*	8 percent

Province	Rate of PST*
Newfoundland*	8 percent
Nova Scotia*	8 percent
Ontario	8 percent
Prince Edward Island	10 percent
Quebec	7.5 percent
Saskatchewan	7 percent

These provinces pay a harmonized sales tax (HST), combining the provincial tax and the GST for a total rate of 15 percent.

Financial Building Blocks

There's no sales tax in Delaware, Montana, New Hampshire, and Oregon. (Alaska doesn't have a state sales tax but does have local sales taxes.) Kids in these states may not realize that if they're on a trip in another state, they pay sales tax on souvenirs and such.

Employment Taxes on Your Child's Earnings

When your teenager gets her first job at a store in the mall or with a company that provides her with a weekly paycheck, she may be in for sticker shock. That great paycheck she was expecting at the end of the week is a lot smaller than she expected. And you know why. It's a good idea for you to prepare your teenager for this reality by explaining what's going to be withheld from her paycheck.

Even though retirement is the farthest thing from your teenager's mind at this time, she may already be preparing for her own retirement. Because she's working, she's required to contribute part of her pay toward Social Security and Medicare. This combined amount is also called FICA. On her pay

Money ABCs

Social Security is a federal system to pay benefits to retired or disabled workers, their spouses, and their dependents. **Medicare** is a federal health care system primarily for those age 65 and older, but contributions to the system are made by all workers, regardless of their age.

73

stub, the taxes may be reported as separate amounts, and these amounts are subtracted from her pay. So, if she has worked for 15 hours at $8 per hour, she'll see withholding for Social Security and Medicare of $9.18. Instead of getting $120 (15 hrs. × $8/hour), she'll get $110.82 ($120 less withholding of $9.18).

What's the amount your child must pay toward Social Security and Medicare? Regardless of age or earnings, all workers pay 6.2 percent of their wages toward Social Security (there's an annual income cap above which no further taxes are imposed—that was $72,600 in 1999) and 1.45 percent of their wages toward Medicare (there's no income cap here). The employer pays the same amount, so if your child pays $10, his employer is also paying $10 under your child's Social Security number.

If your child works in someone's household—for example, as a baby sitter or an au pair—she isn't subject to FICA if her annual wages are less than a set amount ($1,100 in 1999). If she's under 18 and providing household services isn't her main occupation, then all her wages are exempt. If she's not exempt and her wages are more than the set amount for the year, then she must pay FICA. If the employer doesn't withhold your child's share from her pay, then the employer must pay both your child's share and the employer share of FICA.

Piggybank on It

Because income taxes affect what we can keep from our earnings *after* paying taxes (this is called **after-tax return**), we must take taxes into account when deciding how to invest our money. Some types of income are given special tax treatment—the income may be entirely tax free or may be subject to low capital gain rates.

If your child sets up his own business—for example, let's say that you own a lawn mower and leaf-blower and your child advertises that he's a gardener—then he's not an employee. Instead, he's considered self-employed and is solely responsible for paying Social Security and Medicare taxes. A self-employed person pays both the employee and employer share (called self-employment tax) if business profit (the amount if income from your child's services is more than his expenses) is at least $400.

To learn more about Social Security and Medicare and payroll withholding for these purposes, consult the Social Security Administration's Web site at www.ssa.gov/kids. This great site has different activities for younger kids and teens as well.

Income Taxes on Your Child's Wages and Investments

Another tax your child is sure to become familiar with (if he isn't already) is the income tax. There's the federal income tax, and most states also have a state income tax.

The income tax is a series of graduated tax rates levied on income from most sources, such as wages, interest from savings accounts, and cash dividends on stocks. Certain expenses and other subtractions are allowed before the tax is figured.

Federal income tax is a highly complex area. Still, even at a young age your child can master the basic concepts of income taxes. To learn more about income taxes, check out TAXinteractive (TAXi), an electronic learning laboratory at the Web site of the Internal Revenue Service (the government agency that oversees federal taxes) at www.irs.ustreas.gov/taxi.

Paying Income Taxes

One of the most common topics that grown-ups gripe about is taxes. In this case, it's income taxes that they're complaining about. They know it's their civic duty to comply (and not doing it can cost them more money or even a criminal charge), but complaining about how high taxes are is a national pastime. Your child can't help but pick up on the topic—if you're not complaining about it, then the news is reporting how Washington is going to tinker with the income tax system. It's helpful for you to separate truth from perceptions, especially once your child becomes a teenager.

In the United States, we have what's called a system of voluntary compliance. Taxpayers tell the government what their income is and what expenses they have, and they figure their tax accordingly. It's the honor system, but with a catch: Other parties also tell the government about your income and certain expenses. This is called information reporting, and it's the way government checks up on taxpayers. It's not a covert operation; you get copies of everything reported to the government.

Who reports to the government on your child's income and on payments he may have made? Here are some examples:

➤ Employers report on wages and other benefits your child earned on Form W-2. This form also shows federal, state, and local income taxes that he paid on his wages and benefits through withholding.

➤ Banks report on interest your child earned on Form 1099-INT.

➤ Corporations report on dividends they paid to your child on Form 1099-DIV.

Piggybank on It

No matter how young your child is, she may already be a taxpayer. Income taxes are dependent on income, not age. Even though you might do all the mechanics—completing the return, writing out the checks, and filing—your child is still the taxpayer.

Money ABCs

Withholding means that the person who owes you income of some sort, such as your wages, keeps back (withholds) a part of the amount and sends it to the government on your behalf.

➤ Brokerage firms and mutual funds report on proceeds from the sale of securities on Form 1099-B.

➤ Lenders report cancellation of debt of $600 or more, such as forgiveness of certain student loans (whether or not you child is required to report this cancellation of debt as income).

➤ Schools report student interest that your child or you have paid (if it's $600 or more) on Form 1098-E.

The government's computer uses this information to cross-check that what's been reported on the return is correct. If a different amount is reported, the taxpayer will get a notice from the government adjusting the tax bill.

Money ABCs

Liability means that something is owed. When talking about federal income taxes, liability refers to taxes that a person owes.

Money ABCs

A **dependent** is a tax term for someone who's under age 19, or under 24 and a full-time student. Someone who's older (for example, a 21-year-old who's not a full-time student) can still be considered a dependent if that person has income of less than $2,700 and if more than half of the person's support is provided by a parent or someone else.

There's another catch to this so-called honor system of taxes: It's called *withholding*. Most taxes in this country are paid through withholding, primarily on wages.

The government knows that withholding has been made on your behalf because it's done under a worker's Social Security number. Because tax has been withheld, the purpose of filing a return is to figure the exact amount of tax that should be paid, compare it with what was already paid, and settle up with the government (either pay extra or get a refund of an overpayment that has been made).

Opting Out of Withholding

When your child gets a job, she'll learn TAXinteractive (TAXi) soon enough what it means to have withholding taken from her paycheck beyond Social Security and Medicare taxes. Say she works for $6 an hour and works 15 hours. She won't actually pocket $90 from her labors because her paycheck will be reduced for Social Security and Medicare taxes, as well as income tax withholding.

At the time she's hired, she'll be asked by her employer to complete certain government forms. One of the forms is Form W-4, Employee's Withholding Allowance Certificate. This is an IRS form that tells the employer how much federal (and state) income taxes to withhold (subtract) from a worker's paycheck and submit to the government on the worker's behalf. For example, if your child earns $100, she may have $15 withheld for federal income taxes. That $15 is sent to the U.S. Treasury under her Social Security number and is treated as her tax payment. Before your teenager even applies for a job, you might want to go over Form W-4 with her. In this way, she'll be prepared to complete it if a job opportunity presents itself.

Generally, a worker tells the employer how many withholding allowances he wants to claim (none, one, two, or more) and then the employer does the rest. In most cases, someone who's single, such as your child, claims one allowance (for himself). This lets the employer figure withholding on the basis of his single status and his claim for one allowance. Your child also may be eligible to claim exemption from withholding so that no taxes are withheld. To claim exemption, your child must meet both of these conditions:

········· **Cut here and give the certificate to your employer. Keep the top part for your records.** ·········

Form **W-4**	**Employee's Withholding Allowance Certificate**	OMB No. 1545-0010
Department of the Treasury Internal Revenue Service	▶ **For Privacy Act and Paperwork Reduction Act Notice, see page 2.**	19**99**

1	Type or print your first name and middle initial	Last name		2	Your social security number

Home address (number and street or rural route)	3	☐ Single ☐ Married ☐ Married, but withhold at higher Single rate. **Note:** *If married, but legally separated, or spouse is a nonresident alien, check the Single box.*

City or town, state, and ZIP code	4	If your last name differs from that on your social security card, check here. **You** must call 1-800-772-1213 for a new card . . ▶ ☐

5	Total number of allowances you are claiming (from line H above or from the worksheets on page 2 if they apply) .	**5**	
6	Additional amount, if any, you want withheld from each paycheck	**6**	$

7   I claim exemption from withholding for 1999, and I certify that I meet **BOTH** of the following conditions for exemption:
     • Last year I had a right to a refund of **ALL** Federal income tax withheld because I had **NO** tax liability **AND**
     • This year I expect a refund of **ALL** Federal income tax withheld because I expect to have **NO** tax liability.
     If you meet both conditions, write "EXEMPT" here . . . . ▶ | **7** |

Under penalties of perjury, I certify that I am entitled to the number of withholding allowances claimed on this certificate, or I am entitled to claim exempt status.
Employee's signature
(Form is not valid
unless you sign it) ▶   Date ▶

8	Employer's name and address (Employer: Complete 8 and 10 only if sending to the IRS)	9	Office code (optional)	10	Employer identification number

Cat. No. 10220Q

➤ He had no federal tax liability in the prior year (even if he paid taxes, he received a full refund of payments).

➤ He doesn't expect to have any federal tax liability this year. If, in 1999 he earns no more than $4,300, he won't have any federal tax liability. If he's not sure whether he's going to be under or over this limit, he may want to forgo the exemption and pay the tax to make sure he has the funds to cover his liability. He can always get back any excess payments when his 1999 tax return is filed in 2000.

Your child cannot claim exemption from withholding if his income is more than $700 and includes interest, dividends, or other unearned income, and if he can be claimed as a dependent on another person's return (for example, you claim him as a dependent on your tax return). Let's say that your child had investments made on his behalf— bank accounts paying interest, or stock or mutual funds paying dividends. In this case, he may have other income that would require him to file a return, so he would be ineligible to claim exemption from withholding.

Filing a Tax Return

Once a year, taxpayers must go through the annual ritual of filing a tax return with the federal government (a state return may be required as well). No matter how young your child is, a tax return *must* be filed if her income is above what's called a filing threshold. This threshold changes each year. In 1999, a single taxpayer must file a return if she has wages of $4,300 or more, even though she's still your dependent.

Watch Your Step

A child under 14 with unearned income over a threshold amount ($1,400 in 1999) is subject to a "kiddie tax." This means that income over the threshold amount is taxed to the child, but at the parent's tax rates. In effect, it's as if the parent had earned the interest and dividend income instead of the child.

But even if she doesn't have income from a job (earned income), your child may have to file a return if her investment income (called unearned income) is over a threshold amount. This threshold was $700 in 1999. If she has both some earned income and some investment income, a return must be filed if the total of earned and unearned income is more than $700 *or* if her earned income is up to $4,050 and she has unearned income of at least $250.

As a parent, you're responsible for filing your child's tax return if he's a minor. You sign the return as the parent for your minor child. Use this time as a learning tool: Let your child see the tax return, and explain that it's investments in his name that generated the tax. Show what taxes are being paid. Don't worry that your child will think he's rich because of the income shown on the return. It's not his to spend now; as long as he's a minor, that money is still under your control.

The Least You Need to Know

➤ Learning things about the economy can help kids understand why things cost what they do.

➤ Economic forces can have an impact on a child's ability to get a job and how to invest money.

➤ Sales taxes boost the cost of things your children pay for.

➤ Regardless of age, children must pay the FICA tax if they work (or self-employment tax, if they have their own business and net at least $400).

➤ Parents must file tax returns for their minor child if the child's income is over a threshold amount (that amount changes each year).

Part 3
Money Makers for Kids

Kids can and should have their own money, and there are many different ways to get it. You can give it to them in the form of an allowance. They can earn it from a job or even a business they start up. Or, they can receive it as a present for some occasion. Some may even be fortunate enough to receive money as an inheritance from wealthy relatives.

This part of the book looks at the different ways in which your child may acquire money of his own. It's usually this money that helps the child learn to make decisions about spending and saving.

In this part of the book, you'll start with the issue of allowances—when to start them and how much to give. You'll move on to ways in which the child can earn his own money from a job or a business. Finally, you'll consider ways in which the child may come by money in other ways—many of which you have a hand in.

Making Allowances

The subject of allowances is a topic that can fill up a book all by itself. There are many aspects of an allowance to consider: if, when, and how much should be given, whether there should be strings attached, and whether you should tell your child how to spend it. Allowances are also a touchy subject in some families. Mom and dad may have different opinions about it, and money may be tight, with allowances viewed as a luxury rather than a necessity.

In this chapter, you'll get some guidance on when you should start a child's allowance (if you decide you want to start one at all). You'll get some help in setting the amount of the allowance, and you'll learn how to decide whether you should put any conditions on receiving the allowance. You'll also get some ideas on how much influence you should exert over your child about how he should use his allowance.

Allowing Allowances

Despite what your child may tell you to the contrary, the God-given rights enumerated in the Declaration of Independence of life, liberty, and the pursuit of happiness don't necessarily include an allowance. So don't feel that you *have* to give one to your child. However, there are certainly compelling reasons why you might want to start an allowance, besides the fact that your child will probably appreciate you more.

➤ *Instilling a sense of responsibility for money.* Your child must learn to hold on to money and not lose it. For younger children who are always losing gloves and notebooks, this is one way to teach responsibility for personal things.

➤ *Shifting the burden of decision making on spending money to your child.* The choice on how to spend allowance money rests primarily with your child, alleviating your responsibility for most routine money decisions. In turn, this can reduce friction between you and your child on this issue.

➤ *Teaching money concepts.* Having an allowance is good practice for the time when your child will have larger sums, such as a weekly paycheck, to handle. (Guidance on how to use allowance money is discussed later in this chapter.)

At the start, an allowance is usually given weekly. This limits the amount of money your child has to handle. And time goes slowly when a child is young—two weeks could seem forever to a 7-year-old.

But as your child gets into his later teens, you might consider shifting to a monthly amount. This is more in line with the traditional budgeting period and may be good practice for a lifetime of money management. It's also easier on you. And giving your teenager more financial responsibilities makes it possible to meet them. If you expect your 16-year-old to pay her own phone bill, a monthly allowance matches the monthly expense.

Some parents use a credit and debit system: They credit their kids the amount of their allowance each month. Then, as needed, their kids can draw from that amount. Of course, this system requires parents and kids to keep track of money in and money out, but it keeps kids from having a big chunk of money all at once. In effect, it's a way to monitor the money along the way. A more formal arrangement of this credit and debit system is to use a kit called ParentBanc that let's kids write checks against their allotted allowance. The kit can be found at some toy stores (or call 800-471-3000).

Using a credit and debit system has a second advantage: It's a good prelude for your child to see how a bank works. She'll be able to deposit her money in a bank and withdraw it as needed in the same way she did with your own credit and debit system.

Allowance Versus Spending Money

Some parents don't believe their kids need money in the form of an allowance. The reason: These parents may give their kids spending money whenever it's required. In affluent neighborhoods, pre-teens routinely are given virtually unlimited use of their parents' charge cards for a day at the mall.

Let's say that a group of kids wants to go to the movies. Parents who use the spending money route may give their kids enough cash for a ticket and popcorn. Or, if the kids instead want to buy a T-shirt at the mall, the parents give them $20 and expect change.

Financial Building Blocks

According to a survey by *Zillions*, the kids' magazine by *Consumer Reports*, 26 percent of children between the ages of 8 and 14 got spending money for the things they needed to buy. This compared with 43 percent of children in this age category who received an allowance.

You may decide you want to and can do both: give an allowance plus give spending money when required. Where your child is in elementary school, you can't expect her to save for sneakers out of a small weekly allowance. Instead, you'll give her an allowance to use as she wants, plus spending money for the bigger things she needs.

When you expect your child to pay for certain things, then you'll have to rethink the amount of money you might give as an allowance. For example, if you plan to cover the cost of clothing for your child in middle school, then the weekly allowance can be more modest than if you expect your child to buy some of his own clothing. With your high-schooler, you'll have to provide even more of an allowance as the responsibility for

Money ABCs

Spending money is cash given to your child for a specific purpose—a day at the video arcade, lunch at McDonalds, or shopping for sneakers. The money is restricted for its designated use. Generally, excess money over the cost of the designated use is returned to the parent.

paying for things shifts to him. As you'll see in Chapter 12, "Picking Up the Tab"; Chapter 13, "So Many Choices (So Little Money)"; and Chapter 14, "Buying on a Budget," shifting this responsibility is part of your child's education on the money management process.

What's the Norm?

Do most parents give their children an allowance? Depending on what survey you look at, you'll see that a majority of children in this country get an allowance. The thing you'll discover is that there's no one-size-fits-all allowance. You have to make your own decision when it comes to fixing the dollar amount.

Allowances aren't common before the age of 5. Experts and most parents agree that this age is just too young. (One survey actually found that a child as young as 1 was receiving an allowance!)

Most parents begin giving allowances when children start school, usually at 6 or 7 years old. This is when children can be expected to take some responsibility for things. They can hold onto a dollar bill without losing it, and they can make decisions about what to do with their money.

On the flip side, when should an allowance end? Some parents continue an allowance well into a child's 20s. Others end it when the child begins to work as a teenager or goes off to college. Obviously, the decision to end an allowance has just about as many variables as the one to start an allowance. But clearly, once your child is working full-time, there's no longer any need for your financial input.

If you want to see a compilation of a dozen different surveys conducted on allowances to get ideas on how much to give and when to start, click on pages.prodigy.com/kidsmoney/allstats.htm.

Piggybank on It

Whatever your decision, your child's sex shouldn't have anything to do with the dollar amount of the allowance. Boys and girls should be paid the same (and statistics show that they generally are).

How Much to Give

There's no one dollar amount that's appropriate for all kids. The amount you decide on should be sufficient to provide your child with some extra money so he'll learn how to handle it. There's no educational benefit in setting an allowance at an amount at which it's already decided how it will be spent before it's even received.

Many factors go into fixing an allowance. The four main ones are listed here:

➤ *Your child's age.* Obviously, the older your child, the bigger the allowance (up to a certain point, at which your child may become too old for an allowance).

➤ *Your family income.* Only you know how much your family can afford to allocate to allowances.

➤ *Where you live.* Maybe keeping up with the Joneses isn't high on your list of priorities and you frequently tell your child, "I don't care that Jimmy Jones has this or does that." But, realistically, the neighborhood you live in can certainly influence how much allowance you give your child. What your child's best friend receives may not be a deciding factor, but it's a factor nonetheless.

➤ *What the allowance is supposed to cover.* If you expect your teenager to buy all his own clothing from his allowance, then the dollars paid to him each week must be sufficient to allow for this extensive purchase. If you supplement an allowance with spending money, then a less generous allowance may be in order.

Your Child's Age

Young children should get a smaller allowance than older children. While some families give the same allowance to all their kids even though they're of different ages, this isn't the usual approach. Most give more money as to their older kids than younger ones.

Using a rule of thumb to set an allowance is only a starting point. An allowance of $1 per week may be okay for a 10-year-old, but $15 may not be enough for a 15-year-old. You need to make some realistic judgments about what the allowance will buy.

As your child gets older, you'll have to adjust the allowance. Part of this adjustment is simply because of added age. Because your child is older, she must pay for more things and needs more money to do it. For example, being at college means that your child has to pay for many of the things you used to buy when she was at home, such as toiletries and the newspaper. Of course, inflation also puts pressure on you to increase allowances so that your child's buying power isn't eroded.

What if your children are of different ages? Generally, you'll want to give them an allowance appropriate to their age. If they're close in age— say, two years or less apart—maybe you'll give the

Watch Your Step

Forget what you got as a kid—that's out of date. Today, a key rule of thumb in setting allowances is paying a dollar a year: Pay $1 for each year of your child's age. Under this scenario, your 8-year-old would get $8, while your 12-year-old would receive $12. Adjust this general rule for other factors (your family finances or other issues).

Piggybank on It

You may not need to continue increasing a child's allowance when they reach their teens. At that age, you may expect them to supplement their allowance with their own earnings, whether baby-sitting or other after school jobs. If they ask for more money from you, suggest that they go out and earn it.

same amount. A child may complain that it's not fair that her older brother gets more than she does. Fairness doesn't mean that everything has to be equal, though: It's fair to base allowance on several factors, with age being an important one.

Your Family Income

Your head and your heart may want to pay a generous allowance, but your family's limited resources may dictate otherwise. You have to be realistic about what you can afford to pay as an allowance.

If you can't afford to pay an allowance or set it at the amount you really think appropriate, be honest about it. Explain that family finances prevent you from giving your child the amount you'd prefer.

Your Town

You can bet that the kids who live in the real Beverly Hills 90210 don't receive the same allowances as the kids in most inner-cities. You may feel that this is really just another way of saying that a family's income should influence the allowance. But there's more at work: There's peer pressure to get the same allowance that the other kids do.

Of course, you can take your neighborhood into account when fixing your child's allowance, or you might decide that this element shouldn't be factored in. It's your call.

Allowances with Strings

Some parents give allowances with no requirements on the child's part. Others make performing chores a condition of receipt.

Financial Building Blocks

According to the same survey by *Zillions,* about three-quarters of all allowance recipients (of all ages) were supposed to perform chores to get their allowances.

Child experts hotly disagree on whether allowances should be conditioned on performing chores. Each side believes strongly in its position. On the one hand, requiring work for pay prevents a child from believing in entitlement. There's value in doing work and being rewarded for it, and it's good training for getting a job.

On the other hand, others believe that chores should be required just because a child is part of the family. Just as Mom and Dad aren't paid for shopping, cooking, and repairing the broken porch, a child should be required to contribute his time and effort to help with the family work load. Conditioning the receipt of an allowance on performing work can lead to disaster. A child may think that *all* jobs around the house should be monetarily compensated. A child who continually tries to negotiate and renegotiate his workload and allowance may be in perfect training for a job with a union or the NLRB, but he can cause endless friction on the home front.

Obviously, the decision of whether to attach strings to an allowance comes down to what you think best in your family. You may, of course, be influenced by whether you were required to perform chores when you were a child and how you felt about that at the time. Whichever way you come out, make sure that the rules are clear—and be consistent. Think through which alternative you'll use, and then follow through.

There's another string that some parents put on the receipt of an allowance: good behavior. If a kid fights with his brother, breaks a lamp, or talks back, a parent might threaten to dock his allowance for this bad behavior. Some child experts think this type of string isn't a good idea, though: They don't believe it works to create good behavior—it just punishes a child without any benefit. You, of course, must decide on punishment for bad behavior, and you may think that withholding an allowance for a week or a month may be appropriate in certain circumstances.

Piggybank on It

If you decide to condition an allowance on doing chores, you must be realistic in setting the dollar amounts. There's no lesson in having your child work for sweatshop wages. Keep in mind that the current federal minimum wage is $5.15 an hour.

Watch Your Step

Don't condition an allowance on completing homework assignments. You don't want to buy your child's good grades.

Checking on Chores

If you think that chores should be required as a condition to receiving an allowance, spell out just what's expected of your child. Detail what your child has to do and how often. Some tasks may have to be done only once a month; others, such as taking out the garbage, must be done twice a week.

Obviously, chores need to be age-appropriate. You're not going to have your 7-year old mow the lawn, but he can walk the dog or change the cat's litter box. Generally, it's a good idea to keep chores to those tasks that can be performed quickly (say, 15 minutes or so). Also change chores periodically so that boredom and other complaints are avoided. Here are some chores that you might consider asking your child to do and how often to do them.

List of Chores	How Often They Need to Be Done
Baby-sitting siblings	_____
Changing the cat's litter box	_____
Doing dishes	_____
Dusting	_____
Feeding family pets	_____
Laundry	_____
Managing the family's recycling	_____
Taking out the garbage	_____
Vacuuming	_____
Walking the dog	_____
Washing the car	_____

Keep track of how well your child is doing on the chore front—you may have to make reminders. Consider posting the checklist where it'll serve as a reminder to your child (for example, in her room or on the refrigerator).

Watch Your Step

Don't try to track performance with complicated charts and graphs: It's a burden for you to maintain and can make your child feel over-regulated.

Canceling for Nonperformance

What happens if you've laid out an elaborate work schedule for your child and she fails to do some of the chores during the week? Do you reprimand her? Do you adjust or withhold her allowance?

Obviously, if there's no reduction in allowance for nonperformance, your child may come to believe that there are no consequences for bad behavior. On the other hand, it's tough to withhold money if the violations are minor or infrequent. And what do you do when your child is sick or injured and can't do the chores? However you decide to act, make sure that your child knows what will happen, and be consistent about it.

Financial Building Blocks

The same survey in *Zillions* magazine noted that only 20 percent of children had their allowances docked because they failed to do their required chores.

How Your Child Spends His Allowance

Whether or not you put strings on receiving the allowance, once it's his, you really can't make your child use it as you want. That's just not fair (not that everything has to be fair, of course). After all, you want your child to think for himself when it comes to money. According to a survey on teens and money consulted by *USA Weekend*, 75 percent of kids had complete control over their money.

You may want to place some expectations on how your child spends it, but you really can't require your child to use the allowance as you see fit. You can, however, provide guidance on how the money should be used by discussing these issues with your child.

Dictating Your Child's Spending

In receiving an allowance, your child faces a great temptation to spend it all at the first opportunity. But one of the reasons for giving an allowance is to make sure that your child has money for the things she wants when she wants them. To do this, she'll have to think ahead.

You can help your child decide how to allocate her money. Of course, the allocation will vary greatly with a child's age, the amount of allowance, and other factors. Here are some categories that are commonly considered:

➤ *Car.* Obviously, this is only a concern when your child is of driving age. He may be responsible for putting gas in your car when he uses it, or he may be able to save up and pay for the purchase and upkeep of his own car.

➤ *Charity.* When you give to charity, you set an example for your child to follow. Certainly, children learn about giving to charity through the UNICEF Halloween collection program, the Girl Scout cookie drive, and in religious schools. You can suggest she set aside part of her allowance for charity and help her decide how to make her contributions.

➤ *Clothing.* As kids (especially girls) get older, they tend to spend more money on clothes.

➤ *Entertainment.* The extent to which your child uses his allowance for fun is up to him. In the

Piggybank on It

Talks about how to use an allowance should be done periodically. As your child gets older, suggestions on how the money should be used will naturally change. (The topics of spending, saving, and investing are discussed in this book in Parts 4–6.)

Piggybank on It

Some clothes are necessary (such as a winter coat, underwear, and a pair of shoes). Having 15 sweaters, however, may be desired but certainly not necessary. Consider suggesting that your child pay for the extras in this category from his allowance.

past, teenage boys used to get bigger allowances than their female counterparts because boys were expected to pay for dates. Today, teenagers don't have the same dating mores that their parents had. For the most part, they don't have dates in the conventional sense—they may go out in groups or do other activities together. Generally, girls and boys share the cost of entertainment.

➤ *Savings and investments.* It's important that children start at an early age to view saving money as a regular activity. The best way to do this is to suggest that they set aside part of their allowance for this purpose. If you insist that they're responsible for paying for certain things such as the going to the movies, then they'll be forced to save or go without.

➤ *School expenses (extracurricular activities and other expenses).* While school may be public, many trips and other activities at school are certainly not free. You may want your child to be responsible for these things. Again, you may decide to share expenses (for example, she pays the activity fees but you buy the equipment). Should an allowance cover the costs of school lunches? When a child routinely buys lunch at school, adding in the cost of lunches to the allowance may make it easier for a parent (there's only one amount that needs to be given each week instead of two separate amounts). But doing this creates a temptation for your child to skip lunch and use the money for other things. If the one-payment system is used, be sure to talk about how the money should be used.

➤ *Toys and video games.* As with entertainment, kids should be allowed to use their allowance on fun things, as long as allocations have been made for savings and other categories that are necessary.

Watch Your Step

If your child is supposed to pay for his own toys and entertainment, it's not a good idea for you to pay for them whenever he's short of funds. This won't help in teaching responsibility for managing money. He'll just have to forgo a movie it he doesn't have the money for the ticket.

How Much Parental Guidance?

Providing guidance on what your child should do with his allowance is certainly a wise thing on your part. But how much influence should you exert? Can you insist that a certain percentage of the allowance go toward savings? Can you require your child to pay for all her entertainment costs? There are no hard-and-fast rules; decisions here are guided in part by the age of your child, the size of the allowance, your personal beliefs, and other factors. Clearly, whatever you think the allocation should be, getting your child to follow suit requires a little finesse on your part.

At one extreme, you can say nothing and let your child make all his own decisions. On the other extreme, you can set requirements on how the allowance should be allocated among the different categories of expenditures. Somewhere in the middle is where you'll probably want to fall, providing guidance without making the child feel like there's no point to receiving the allowance in the first place. Of course, it goes without saying that your child should know without a doubt that the allowance would stop in a second if it were to be used for drugs, alcohol, or other illegal activities.

Helping your child make spending decisions by setting up a budget and allocating a portion to savings is discussed in the next part of this book.

The Least You Need to Know

➤ While your child's birthright doesn't include receiving an allowance, most kids do get one.

➤ An allowance can be supplemented or supplanted by spending money.

➤ Deciding when to start (and stop) an allowance is up to you.

➤ The dollar amount of the allowance depends on age, family income, and what the allowance is supposed to pay for.

➤ There are pros and cons for conditioning an allowance on the performance of chores.

➤ You can and should guide your child on how to allocate his weekly cash.

Chapter 9

Junior Job Market

In This Chapter

➤ Working for the experience

➤ Working for the money

➤ Locating job openings

➤ Landing a job

No one's suggesting that you send your child to a sweatshop to labor 10 hours a day. Still, working—even at a young age—can prove to be a good thing for your child. He can learn about the work ethic, develop skills, and earn money to boot—and he may even have fun at the same time.

In this chapter, you'll learn about the benefits—monetary and otherwise—that working can have for your child. You'll learn about job opportunities for kids of all ages, and you'll find out about restrictions on child labor. You'll also learn about what your child should know to locate job openings and nail down a position.

Working for Fun and Profit

On the old *Dobbie Gillis* show, Maynard G. Krebs' voice used to crack every time he said the word "work." To him, work was a dirty word. Today, things are different; kids work, even at a young age, and each kid has his own reasons for working.

Some do it only (or mainly) for the money—they need or want extra money, and working is the way to get it.

Others do it for a variety of other reasons—they want to fill up their time, gain experience, or just get out into the world.

Financial Building Blocks

According to a survey reported in *USA Today,* about two-thirds of college students work to earn money while they're in school. About a quarter of them earn between $200 and $400 a month; more than a quarter of them earn even more.

Of course, before your child takes a job, it's a good idea for you to discuss certain parameters about working: how many hours a week you think is appropriate, how far you'll let your child travel to a job, and what type of work you think is acceptable (or unacceptable). You don't want your child commuting and working long hours at the expense of the time needed for school work or other activities.

Non-monetary Benefits of Working

Working can do more for your child than provide spending money. Many of these benefits also may translate into dollars down the road:

➤ *Instilling a good work ethic.* It may sound old-fashioned, but there's nothing wrong with having a strong sense of responsibility when it comes to work. Understanding what's required to get and keep a job or to earn a promotion are just basic parts of being a responsible adult. The earlier a child starts to learn this responsibility, the more natural it becomes. Taking responsibility for work also can carry over to taking responsibility for money, too.

Piggybank on It

Children too young to work can begin to learn about the work ethic at home by doing chores. They'll learn how to start and finish an assigned task, which is a good foundation for getting a job.

➤ *Learning skills.* Okay, so stocking shelves at the A&P or flipping burgers at McDonalds doesn't exactly supply the job skills of a lifetime. But it can help a child learn to pace herself to get work done and gain self-confidence in doing something well. Some jobs can offer a child the chance to learn things that can be helpful in landing better jobs later, and working at any job can teach time-management skills. It's the old cliché of asking a busy person to handle a job that needs to get done. Working will help a child learn to manage her time more effectively.

➤ *Gaining experience.* It's the old catch 22: The job requires work experience, but your child can't get that experience without getting a job. Starting at a job—any job—is the first step in building up work experience that can be used to catapult your child later into a better job.

➤ *Trying out work environments.* Does your child think he'd enjoy working in a hotel? In television? He can use a job to test possible career paths. When my daughter was in high school, she thought she wanted to be a scientist until she worked for a summer in a physicist's lab. This job convinced her that she did not want to spend her working years cooped up in a lab.

➤ *Testing aptitude.* Getting a job now not only can show your child that she likes a particular field, but it also can show her whether she's good at it. She may want to go into radio, but working at the campus radio station can show her whether she has the voice quality and the gift of gab needed to pursue her dream. It's better to learn early that she's headed down a dead-end career path so that she can change her dream and go off in another direction.

Earning a Paycheck

One of the biggest benefits your child can have from working is the chance to earn his own money. This money can be used to gain a measure of independence for your child: He can support an active social life, buy a car, or go to college.

Working may become necessary as your child gets older and his tastes become more expensive or you decide that you are no longer going to pay for certain things. If your child wants these items, he'll have to earn his own money.

Piggybank on It

Earning a paycheck is the quickest way to teach a child the value of a dollar. When she has to work for it, she's less apt to take the money for granted. A $15 CD has more meaning when a child realizes that she has had to work three hours to pay for it.

Financial Building Blocks

The federal minimum wage rate started in 1938 at 25¢ an hour. It's currently $5.15 an hour for most workers, but there's a subminimum wage of $4.25 an hour for workers under 20 years of age during their first 90 consecutive days of employment. Some states, however, have higher minimum hourly rates. There's talk in Congress of increasing the rate in the future (the last increase was in 1997).

Working can be the start of a meaningful financial education. It can give your child enough money to allow him to start a checking account and a savings program. It can also give your child a true understanding of what jobs really pay—something that the majority of kids seem to lack. According to a survey on teens and money by *Weekend USA*, 42 percent of teenagers expect to earn $75,000 a year by the time they're 30. The average 30-year-old today earns about $27,000.

For general information about the federal minimum wage and labor laws, go to the Department of Labor's Web site at www.dol.gov. You can also call DOL's Teen Safety Hotline at 800-959-3652.

Where the Jobs Are

There's good news for young people today: There are plenty of jobs out there. And with openings galore, even some formerly minimum-wage jobs are paying higher wages to attract job applicants.

Financial Building Blocks

According to the Bureau of Labor Statistics, in the summer of 1998 a total of 21.6 million youths age 16–24 were employed—this is nearly 65 percent of all people in this age group. Most worked in retail and service companies, but a large number also were employed in manufacturing and construction. About 1.5 million also worked in government jobs, mostly at the local level.

Jobs can be found in many places:

➤ *Doing work around the house.* Although to some farm families, working at home still might mean working the fields and feeding the farm animals at times, it usually means doing chores or even helping a parent in a home-based business.

➤ *Working for a paycheck.* Businesses today are looking for help, particularly in low-end jobs to which teenagers are well-suited.

➤ *Working to gain experience.* Internships and volunteer positions can offer something money can't buy: work experience.

Working at Home

When my friend lived above the candy store her parents owned, working at home meant clerking behind the counter in the store. Today, working at home has a whole new meaning. Technology and other factors have spawned a home-based business revolution. If you're part of that revolution, you may be able to provide a job opportunity for your child. My kids have worked for my home-based business since they were young, spending hours filing papers in my library, photocopying reports, and collating materials.

Putting your child to work for you offers benefits for both of you. There's probably no zoning problem because your child/employee is a member of your household. And there are tax benefits as well: As a self-employed person, you don't owe any FICA on wages paid to your child under age 18, and you can deduct the wages you've paid her.

But even if you don't run a business out of your home, you can still put your child to work there. You may want to compensate your child for doing regular chores (such as starting dinner for the family each night because you work outside the home) or special chores (such as painting the porch railing).

Be very clear on what work you expect your child to do just because she's part of the family, what work is tied to her allowance, and what work is over and above that (such as special jobs around the house or work in a family business). It's not always easy to draw the distinction (see a related discussion in Chapter 8, "Making Allowances").

Piggybank on It

With nearly one in three households having (or starting up) some type of home business, there's new opportunities for kids to find work close at hand.

Watch Your Step

While you can turn a nondeductible weekly allowance into a deductible business expense for yourself by putting your child to work for your business, use caution. Be sure that you keep good records of the actual hours he has worked and the tasks he has done for you (in case the IRS questions this deduction).

Delivering Papers, Flipping Burgers, and Beyond

The type of job your child seeks out in the world depends on his age and his abilities. As a practical matter, it may also depend on whether he has a driver's license and the use of a car. Also, state labor laws may limit the type of work that your child can do and hours that he can put in.

For younger kids (those who don't have a driver's license), job choices may be limited. Here are some ideas for openings that may be available in your area:

➤ *Baby-sitting.* Depending on customs in your area, kids as young as 11 and 12 start to baby-sit as a way to earn money. Baby sitters are usually in big demand, especially on Saturday nights, open school nights, and holidays when parents want to go out. Older teens also have opportunities to watch other children after school until parents return from work. The money's good, too—in my neighborhood, the going rate is now about $7.50 an hour.

Financial Building Blocks

If your child is under age 18, she may need certain papers or documents to show that she's allowed to work. For example, in New York, a child who has not reached 18 must have a full-time Employment Certificate to work even though she has graduated from high school. Papers are also required for those under 16, even when working as a camp counselor or such. Check with the Department of Labor in your state to see if your child needs any type of working papers. Generally, your child can get the necessary papers from her high school.

Piggybank on It

While job openings may be limited, a young child can make his own opportunities by starting a business. This is discussed in Chapter 10, "Business Basics for Kids."

Piggybank on It

Special businesses or industries in your area may offer unique work opportunities for kids. An amusement park, a factory, or a computer company may have openings for youth, particularly those of college age. New York City, for example, offers kids of all ages the chance to get into television and commercials or to work on Broadway.

➤ *Pet care.* Neighbors have dogs that may need to be walked during the afternoon when they're at work. Even at a young age, kids can usually handle the task of walking, feeding, and playing with pets. Pet owners may also need pet care when they're away on vacation.

➤ *Paper delivery.* Kids don't hawk papers on street corners anymore, but newspaper delivery routes are still available in some areas. In fact, some routes are so prized that they're passed down in families from older to younger kids.

➤ *Snow shoveling and yard work.* Both winter and summer, there's always work to be done around a house. Neighbors—particularly elderly ones—may be more than happy to have the help.

When your child is older, there's usually a much larger pool of jobs to choose from. This is especially true if he has a driver's license. Here are some ideas:

➤ *Camp counselor.* Your child may be able to find a summer job at a day camp near you or at a sleepaway camp. The pay is modest, but if your child likes working with kids and being outdoors, the match may be ideal.

➤ *Store clerks and other mall positions.* Clothing stores, book stores, and drug stores in your area may need someone to man the cash register, stock shelves, and help customers. Movie theaters, fast food chains, and supermarkets are also places to look for jobs.

➤ *Delivery person.* Pizza and other food deliveries are often made by teenagers. Usually, the business provides the vehicle for this job.

Investing in Their Future

While money is always a strong motivation for working, sometimes it may pay to work for free. You child can take part in certain work arrangements that will pay off big-time in the future. She'll gain work experience, make important job contacts, and a whole lot more.

➤ *Internships.* Your child may find a position through his school that offers him work in a field that interests him. Many college programs now require students to do some sort of internship as part of the degree program. Internships are even open to high school students. While there may not be any money involved, your child receives supervision for this invaluable learning experience. He also may receive a stipend at the completion of the internship, or he might receive money to reimburse him for his transportation or lunches. Internships are a great way for a child to meet professionals and make contacts that can be used in the future to get a paying job.

➤ *Volunteering.* Nonprofit organizations, such as food banks and hospitals, are almost always looking for more help with their projects. Your child generally can put in as much or as few hours as she wants and may be able to work in an area of interest to her. For example, your child may want to work as a candy striper at your local hospital to test out an interest in nursing. Or, she may be able to create her own volunteer position by contacting a business where she's interested in working, even though that company offers no paid position for her.

Watch Your Step

If your child uses a family car for business purposes, make sure that your insurance will cover any accidents that occur while he's on the job.

Money ABCs

A **stipend** is a payment for services that's typically made in one lump sum.

Piggybank on It

Girl Scouts who participate in the annual cookie sale may not view this event as work, but it teaches important job skills: The girls learn to sell, collect the money, and deliver the cookies.

Landing a Job

Unless you have connections—you own a company or know someone who's looking for help—your child will have to find a job on his own. Fortunately, the jobs are out there.

Your child just has to learn how to find them and how to get hired—but these two things are not always simple.

Where to Look

The job your child wants may be right under her nose. Here are some of the more common places to check out first:

➤ Job listings at school employment offices.

➤ Signs in stores and shops in the neighborhood. It's difficult these days not to see "help wanted" signs all over town.

➤ Ask neighbors and friends for possible openings. Those in high school can talk to kids about to go off to college. As job openings are created by kids going off to college, high schoolers may be able to fill those openings.

➤ Look at local newspapers. Job openings are listed daily in the want ad or advertisement section.

➤ Check out the state employment office. There may be a youth employment division that your child can check into for possible positions.

Money ABCs

A **reference** is a person who can vouch for your child. Generally, a reference is a former boss who can attest to the period of your child's previous employment and tell whether he was a good employee. Sometimes your child also will be asked for a personal reference, which can be a neighbor or friend who knows him well, or a teacher or professor he's had in school.

What to Do

Jobs may be plentiful, but your child still must know his way around the job application process to nail down a position. He can't just present himself and expect immediate and positive results.

Your child must come prepared. For most jobs, he'll have to complete a job application. Typically, this is a one-page form that asks him to list his name, address, telephone number, Social Security number, previous jobs (if any), and who can be contacted as a reference.

Your child should be ready with all the information asked on the application. By anticipating what's asked, he'll be able to have the information on hand and provide it quickly and accurately. If he has never applied for a job before, then it's up to you to prep him on what questions will be asked and what information he needs to respond.

As your child gets older and moves up the job scale to better positions and gets some work experience under his belt, she may be asked to provide a *résumé*. This usually happens once kids hit college and start to look for jobs in their intended field. It's a good idea for your child to make a résumé even before she reaches the job market and to keep it handy and update it as necessary. You can help your teenager by letting her know that she should have a résumé and helping her to prepare one.

Even if she may not be asked to provide a résumé when she applies for a job, going through the exercise of making a résumé isn't a waste of time. The résumé will include all the information she needs to complete the job application, so she can bring it with her as a reminder of this information.

There's no single résumé formula that your child must use. Books in the library can provide her with many ideas on how to write a resume.

Even easier, your child can write a résumé using a template in a word processing program. For example, Microsoft Word allows users to tailor a résumé according to specific needs. Your child can list her education before work experience if she want to emphasize her academic credentials. Or, she can list her work experience before noting her school background when her job experience becomes more impressive. The idea of the résumé is to emphasize the positive and minimize the negative.

To make a résumé using a template in Word, simply answer the questions posed by the Résumé Wizard found under "Other Documents"—first select New from the File menu.

For more professional-looking, custom-tailored résumés, consider investing in a résumé software program, such as Résumés That Work (contact Macmillan at www.macdigital.com).

After your child is hired, she'll be asked by her employer to complete Form W-4, Employee's Withholding Allowance Certificate. This is an IRS form that tells her employer how much federal (and state) income taxes to withhold (subtract) from her paycheck and submit to the government on her behalf. For example, if she earns $100, she may have $15 withheld for federal income taxes.

Piggybank on It

If he doesn't already know his nine-digit Social Security number by heart, your child should memorize it now. He'll be asked to provide this number very often throughout his life. Even more than a name, a Social Security number is a person's identifier. It's the number used by the government to know who you are despite job moves, new residences, and even name changes. If your child can't memorize it, then he should carry it in his wallet.

Money ABCs

A **résumé** is a summary of personal information (name, address, and telephone number), jobs a person has already held (what work was performed and when), and education level (including any degrees expected to be earned).

The $15 is sent to the U.S. Treasury under her Social Security number and is treated as her tax payment. She must complete it, and she doesn't want to appear ignorant about the form when she's hired. It's up to you to explain things beforehand.

Piggybank on It

Be sure that your child updates her résumé after each new job, school award, or other accomplishment worth noting.

Money ABCs

Liability means that your child owes something. When talking about federal income taxes, then liability refers to taxes he owes.

Generally, your child tells the employer how many withholding allowances he wants to claim (none, one, two, or more) and then the employer does the rest. In most cases, he'll claim one allowance (for himself). This lets the employer figure withholding on the basis of his being single and claiming one allowance. He may be eligible to claim exemption from withholding so that no taxes are withheld. To claim exemption, he must meet both of these conditions:

➤ He had no federal tax liability in the prior year (even if he paid taxes, he received a full refund of his payments).

➤ He doesn't expect to have any federal tax liability this year. If in 1999 he earns no more than $4,300, he won't have any federal tax liability. If he's not sure whether he's going to be under or over this limit, he may want to forgo the exemption and pay the tax to make sure he has the funds to cover his liability. He can always get back any excess payments when his 1999 tax return is filed in 2000.

Your child cannot claim exemption from withholding if his income is more than $700 and includes interest, dividends, or other unearned income and if he can be claimed as your dependent on your tax return. If any investments have been made on his behalf, he may well have bank accounts paying interest, or stock or mutual funds paying dividends to him that will prevent his claiming exemption from withholding.

He may not know that his grandmother has a savings account for him or that you've set up a custodial account in his name to save for college. These investments may generate enough income to prevent him from claiming exemption withholding. When you know he's job-hunting, be sure to review the W-4 process and explain how many withholding allowances he should claim, or whether he's eligible for exemption from withholding. When my oldest child got her first job, she asked with some embarrassment to bring the W-4 home for me to look at. You can bet that my other kids knew what to do with this form when they got their first jobs.

Your Name

Your home address City, State Zip Code Phone number e-mail (if you have it)	Address at school City, State and Zip Code Your phone number at school e-mail (if you have it)

WORK EXPERIENCE

Name of Company   *Period of employment*
City, State
> Your position (or what you did) [Example: Summer Intern in Marketing Department]
> Add anything special you did (awards or recognition you received)

Name of Company   *Period of employment*
City, State
> Your position (or what you did)
> Add anything special you did (awards or recognition you received)

Name of Company   *Period of employment*
City, State
> Your position (or what you did)
> Add anything special you did (awards or recognition you received)

EDUCATION

Name of college/university, City, State   Degree/Date received (expected)
> Your major

Name of high school, City, State
> Any special honors/awards you received

EXTRACURRICULAR ACTIVITIES

List activity/date of participation
List activity/date of participation
List activity/date of participation

SPECIAL SKILLS

Anything that may help you stand out (language proficiency; computer skills)

Sample résumé

- - - - - - - - - - - - - - - Cut here and give the certificate to your employer. Keep the top part for your records. - - - - - - - - - - - - - - -

Form **W-4**	**Employee's Withholding Allowance Certificate**	OMB No. 1545-0010
Department of the Treasury Internal Revenue Service	▶ **For Privacy Act and Paperwork Reduction Act Notice, see page 2.**	**1999**

1 Type or print your first name and middle initial Last name	2 Your social security number

Home address (number and street or rural route)	3 ☐ Single ☐ Married ☐ Married, but withhold at higher Single rate. **Note:** *If married, but legally separated, or spouse is a nonresident alien, check the Single box.*
City or town, state, and ZIP code	4 If your last name differs from that on your social security card, check here. **You** must call 1-800-772-1213 for a new card . . . ▶ ☐

5	Total number of allowances you are claiming (from line H above or from the worksheets on page 2 if they apply) .	5	
6	Additional amount, if any, you want withheld from each paycheck	6	$

7 I claim exemption from withholding for 1999, and I certify that I meet **BOTH** of the following conditions for exemption:
 • Last year I had a right to a refund of **ALL** Federal income tax withheld because I had **NO** tax liability **AND**
 • This year I expect a refund of **ALL** Federal income tax withheld because I expect to have **NO** tax liability.
 If you meet both conditions, write "EXEMPT" here . . . . ▶ | 7 |

Under penalties of perjury, I certify that I am entitled to the number of withholding allowances claimed on this certificate, or I am entitled to claim exempt status.
Employee's signature
(Form is not valid
unless you sign it) ▶   Date ▶

8 Employer's name and address (Employer: Complete 8 and 10 only if sending to the IRS)	9 Office code (optional)	10 Employer identification number

Cat. No. 10220Q

Form W-4

The Least You Need to Know

➤ Earning a paycheck is a quick lesson for your child on the value of a dollar.

➤ If your child does work around the house, be sure to coordinate any payments with an allowance you may already be giving.

➤ Make sure your child has any necessary working papers.

➤ Working for free (at an internship or volunteering) can provide good work experience for your child.

➤ Jobs for kids are plentiful, but it's still necessary for them to know where to look and how to land the job.

➤ Kids should come prepared to job interviews armed with a working permit (if necessary), information about prior work experience, and a Social Security number.

Chapter 10

Business Basics for Kids

In This Chapter

➤ Finding a good business idea for kids

➤ Deciding whether they have what it takes for business

➤ Learning business skills

➤ Getting a business off the ground

The entrepreneurial spirit isn't restricted by age. Even kids of any age (with parental help) can start up businesses to earn extra money. Today, kids have come a long way from the lemonade stand—some are getting into all sorts of businesses, which might develop into life-long pursuits. Michael Dell started his computer sales business out of his college dorm room, and today he's now one of the richest people in America.

In this chapter, you'll see what business opportunities exist for kids today. You'll learn to help your child decide whether he's got the ability to commit his time and effort to a business. You'll find out about some places kids can go to learn about business skills, and you'll learn about what they should know before trying to run their business.

Today's Businesses for Kids

A 1994 Gallup poll revealed that 7 out of 10 high school kids wanted to start their own businesses. Some of these kids don't wait until they're adults to get going on their dream. They may demonstrate their entrepreneurial spirit of innovation, self-reliance, and hard work by starting a business while they're still kids.

There's good reason for the high level of interest in being an entrepreneur. Some kids may have seen their parents downsized from corporate America and want to avoid being in a similar situation later in life. They may think that when they grow up, they'll have their own companies and create their own job security. And what better way to prepare for that status than to start a business while they're still kids.

Today there are good reasons why kids can and should get started early in pursuing their dreams of owning their own businesses.

Money ABCs

An **entrepreneur** is someone who starts and runs a business. An entrepreneur assumes the risk for the opportunity to turn a profit.

➤ *Opportunities are there.* Thanks to expanded computer programs in the schools and the reduction in the price of home computers, kids today are almost all computer-literate. Computer technology has made it possible for kids, like many adults, to start up businesses without leaving home.

➤ *Information and help is available.* Kids aren't left entirely to their own devices. They can get assistance from many organizations and other sources to learn business skills and get started.

Talents Needed for Running a Business

Adults know that entrepreneurs are a breed apart and must possess certain attributes to succeed. Before your child starts a business, she should ask herself whether she has what it takes to make it in business. Here are some questions your child should ask herself if she thinks she wants to start a business:

➤ *Is she a responsible person?* No one (other than you) will be there to remind her of what has to be done. Being in business means keeping promises to customers that she'll do what she says she'll do. For example, if she promises to walk a neighbor's dog every afternoon, she *must* be there, even if it's bad weather, if she doesn't feel good, or if there's a big game after school.

➤ *Does she have the special skills that her business entails?* If she wants to teach computer use to seniors at a senior center, does she know how to operate the word-processing program on the center's computer? If she plans to make jewelry, is she artistically inclined?

➤ *Is she organized?* Being in business requires a child to keep things straight. She must be able to know what to bill, to collect money, to buy supplies, and to schedule jobs at times that can be kept.

➤ *Does she have the time needed for the business?* Today, kids are highly scheduled with after-school activities, such as piano lessons and basketball practice. These activities may not leave much time for other things, including running a business. Your child must have some idea of when she'll conduct business. After school? On the weekends? Only in the summer?

Ideas for Businesses That Kids Can Start

After some second thoughts, your child might decide that he prefers to go out and get a job working for someone else. Or, he may think that he has what it takes to be his own boss and wants to start his own business. The opportunities are boundless.

The type of business kids can start is limited only by a few things: their imagination, the money it takes to start the business, their talents, and their ability (or inability) to get around. Maybe your child already has a good idea of what he wants to do. Here's a sampling of the ideas that have already been put into practice by enterprising youth:

➤ One talented teenager started (with the help of her mother and financing from interested people) manufacturing a successful line of clothing she designed.

➤ Another perceptive teen recognized a growing market niche for Christian religious products for kids her own age. She created an online catazine (a combination catalog and magazine) to sell T-shirts, jewelry, and other items.

➤ One 10-year old (with the help of his father) started a toy company to manufacture a water toy of his design that has already sold more than a million units worldwide. Three years later, his company was bought out by Wild Planet Toys for millions.

➤ A number of kids are getting into computer and Internet-related businesses, designing Web sites, setting up computer systems, and teaching computer use.

➤ One teenager who immigrated from El Salvador at age 8 started a customized framing business that provides frames for special occasions. With more work than she can handle, she continues to advertise by distributing flyers in malls, schools, grocery stores, and even laundromats.

But if your child doesn't have any idea of what he'd like to do, here are some businesses that kids can start with virtually no seed money:

➤ *Car cleaning.* This business provides car washing and inside cleaning. It may be impossible to get your child to clean your car, but she may be more than willing to do it for the neighbors if they'll pay her for it.

Piggybank on It

Labor laws limit the hours that kids can work as employees for someone else. There are no limits on the time kids can spend working for themselves, but school work and other commitments surely limit the time they can devote to their businesses.

Money ABCs

Seed money is the cash needed to get a business off the ground. Also called start-up funds, this money usually is raised through savings and getting loans from family, friends or a bank.

➤ *Computer instruction.* This business provides teaching of computer literacy. It might focus on senior citizens or other groups in need of help, or it might be private tutoring for other kids who are having trouble catching on.

➤ *House sitting.* This business provides mail and newspaper pickup, waters house plants, and keeps an eye on things. I used to pay $20 a day for a teenager to sleep in my house (and eat whatever he found), walk my dogs, collect the mail, bring in the newspaper, and generally give the house a lived-in look.

➤ *Making jewelry and crafts.* This business makes and sells jewelry and craft items to sell to craft stores and at craft fairs. Use things around the house (if parents approve) to get started, and then reinvest sales proceeds in supplies for new projects. One girl who did this just to make pocket money in high school later went on to a career with Avon designing their costume jewelry.

➤ *Lawn and garden care.* This business provides lawn mowing, leaf raking, weeding, and other garden services. If your child uses his own mower and other equipment, he can charge more than if he uses the homeowner's equipment. It's easy to find out what the going rate is in your area for this type of service by asking around.

➤ *Party assistance.* This business provides maid service to neighbors during their parties and offers assistance in setting up, collecting glasses and plates, washing dishes, and performing other related tasks. Your child should charge either an hourly rate or quote a flat fee per party.

➤ *Pet care.* This business provides dog walking, cat litter changing, pet feeding, cage cleaning, and other pet care services. These services can be performed on a regular basis or just when customers are away from home.

➤ *Tutoring.* This business provides academic help in subjects in which your kid shines. While kids usually can't charge the same hourly rate as grown-ups, they make great teachers because they can relate to other kids. A high school math whiz can provide after-school help to someone in a lower grade.

Piggybank on It

Kids proficient with computers can start many types of businesses. My daughter's friend has a business designing Web pages. His revenues, which are impressive, are helping to pay his way through college.

Piggybank on It

A party helper can also provide services at kids' birthday parties as extra hands for parents, as clowns or other entertainment, or simply as maid service.

Learning Business Skills

What a kid must know before starting up a business isn't something that's usually taught in the sixth grade. In fact, even in post-graduate business schools, it's usually more theory than practice—there's more attention given to macroeconomics than to simple advertising ideas. But learn she must before investing any time and effort in a business she'd like to start.

Financial Building Blocks

Business schools that grant post-graduate degrees have only recently begun to offer courses in entrepreneurship. In the past, most MBA graduates wanted to run Fortune 500 companies. Today, they want to start their own businesses (which they hope may someday become a Fortune 500 company).

Many ways exist for learning some fundamentals on business operations. However, most books and courses are geared to adults; kids are more or less on their own when it comes to learning business skills. They can teach themselves business skills by using resources found through the Internet (for example, at www.kidsway.com and www.youngandsuccessful.com) and by staying current through periodicals such as *Young Entrepreneur* (888-KIDSWAY). Still, there are two other good ways that kids can and do learn about business:

➤ *Working in a family business.* If you or a relative owns a business, your child can learn things from the ground up by working there.

➤ *Joining business-related clubs and organizations.* School clubs and extracurricular activities can provide a place to learn and practice business skills.

Like Mother (and Father), Like Daughter (and Son)

It used to be common to see store signs that read something like, "Smith and Sons." Children worked alongside their parents and then became part of the family business. My cousins starting working in their parents' neighborhood art supply store when they were still in elementary school. Now they own the business, which has expanded into several stores and a catalog business nationwide.

Today, fewer children are following in their parents' footsteps. Parents have pushed their kids to become executives instead of storekeepers, and doctors instead of plumbers. But for those kids whose parents own a business, there's still plenty of opportunity for them to learn business skills.

If you have an office in your home and run a business from it, as more than 26 million people now do, you can show your child a thing or two about how to run a business. You'll be able to teach her that a multitude of skills are required to run a business.

If you're a business owner, you know that you must wear many hats and be good at all of them to succeed. You have to not only be skilled at the service you're offering, but you also must know how to handle marketing, billing, collections, and more. You can expose your child to these aspects of business operations by having her work for you.

Piggybank on It

Even if you don't own the company, you can certainly expose your child to the business atmosphere by bringing him to the office on occasion. Don't overlook annual events such as "Take your daughter and son to work day" (sponsored by the National Organization of Women [NOW]) and "Groundhog Shadow Day" (sponsored by the U.S. Chamber of Commerce).

Whatever your business, there's always photocopying, filing, mailings, and other jobs that a child can help you with.

Even by just being there, she will see you in action at your different jobs. She'll hear you on the phone handling business problems, and she'll also see the hard work (and sometimes frustration and anxiety) that running your own business entails.

Clubs for Practice

Clubs and organizations, both in school and after school, can provide kids with guidance on learning about businesses and business skills. Here are some of the most popular national organizations that provide business programs for kids.

➤ *Distributive Education Clubs of America* (DECA) helps to improve the education and career opportunities in marketing, management, and entrepreneurship for kids in secondary and post-secondary school. Each year there's a national competition for DECA members, with prizes of more than $25,000 in cash and stock awarded to winners. DECA also awards scholarships annually. Contact DECA at www.deca.org.

➤ *The Entrepreneurial Development Institute* is a nonprofit organization that has been helping teens since 1991 to realize their entrepreneurial dreams. Contact the organization at www.bedrock.com/tedi/tedi.htm.

➤ *4-H clubs* give kids the opportunity to learn about agricultural science and technology in a closely

Piggybank on It

If there's no club or organization in your area, consider starting one. Contact the national headquarters of an organization that you would like to see in your area to find out what needs to be done to get a club started.

supervised environment. These clubs aren't restricted to rural areas. Contact 4-H at www.4h-usa.org.

➤ *Future Business Leaders of America–Phi Beta Lambda* (FBLA-PBL) helps prepare kids for careers in business. Programs for promoting competitive, aggressive business leadership and understanding American business enterprise are geared for junior high and intermediate students, high school students, and post-secondary students. (There's also a Professional Division for parents and other adults who want to support the goals of the association.) Contact FBLA at www.fbla-pbl.org.

➤ *Junior Achievement* teaches more than 3 million students each year about the Free Enterprise System. Different programs are provided for those in grades K–6 (elementary school program), grades 7–8 (middle school program), and grades 9–12 (high school program). In one of the high school programs, called Company Program, kids learn how to operate a business. During a 15-week cycle, they sell stock to raise capital, market their product or service, and finally liquidate the company at the end. In another program, called GLOBE, kids learn the basics of running an international company. They also get to work with kids from other countries and learn about their business cultures. Contact JA at www.ja.org.

Financial Building Blocks

Former Junior Achievement participants who've made it big in the business world include Frederick A. Deluca, founder and CEO of Subway; Dick DeVos, president of Amway; Marshall Loeb, financial journalist and currently the editor of the *Columbia Journalism Review*; and Thomas S. Monaghan, president and CEO of Domino's Pizza, Inc.

Other Learning Activities

Clubs aren't the only way your child can learn entrepreneurial skills to start a business. Summer programs also are designed for this purpose.

For example, there's Camp Start-Up, a two-week summer camp for girls 13–18. There's one program for girls who don't know a thing about running a business, and there's another program for returning teens to hone their entrepreneurial skills. These programs are held in various locations nationwide. For information, contact www.independentmeans.com/camp/programs.html.

Look Before Your Kid Leaps

Let's say that your kid has what he thinks is a great idea for a business. Before he puts in time and money, clear some hurdles first.

➤ *Make sure it's legal.* If he wants to run a business from home, check local zoning regulations to see that the business is permissible. You may need to get permits or obtain a variance to operate, and you may have to pay fees for the privilege of doing so.

➤ *Make a business plan.* Your child doesn't have to write a lengthy or formal term paper. The purpose of making a business plan is to map out a course of action that he can take to start up and grow the business. Make sure that the plan contains certain key elements: a good description of what the business is all about, how much money it will take and where it's going to come from, and how the business will function from day to day. There's a business plan helper on the Web at www.independentmeans.com/bizplan/helper.html.

➤ *Get all necessary licenses.* Check with your town hall or county clerk to see whether the business must register. This is called a *DBA* (doing business as). You tell the government the name of your business (it can be different from your child's own name) and who owns the business. For example, your child might call his pet care business Animal Friends. You don't need a lawyer to file a DBA; the county clerk can provide the forms and tell you how to fill them out.

➤ *Check with your insurance company.* If your child's business will be run from your home, make sure that your homeowner's policy will cover things. You may need to add coverage for liability and equipment, or you may have to buy separate business insurance to cover things.

➤ *Make partnerships official.* If your child thinks that two heads are better than one and decides to team up with someone else, make sure that they think through the arrangement, called a *partnership*.

Money ABCs

A **variance** is a change or alternation of a zoning rule granted specifically to the homeowner asking for it.

Money ABCs

A **partnership** is a business formed by two or more people who work together with the goal of earning a profit.

On the positive side to having a partnership, both people can share responsibilities and may have complementary skills to make the business a success. On the negative side, they may not always agree on how things should run, or one partner may do more work than the other. Partnerships are no guarantee of success.

Also be sure to consider these issues before setting up a business:

➤ *Deciding to incorporate.* For a 14-year-old's lawn care business, it's probably not necessary to go through the legal steps of setting up a corporation. But if your 21-year-old is starting a full-time business, think again. A corporation doesn't come into existence until it's formally set up (*incorporated*) under state law. Corporations cost money: There are fees to incorporate, annual state franchise taxes to be paid, attorney's fees for preparing the corporation's minute books and issuing stock, and accounting fees for preparing the company's financial books and tax returns (unless your child does this himself).

➤ *Setting up a limited liability company.* Instead of incorporating the business, you can have it organized under your state's limited liability company laws. In this way, your child enjoys the same personal liability protection offered by the corporate umbrella, but business profits (or losses) are taxed in the same way as a partnership (they're passed through to partners and taxed on their individual income tax returns).

➤ *Put the money together to start up.* Whether it's going to take $100, $1,000, or even $10,000 to get started, decide where that money's coming from. Your child may have saved up from a job or gifts to get started, or you may become an investor in your child's business and make a loan of seed money.

➤ *Make a marketing plan.* Big businesses have formal plans in which they plot out how they'll bring their company to the public's attention. But even the smallest business needs a plan on how it's going to get customers. Spread the word. The best form of advertising is word of mouth. Tell neighbors and friends what your child has to sell. Ask existing customers for referrals. Another cheap and effective way to get customers locally is to post signs in the supermarket and other local stores. A third, although slightly more costly, way is to advertise. Local *Pennysaver* or other weekly circulars in your neighborhood can

Watch Your Step

While there's no legal requirement that a partnership have a formal agreement, it's a good idea to put in writing some terms to protect both partners. As a minimum, decide how profits are to be split (50-50 or otherwise), what happens if one partner wants out, and how deadlocks are to be broken.

Watch Your Step

Once there's a corporation, formalities must be observed. Special accounting and tax filing rules apply, and you can't just walk away from it, even if the business isn't profitable. You'll have to take legal steps to end the corporation, formally dissolving it under state law.

bring attention your child's business. The cost of a weekly ad may be about $15, but you'll probably have to run the ad for some time before the business has an established clientele. Yet another way is to advertise on the Internet. Your child can post her own Web page about her business for free (see www.independentmeans.com/aioho_teenbiz.html).

Money ABCs

Marketing is the process by which people get what they want through creating and exchanging products or services with each other for value (money, products, or services). It includes advertising and promotion.

Your child can learn about the different facets of running a home-based business by reading *The Complete Idiot's Guide® to Starting a Home-Based Business.* Also check out a Web site called Independent Means (www.independentmeans.com) designed to help females under 20 start up businesses and handle money matters.

Finally, as a parent, be prepared to help your child overcome the practical limitations of his age in running his business. For example, you may have to drive him to see customers or suppliers or to deliver his wares. You may have to sign purchase orders or other agreements because your child is under the legal age for making a binding contract and sellers may not want to risk having only a child's promise to pay or perform.

The Least You Need to Know

➤ Age is generally no barrier to starting a business.

➤ Kids need to understand the responsibility involved in running a business.

➤ Working in a family business can give a kid the opportunity to learn things from the ground up.

➤ Clubs and organizations at school or after school can teach your child business skills.

➤ Make sure things are legal before your child opens his doors for business.

➤ Think through how much cash is needed to get started and what means of advertising will be used.

Chapter 11

Getting Money Out of the Blue

In This Chapter

➤ Getting gifts

➤ Winning awards

➤ Taking in trust fund money

Until now, the chapters in this part of the book have concentrated on what your child can do to make money. But your child may come into money through no effort on her part. You and other relatives may shower her with gifts. She may be a lucky winner in a contest. Or, she may be heir to some great wealth.

In this chapter, you'll see other ways in which your child may come into money. You'll find out about different types of gifts that may be given, you'll learn about awards that can be earned, and you'll find out about trust funds that may be set up for kids. In the parts of the book that follow, you'll learn about what your child can or should do with the cash she gets as a gift or award.

Gifts Are Golden

You probably give things to your kids each day, and you may also give presents on special occasions. Chances are, you don't think of this as being generous or making gifts—still, they're gifts just the same. Maybe it's only a visit from the Tooth Fairy, a reward for a good report card, or a birthday present: All are gifts.

In addition to the little things you give your kids, there may be times you give more significant gifts, such as cash or securities. These larger gifts are perhaps motivated more by your own estate planning concerns than thoughts of generosity, but whatever the motivation, it's important to understand what making gifts to your kids can mean. It's also necessary to understand the impact of gifts given to your kids by other people.

Making Gifts to Kids

How generous should you be to your child or other kids? When it comes to your own child, there's always a concern that giving too much will spoil him or that you'll give too much and it will be taken for granted.

Concerns about spoiling aside, your generosity to your child is guided by your financial abilities. You can give only what you can afford and what you think is appropriate under the circumstances.

Certainly, at times gifts are standard operating procedure (and maybe even expected). Often, these gifts are made in cash.

➤ *Tooth fairy offerings.* Payments left under the pillow for the first tooth or two your kid loses may come as a big surprise. Unfortunately, kids become knowledgeable very soon about who the Tooth Fairy really is and come to expect payment for each lost tooth. Usually, the first tooth warrants a big surprise— $1 or even $5 in some neighborhoods is the going rate. Then, each successive tooth may fetch a 25¢, 50¢, or $1. In other neighborhoods, the traditional cash left under the pillow is being replaced by small things, such as stickers.

Piggybank on It

According to child-care expert Dr. Spock, kids are spoiled as babies from overattention. They learn to always put their needs first. Money itself doesn't spoil a child (rich kids aren't necessarily spoiled); it's only how you use the money with your kid that can continue early childhood lessons in how to be spoiled.

➤ *Birthday presents.* There's no standard on what's appropriate for a birthday gift, and the size of the gift can vary greatly. The amount may differ depending on whether it's a gift to your own child, a grandchild, a niece out of town, your child's classmate, or his best friend. You may spend $10, $15, or $20, depending on what's customary in your area and what you can afford. It's not common for a parent to give his own child cash for his birthday (at least until he's more adult), but cash may be appropriate if you're sending a gift by mail to a relative out of town. Sometimes, birthday gifts are made in the form of savings bonds to mark the occasion.

Piggybank on It

Gifts of U.S. Savings bonds (Series EE or I) can be made in a child's name, with a child's Social Security number listed on the bond. You don't need a custodian to hold the bond, no matter how young the child may be.

➤ *Gifts on religious occasions.* Gifts given to a child to mark a religious milestone—a bar or bat mitzvah, or a confirmation—can be nominal in amount or quite large. The going rate in gifts these days varies from place to place, but the total gifts your child may receive on such occasions can add up into the thousands.

➤ *Graduation presents.* A decade ago, a lucky high school senior off to college may have received an electric typewriter. Today, it's a computer. But cash gifts from family friends or other relatives also may be given.

Serious Gifts

If you are financially fixed enough to seek estate planning guidance, then you're probably in a position to make larger gifts to your child. You are encouraged by the tax laws to make gifts to your kids for several reasons:

➤ *You reduce the size of your estate.* Everything you have will be taxed after you die, but a person can die owing no federal estate tax if his assets don't exceed a certain amount ($650,000 in 1999, increasing in stages to $1 million by 2006). In effect, married people can have twice as much in the family without any estate tax concerns. But if there's more involved, it becomes important to find ways to transfer assets to children or others without any transfer tax costs. If such planning isn't undertaken, then inheritances for children will be needlessly reduced by estate taxes.

Watch Your Step

Before you dump lots of money in your child's name, make sure that you understand the impact it may have on his ability to qualify for college financial aid. Currently, money saved in the child's name is counted more heavily (35 percent) than that in the parent's name (5.6 percent) in figuring financial aid eligibility. Colleges expect that kids will spend their money on their own education.

Financial Building Blocks

Under the United States' federal unified estate and gift tax system, transfers over a certain amount are subject to the same tax whether they're given during life or at death (there's one tax rate schedule for both gifts and estates). Only a handful of states have any gift tax, although most states have some type of death tax (either a tax on the estate or an inheritance tax on heirs).

➤ *You can save income taxes within the family.* If income-producing assets such as stocks and bonds are given to children, the recipients may pay tax on the income from these assets at a lower tax rate. This is called income-shifting, and it saves the total taxes paid by all family members.

119

For example, if you give your teenager stock you've owned for a while that has appreciated, your teenager may pay only half the tax you'd have paid on the sale of that stock. You'd pay 20 percent capital gains tax; she'd pay only 10 percent (if she's in the 15 percent tax bracket on his other income).

If you set up a trust for your child and funds in the trust are used to satisfy your parental obligation of support, then you—not your child—are taxed on the income from the trust, which defeats the income-shifting purpose of the trust.

Financial Building Blocks

Kids pay tax on income they receive. However, for children under the age of 14, income may be subject to a "kiddie tax." This means that income over a set amount ($1,400 in 1999) is taxed to them at their parent's highest tax rate. It's as if the parent had received the income instead of the child. However, careful planning, such as putting money into appreciating assets that don't throw off current income, can avoid the impact of the kiddie tax.

➤ *There's little or no gift tax cost to you or your child for making a gift.* Each year you can give up to $10,000 to your child, and your spouse can also give $10,000 (for a total of $20,000). You can give each of your children up to this amount each year. This is called the *annual gift tax exclusion* (and may be adjusted for inflation in the future). For example, if you're a single parent with three children, you can give away up to $30,000 each year if you give each child $10,000. Over five years, this can total up to $150,000 in transfers that are completely tax-free. Gifts over the annual exclusion may also be tax-free because of the exemption amount mentioned earlier. However, to the extent the exemption amount is used for gifts, it's not available for a person's estate.

Watch Your Step

You can't deduct gifts you make to your kids or others. While they may be free from gift tax if they're under a certain amount, you don't get to claim a deduction for them on your income taxes.

You can benefit your child even more without triggering any gift tax. You'll allowed to make payments of medical and educational expenses in any amount as long as they're made directly to the service provider (such as the doctor or the school). And, if you put money into a qualified state tuition program for their college education, you can treat the gift as if it were made over five years. So, if you put in $100,000 (the limit allowed in some states), you can treat it as though $20,000 contributions were made each year, which allows a couple to avoid all gift tax.

For more information about the kiddie tax and other tax matters, see IRS Publication 929, Tax Rules for Children and Dependents, which can be downloaded from the IRS Web site. Click on www.irs.ustreas.gov. Or you can have the publication sent to you by calling 800-TAX-FORMS.

How to Make Gifts to Your Child

Let's say you decide you want to give your child expensive gifts for the reasons mentioned previously. Expensive here doesn't just mean a color TV; it means something more like a stock portfolio. How should you do it? You don't want to hand over $5,000 in large bills to a 7-year-old—or, for that matter, even a 17-year-old.

Generally, gifts to a child under 18 of this magnitude should be given in one of two ways:

➤ *Custodianship.* State law allows gifts to be made to minors under the Uniform Gifts to Minors Act (called UGMA, for short) or the Uniform Transfers to Minors Act (called UTMA, for short). The Act you use depends upon which one applies in your state.

Title to bank and brokerage accounts, stock certificates, and other property is held in the name of an adult as custodian for the child. The property is listed under the child's Social Security number, and the child (not the custodian) pays tax on the income from the property. Custodianships are easy to set up and don't require the services of a lawyer. Still, your child has an absolute right to the money when the custodianship ends at age 18 or 21. If he wants to blow it on a Mustang instead of using it for college as you'd hoped, there's nothing you can legally do about it.

➤ *Trust.* When assets are very significant, or when you don't think that your child should have control of them at 21, you may want to use a trust to hold property you give to your child. Trusts are discussed later in this chapter.

Piggybank on It

To determine whether UGMA or UTMA applies in your state, ask a local attorney or call the Commissioner on Uniform State Laws at 312-915-0195.

Watch Your Step

Trusts are a very complicated subject, so don't try to do this yourself. Get the help of an attorney who's experienced in trust matters. The size of the lawyer's bill for this help will depend in part on the complexity of the trust you want.

Financial Building Blocks

UTMA is now the law in 46 states and the District of Columbia. The differences between UGMA and UTMA generally are that UTMA doesn't have any limits on the types of property that can be held in custodianship; UGMA is usually limited to bank and brokerage accounts and securities. Also, custodianships under UTMA don't end until the child is 21; under UGMA, they can end at 18.

In deciding whether to use a custodianship or a trust, consider several factors:

➤ *Size of the gift.* The bigger the gift, the more you should look into trusts. It's a way to put lots of assets in one place and manage them together, and this can make for better investment decisions.

➤ *Age of your child.* Even if gifts are modest, you may expect that the funds will appreciate over the years and can grow substantially if you start when your child is young. Your child can wind up with a fund that you'd have wanted to place in a trust from the beginning.

➤ *Personal wishes.* You may want to tailor an arrangement to limit a child's access to funds. For example, you might not want him to get *all* the money at 21. A trust can limit distributions to age 25, 30, 35, or whenever and to whatever extent you want. To do this, you'll need to use a trust.

Watch Your Step

Gambling can get out of control for some kids. Compulsive gambling can cause them to miss school, lose sleep, and suffer in other ways. Yes, even children can become compulsive gamblers who need help. For information about Gamblers Anonymous, click on www. gamblersanonymous.org.

Your Kid's Winning Ways

When Powerball fever infected the country in the summer of 1998 because of its nearly $200 million jackpot, kids couldn't help but hear about this event. They, too, may have fantasized about what they'd do with a winning of this amount.

But winnings for a kid are probably much more modest: They may be nominal awards for successfully competing in contests or impressive awards in the form of scholarships for their education.

In thinking about winning, it's impossible to ignore how pervasive gambling has become in our country. Casinos are everywhere. States run lotteries; churches run bingo. Gambling is an activity that knows no age boundaries.

Some kids in school play poker and bet on professional football games. For some of these kids, it may be a harmless activity (unless you are fundamentally opposed to gambling in any form). But for some of these kids, gambling may develop into a problem that can ruin their financial well-being.

Contests for Kids

Spelling bees and essay contests are just a couple of the ways your child may become a winner. Usually these contests pay small amounts in cash or other awards, such as books or subscriptions. Sometimes, awards paid to kids are given in the form of U.S. savings bonds. Here are just a few money-related contests open to kids:

➤ *National Savings Month Contest*, sponsored by Merrill Lynch. Winners in two divisions (grades 4–7 and grades 8–12) receive savings bonds for essays, posters, or videos on the topic of why saving is important (for information, call 800-637-7455).

➤ *Stein Roe Young Investor Essay Challenge*, sponsored by Stein Roe Mutual Funds (call 800-586-5437). Winners here win shares in the Stein Roe Young Investors mutual fund.

➤ *Kids Speak Out About Taxes Contest*, sponsored by TurboTax. Open to kids in grades 3–5, entrants must submit an essay on how they think the government should be spending tax dollars. Winners receive U.S. savings bonds or contributions to education IRAs in their name, and the best entry is sent to Congress. Kids can enter online by going to the Taxes area of Quicken at www.quicken.com.

➤ *High School Financial Literacy Awards*, sponsored by the National Endowment for Financial Education. This contest, restricted to high school students, gives prizes totaling $30,000 to winners in essay and poster categories. Kids can enter online by clicking on www.nefe.org/hsfla/default.htm.

Watch Your Step

Kids under the age of 18 generally can't enter most contests or try for most awards, such as Publisher's Clearinghouse Sweepstakes or your state lottery. If your child does try to enter and is lucky enough to win, she won't be able to collect her winnings.

Winners in School

As your child gets older, he may become a winner in another way. He may earn a scholarship for primary, secondary, or prep school or for or college. Just attend a high school graduation awards dinner, and you'll hear a long list of gifts, big and small, awarded to deserving graduates. Some scholarships may be large enough to cover the entire cost of a college education.

Scholarships are given out by schools, corporations, organizations, private individuals, and even the government for various reasons. Whatever the reason for winning the scholarship, it certainly helps in paying for the child's education.

Money ABCs

A **scholarship** is a monetary award to cover the cost of education. It's free, and the student never has to repay it.

Piggybank on It

Scholarships aren't taxable income to your child if awarded for tuition, fees, books, supplies, and other course equipment—*and* if he's in school pursuing a degree or a vocational training program. However, any amounts awarded for room and board or paid for services required to render are treated as income to him.

Watch Your Step

Before paying any money to a scholarship search firm, be sure to check it out with your local Better Business Bureau (the number is listed in your Yellow Pages).

➤ *Financial need.* Most schools award money each year to students who would not be financially able to attend without help. Find out about scholarships for financial need through www.fidalgo.net/~clifford/scholar1.html.

➤ *Abilities.* Some scholarships are awarded for certain outstanding abilities or conduct, such as athletic scholarships for football players and National Merit Scholarships and the Westinghouse Science Talent Search for brainy students. Scholarships for top academic students can be located your child's high school guidance, career, or college office and through sandburg.unm.edu/scholarships/scholars.html.

➤ *Profile.* Some scholarships may be given because your child fits a certain profile (for example, she's an African-American who meets the qualifications of a scholarship set up by a certain family in the neighborhood). For links to various scholarships for women and minorities, click on www.aol.com/ox13qu/webpages/eyfswm1.html. Scholarships for minorities also can be located through www.fie.com/molis/scholar.htm. Also check out scholarships offered for community service, such as the Coca Cola Scholarship Foundation and the Johnson & Johnson's Tylenol Scholarships.

Typically, the scholarships awarded by sources other than the school itself are paid directly to the school. Sometimes a child is given unfettered use of the funds, with the expectation that she'll use the money for school.

Some other expectations sometimes accompany scholarships. For instance, all the military academies are free, but the catch is that your child must complete a certain term of service to that branch of the military. Reserve Office Training Corps (ROTC) also offers full or partial scholarships (including a monthly spending allowance) to applicants who agree to serve four years of active duty, plus two years in the reserves.

Some search firms will match your child's academic record, special talents, or other abilities with available scholarships. These firms charge a fee. Some are good, but a number may provide only a listing of all scholarships, leaving you to track them down, or giving you information readily available to everyone. Two scholarship search firms to check out yourself are College Quest (609-243-9111) and National Scholarship Research Service (707-546-6777).

Little Rockefeller's Pot of Gold

It used to be that only the Rockefellers set up trust funds for their children and grandchildren. Today, with ordinary people becoming millionaires through the increased property value of their homes and stock market-driven accumulations in their company retirement plans, trust funds are becoming more commonplace. Parents and grandparents in this category are undertaking estate planning to preserve their wealth and minimize death taxes. This means good news to the younger generations.

Trusts are set up to provide certain benefits for all concerned:

➤ *Protection of assets for the beneficiary.* The property in the trust is managed by a trustee. Usually, this is someone who's good at handling money. It can even be a parent (although this may not be a good idea tax-wise) or a trust company. Having a trustee in charge means that the beneficiary can't squander the property; it's protected for his benefit.

➤ *Tax savings for the person setting up the trust.* There are income, estate, and gift tax advantages to using a trust.

Grandparents who are wealthy may be especially interested in making gifts in trust to their grandchildren. Grandparents can do this while they're alive or can leave money in trust when they die. Grandparents whose own children are wealthy in their own right might not want to complicate the estate plans of their kids, so they leave money to the grandkids.

Money ABCs

A **trust** is a legal type of ownership in which property is held by a fiduciary, called a **trustee**, for the benefit of someone else, called a **beneficiary**. The trustee runs things; the beneficiary gets things from the trust. The person who gives the money to the trust is called a **grantor** or **settler**.

Piggybank on It

Instead of using a trust to gift property to kids, you can use a custodial account. The key difference is that kids are entitled to all the funds from a custodial account at 18 (or 21, depending on state law), as explained earlier in this chapter. In contrast, trusts can restrict when and how much is given out.

Financial Building Blocks

Gifts from grandparents to grandchildren may fall victim to a special transfer tax because the gifts skip a generation (that of the parents). However, each grandparent has a $1 million exemption (that's indexed annually for inflation) that can be used to make gifts to grandchildren without the generation-skipping transfer tax. This tax is complex, and wealthy people should talk to their tax advisers before making any large gifts.

Types of Trusts for Kids

When you make gifts to a child in trust, you want to do it in such a way that your gifts qualify for the annual gift tax exclusion. This isn't automatic because your kid can't touch the money until she's an adult. Under the gift tax law, this is viewed as a gift of future interest, which doesn't automatically qualify for the annual gift tax exclusion. But the law allows two types of trusts for minors to qualify for this exclusion. Both types get their names from the provision in the Internal Revenue Code that creates them.

➤ *Section 2503(b) trust.* In this type of trust, income *must* be distributed at least annually to your child while he's a minor. It doesn't actually have to be put in his hands; it can go into a custodial account if the child is too young to handle things or if the funds are too great. Alternatively, he must be given the right to withdraw an amount at least equal to the annual gift tax exclusion. Of course, because he's still a minor, it's you, his parent, who decides whether to exercise this right.

➤ *Section 2503 trust.* This type of trust must allow trust income and principal to be used for the child until she's 21. At that age, all the money still in the trust must be paid to the child. At that time, the child is allowed to decide whether to extend the trust.

A Kid's Rights in the Trust

Once you put money in a child's name, it's his. You can't get it back, even if you need it. (Of course, the same is true of any gift you make.) As beneficiary of the trust, your child is entitled to whatever income and principal from the trust that the trust document says he's entitled to. Usually, this is only the income while he's a minor.

When do you tell a child about being a beneficiary of a trust? There's no magic age because it depends on your circumstances. Does he need to know? What would happen if he knew? As a general rule, it's always a good idea to give as much information about financial matters as your child can handle. There's no point in telling a 10-year-old that there's a million dollars sitting in trust that Grandma funded for him. But as a child gets older, this can ease concerns about being able to pay for college or do other things—plus, you can start to prepare him to handle his money.

When the trust ends and whatever remains in it is distributed to the child, he's usually entitled to an accounting from the trustee. This means that the trustee must show how the money has been spent over the years. If the trustee has acted in violation of the terms of the trust or state law, then your child has a lawsuit for damages against the trustee.

The Least You Need to Know

➤ The amount of gifts you give your child depends on your circumstances.

➤ The tax laws encourage gift-giving.

➤ The kiddie tax limits your ability to shift your income to your kids if they're under age 14.

➤ Sizable gifts should be given through a custodianship or in trust.

➤ Trusts are becoming more common today as the size of people's wealth has increased through property values and the stock market.

➤ Gifts given to a child belong to him and cannot be taken back.

127

Part 4
Big (and Little) Spenders

Getting money, through work or otherwise, is only the first step in money management. By far the more complicated lesson is what to do with it once your child has it. Here's where you, as a parent, come in. Learning to spend wisely is no easy task; it requires decision-making and personal character. It's up to you to provide guidance and assistance in making choices and learning to live within a budget.

When a child comes into money, there are basically two things he can do with it: spend it or save it. Obviously, there's an important balance between these two demands.

In this part of the book, you'll find out about the first alternative—spending. In the next part of the book, you'll look at saving money. In this part, you'll see how to share the responsibility for expenses as your child gets older. You'll help your child make spending choices, and you'll learn how you can guide your child to set up a budget as practice for a lifetime of handling money. You'll be able to help your child learn how to give money away to worthy causes.

Chapter 12

Picking Up the Tab

In This Chapter

➤ Shifting spending responsibility

➤ Shopping for clothes

➤ Gassing up the car

➤ Moving on to college

➤ Dealing with problems

When your child is young, you naturally pay for everything. You pay for the roof over his head, the food that goes into his mouth, the clothes on his back, the medical care he receives, and everything else. But as your child gets older, he starts to have his own money. From then on, he becomes a consumer, and it's up to you to guide him on how to become a smart consumer.

One important aspect to his consumer status is knowing what he's responsible for. What will you continue to pay for? What must he now buy? Who makes these decisions—you, him, or both of you?

In this chapter, you'll get some ideas about when and how to shift spending responsibility to your child. You'll learn about the three C's—clothing, car, and college—in which parents typically share spending responsibility with their kids. You'll also learn what to do if you find that your child is getting things illegally.

When You No Longer Pay

It used to be that kids grew up, moved out of their parent's house, and became self-supporting at what we might view as a young age. Self-support starts when adolescence ends.

Today, many kids stay in school longer. Once they graduate, they may become "boomerang kids" who live at home until they're married or can afford the high cost of housing in some parts of the country. Even if the child pays rent, a parent with an adult child living at home still effectively provides support for her.

Money ABCs

Adolescence is the period from puberty to maturity. It may or may not coincide with the teenage years (those from 13 through 19).

As a parent, however, you don't want to support your kid forever. At some point, you want to be able to see that she is financially independent. This is a desirable goal for both you and your child. She gets to enjoy self-reliance, and you can concentrate on yourself, taking the vacations you have put off over the years, saving for your retirement and old age, or just being able to work a little less. To do this, you need to start teaching the value of independence when your child is young. One way to start letting her make spending decisions is by putting the responsibility for certain purchases on her shoulders.

Financial Building Blocks

How long are you *legally* required to provide support for your child? The answer depends on the law in your state. Typically, this legal responsibility ends when your child reaches the age of majority (18 or 21) or becomes emancipated (moves out, marries, or joins the military). Parental support may go longer if required under the terms of a divorce agreement.

What are you required to pay for? Generally, you have to pay for necessaries (food, shelter, and medical care). But you have to pay for the extras only if they're consistent with your standard of living. So, Bill Gates will certainly be required to pay for his child's education, but the law won't make you do it if you can't afford to pay for it.

You must settle two things if you're going to shift spending to your child.

➤ You have to know who's going to decide whether you or your child is responsible for certain types of expenditures.

➤ You need to know when you'll shift spending for these expenditures to your child.

Who Decides?

The parent-child relationship isn't a democracy; it's more like a benevolent dictatorship with you in the role of despot. But just because you make the final decision doesn't mean that you can't talk about things before that decision is made.

The discussion isn't just you asking your child, "Do you want to pay for your entertainment?" Such a question would probably just produce a "no" answer. After all, who would *want* to pay for things voluntarily?

But there's a point to having a discussion. Giving your child responsibility for certain types of expenses is a way of giving him independence. He, not you, decides what to spend the money on. For example, if you tell your teenager that he's responsible for clothing purchases, then he can decide what he'll wear.

Obviously, the responsibility to pay for things must be coupled with the ability to do it. This ability can come in the form of a spending allowance from you or through earnings from a job your child has taken. The responsibility also must be sensitive to your ability to provide the things that your child wants; you may not be able to buy all those video games he so desperately desires. Here's where a shift in responsibility makes sense: If he wants it, then he'll have to figure out how to buy it.

The decision on who buys what isn't set in stone. It should be adjusted periodically and should be accompanied by discussions on the subject. Revisit the topic at any or all of following events:

➤ Once a year (or every six months)

➤ At the start of each school year (or school transitions, such as from middle school to high school or from high school to college)

➤ When you adjust your child's allowance

➤ When your child starts working

Age-Appropriate Responsibility

When your child is 5, you can't expect her to pay for her shoes or even her toys. That's up to you (and your pocketbook). But as she gets older, things change. There are no magic ages for giving your child responsibility, but here are some guidelines on when you might consider shifting spending responsibility to your child.

➤ *Candy and snacks*. As soon as your child is old enough for an allowance, he's old enough to start making spending decisions. At that time, you should begin to place spending responsibility on him for the little things, such as a

Piggybank on It

Most kids start to receive an allowance when they're in school, usually by 6 or 7. From this age on, they'll become consumers. Starting and fixing allowances are discussed in Chapter 8, "Making Allowances."

candy bar or a soda. These decisions come naturally as your child has access to vending machines at school. As he goes places by himself, he'll have an opportunity to spend his money on a slice of pizza or a burger.

➤ *Toys and games.* As with candy and snacks, the responsibility for buying toys and games can begin to shift once your child starts receiving an allowance.

➤ *Entertainment.* The time for shifting responsibility for paying for the movies, a trip to the video arcade, or a date depends on when your child starts to do these things without you tagging along. Depending on the neighborhood you live in, kids may start to travel on buses and subways to get to movie theaters on their own when they're young. Growing up in Queens (a borough of New York City), my friends and I used to take a bus and subway to get into Manhattan from the age of about 11. In other places, it's tough for kids to get anywhere unless you drive them. Growing up in the suburbs, my kids couldn't get to the mall unless I dropped them off. It seems to follow that if they're transportation-independent, then they become responsible for deciding where to go (and that they have to pay for it).

➤ *Private telephone line.* Teenagers are notorious for talking on the telephone, and many of their parents can't gain access to the phone in the post-school hours of the day. It's not uncommon to add a second home phone line for their use. Responsibility for the payment of this second line may be given to teenagers.

➤ *Clothing.* As kids get older and enter their teens, their tastes become more fixed. What you like won't necessarily coincide with their tastes, though, so shifting responsibility for buying clothes can make both financial sense (teaching them how to do it) and personal sense (ending constant squabbles about what to buy). Shifting responsibility for clothing is discussed later in this chapter.

➤ *Car.* The issue of whether your child should have a car and who should pay for it doesn't come up until she's past driving age, typically 16 or older. But once the issue arises, you'd better be prepared to deal with it. A car is a costly item: A parent who can afford it may provide the child with a car and pay for its upkeep. A parent who can't may still be able to split expenses; shifting responsibility for a car is discussed later in this chapter.

➤ *College.* Kids may have the right to vote at 18, but there's no law giving them the right to go to college. Still, we're all in favor of education—the only issue is how to pay for it. How much do you pay? How much does your child pay? Shifting responsibility for college is discussed later in this chapter.

Shopping for Clothing

Whether your child pays for his clothes out of an allowance, spending money specifically for clothes, or personal earnings, having the responsibility of purchasing his own clothes will teach many things.

➤ *Budgeting money.* If your child has to buy a variety of clothes, she'll have to learn that she can't blow it all on a fancy pair of boots, leaving nothing in reserve for underwear. Or, he'll have to decide whether to spend a lot on one good pair of pants or several less pricey ones.

➤ *Shopping for values.* If your child knows that there's only so much to spend on clothes, he'll become a better shopper. He'll look for sales, compare prices, and avoid impulse buying. Today, it's easy to buy even name brands at a discount through outlet malls, through catalogs, and even on the Internet.

Big Things Versus Little Things

According to a survey on teens and money by *Weekend USA,* only 9 percent of teens thought they should be responsible for the cost of their clothes and shoes. As a parent, you may feel differently. Clothing is a big category, and you might want to shift some spending responsibility to your child without dumping the whole category on his shoulders.

Here are some arrangements you can use to split clothing purchase responsibilities:

➤ *Start little.* Let your child shop for one needed item, and see how well he does. If he needs sneakers, you might give him a spending allowance of up to $100 and then let him decide on the pair to buy. Maybe he'll find a $50 pair he wants, or maybe he'll find a $100 pair on a 50 percent sale. Or, maybe he won't find anything in the price range you've targeted and will have to face doing without what he wants.

➤ *Season by season.* Consider giving your child a wardrobe allowance for a season (for example, $500 for back-to-school clothes, if you can afford this amount). She'll have to decide what she needs and how to fill that need.

Watch Your Step

Don't be overly critical of your child's taste in the clothing she's bought (as long as it doesn't involve choices that you really object to, such as bustiers for a 14-year-old). This is part of her chance to express herself. In general, limit your comments to the financial aspects of her choice. Did she spend too much for what she bought? Did she find good value?

Piggybank on It

You can combine strategies, letting your child shop for a season's wardrobe that you pay for but making him buy any extras he wants.

Piggybank on It

Suggest that your child try on what's in his closet to see what still fits and then make a list of what's needed. This will keep him from spending all the allotment on jeans and sweat shirts when what he really needs is a new sports jacket.

135

➤ *Split responsibility.* Maybe you'll pay for the big-ticket items, such as a coat. Your child then becomes responsible for the smaller things, such as jeans or socks.

➤ *Extras.* You might agree to continue paying for needed clothing, such as a new pair of shoes. If your child wants anything above and beyond the basic wardrobe, he's on his own.

Gassing Up the Car

In most places in the country, a 16th birthday marks a rite of passage. This is the date on which a child can get a learner's permit and eventually a driver's license. This also is the time you'll have to address the question of the car.

Money ABCs

A **depreciating asset** is one that grows to be worth less over time. Unlike a work of art or real estate that can grow in value, a car (other than certain antique or specialty cars) is almost certainly guaranteed to be worth less over time than on the day it was bought.

Piggybank on It

Look for ways to cut insurance costs. State Farm offers discounts for good students (a report card must be provided to the company), while Allstate lowers its rates if a child's college is more than 100 miles away from home.

Depending on where you live, a car may be a necessity. Your child might not be able to get to school, a job, or friends without one. So, you'd better help your child know what car ownership is about in terms of dollars and cents. You'll also have to decide how much of this financial burden you're willing and able to share.

Reality Lesson in Car Costs

Your child may not fully understand the exact dollars involved. By the time your child is 16, she may understand it costs money to buy a car, and she may also know that it costs money to own a car. But she probably realizes this only in abstract terms, not exact dollar amounts. She needs to know the hard facts so that she knows what she's getting into if she takes on the responsibility of a car.

Here's a list you might want to share with your child to open her eyes to the types of expenses involved in having a car.

➤ *Purchase price.* Whether you buy a new or used car, you're talking in the thousands today. A car can be one of the largest purchases your child will ever make (although he'll probably make it repeatedly throughout his life). No matter which type he opts for, a car is a depreciating asset. It's not an investment in the usual sense.

➤ *Sales tax on the purchase price.* If your child saves up for a used car costing $2,000, she had better understand that when she goes to get plates for the car in most states, she'll have to pay sales tax on the purchase price.

➤ *Registration and license fees.* As with a sales tax on the purchase price of a car, registration fees are a way that states extract money from car owners for the privilege of being an owner. Rates vary considerably from state to state.

➤ *Insurance.* A car owner *must* carry car insurance because he can't register a car without it. Insurance is costly, especially for drivers under the age of 25. This is because drivers in this age group are considered inexperienced. Rates for male drivers under the age of 25 also are higher than for females of the same age. This is because boys generally have a higher incident of accidents and cost insurance companies more money. Your child can reduce his insurance costs by taking a drivers' education class or a defensive driving course, by not speeding, by keeping a clean driving record, and by forgoing the sports car until he's older (even if he or you can afford it).

➤ *Gas.* Gas prices in recent months have been low. (Adjusted for inflation, 1998 gas prices were as low as they were in 1958.) But there's no guarantee that they'll stay low in the future, so your child should be prepared for fluctuations in gas prices. When shopping for a car, she also should consider the car's MPG. The more your child drives, the more it costs to gas up the car.

➤ *Maintenance.* With new cars, maintenance can be low. With a used car, however, the ongoing cost of keeping it in operation can run high. For example, the car may use a can of oil at nearly every fill-up. Even a new car requires routine maintenance periodically, such as oil changes and new tires.

Money ABCs

Miles per gallon (MPG), is a way of expressing how efficient a car is when it comes to using gas. Technically, this refers to how far the car can be driven for each gallon of gas in the tank (for example, 25 MPG means that you can go 25 miles for each gallon of gas). The higher the MPG, the better the gas efficiency and the cheaper it is to run the car.

Piggybank on It

Look for a car with a generous warranty that will cover the cost of certain repairs. Even if a car is used, the original warranty may still be in effect or a dealer may offer a special used car warranty.

Sharing the Cost of a Car

You may not be in a financial position to pay for all or some of your child's car. If he wants one, he'll have to work for it.

But you may be able to decide how much of the cost of a car you're going to share with your child.

137

➤ *The family car.* If you allow your child to use the family car, you'll want to decide whether she's responsible for putting gas in it and contributing to its upkeep. At a minimum, you can require that she keep it clean.

➤ *Family car hand-me-down.* You may be able to give your child your old car and get yourself a new one. Once the car is his, however, the lines must be drawn on who pays for ongoing costs. I was able to give my kids a used car with the understanding that they pay for half the insurance and all the gas and maintenance. Other parents I know continue to pay for insurance and maintenance but shift responsibility for gas and oil.

➤ *Kid car.* Your child may be able to buy her own car with savings and earnings, and some parents may split the cost of a car in some way (for example, each pays half the purchase price). Some well-heeled parents buy their child her own car. After you and your child know what you both can afford, the next decision to be made is whether to buy a new car or a preowned one.

Buying a new car has its upside and its downside. The good part about a new car is that repairs should be cheap—things that generally shouldn't break, such as the transmission, are covered by warranty if they do. The bad news is the sticker price: You pay top dollar for new cars.

Money ABCs

A **preowned car** is just another name for a used car; it's a new word for an old car.

Piggybank on It

Even if your child pays her own way through school, you can still provide some help in the form of a spending allowance or even loans to meet financial aid shortfalls.

Buying a used car may be all that your child can afford, but that doesn't mean that he can't get a good car for his money. It just takes a little extra effort on his part.

However you work out the acquisition costs with your child, you'll still have to settle responsibility for the ongoing costs. Again, cost sharing can take many forms, as discussed earlier.

Moving On to College

After the car hurdle, it's on to college for many kids. It has become increasingly common to take a college education for granted because it has become expected that a child will pursue a higher education. There are sound financial reasons for doing this: College grads, as a whole, earn more than high school graduates. (Don't let your child talk his way out of going to college by telling you about how Bill Gates made it even though he never finished college.)

Still, paying for college isn't easy these days, and a college education can be one of the most expensive things a person ever pays for. You may not be able to pay for all of it, or even some of it. You may even have more than one child in college at the same time. Joseph

Califano, who served as Secretary of HEW, the forerunner of today's Department of Education, called this "sibling overlap." According to one survey, the majority of teens believe that the cost of college should be shared between parent and child; only 30 percent think their parents should pay for it all.

Financial Building Blocks

Statistics from the U.S. Department of Education show that male college graduates earn 39 percent more than male high school graduates. For women, it's 28 percent more with a college degree.

Bargain Hunting for a College Education

If you can't afford to pick up the tab on your child's college education—and most parents can't—there are certainly ways for your child to reduce her costs. It's a good idea for you to work with your child through the college payment process.

Consider the following types of schools to stretch college dollars while gaining a quality education:

➤ *Community colleges.* The cost of attendance at a state-run community college is generally modest. Usually, your child lives at home while attending, so he doesn't incur the added costs of living away. After he completes the two-year program at a community college, he can continue to earn a bachelor's degree at a four-year college or university. Even if he goes private at that time, he'll have saved a lot from his two-year community college experience. A former babysitter for my kids attended the county community college and then finished her bachelor's degree at Cornell, an Ivy League school.

➤ *State colleges.* If your child attends a college or university run by the state in which you live, tuition generally is modest compared to a private school. State colleges also charge higher tuition to out-of-state students, but even then, a child may pay less to attend a state school from a different state than she would for a private school.

➤ *Bargain schools.* Some schools may have little or no costs for attending. For example, the U.S. military academies are free. You can find a listing of bargain schools by checking with your child's school's guidance or college office.

Other ways exist for reducing the cost of a higher education. Your child can also cut the costs of higher education by getting through school quicker, eliminating the need to pay tuition for the extra time. Here are some ways to do this:

➤ *Take advanced placement courses in high school.* AP exams, administered by the same Educational Testing Service (a nonprofit organization in Princeton, N.J.) that oversees SATs, are offered in more than two dozen subjects. If your child earns a certain grade on the exam, his college will give him credit for the subject. This may allow him to skip an introductory course or meet other course requirements.

➤ *Take extra courses each semester.* Generally, full-time students pay tuition for a semester regardless of the number of credits taken (though there may be a limit of 21 credit hours per semester). By adding just one extra course each semester, your child can easily save a semester of school. By attending summer school or a winter term (between fall and spring semesters), she may cut a full year off her program.

➤ *Look for combined degree programs.* If your child is thinking now about getting a graduate degree after college, he should think about combined degree programs. For example, if he plans on getting an MBA—which normally takes two years in addition to a four-year undergraduate degree—his university may offer a five-year program that combines the undergraduate and graduate program. He'll save at least a year of time and education costs.

Paying for College

If it's primarily up to your child to pay for school, you can help him with the arduous task of doing so. You can assist financially, but more importantly, you can assist by guiding your child through the financial aid process.

Most kids use some type of financial aid (also called student aid) to make ends meet. Most aid comes from the federal government (nearly 70 percent), but there's also state aid and aid from schools and even private sources.

This aid can take the form of scholarships, loans, grants, or school-arranged part-time work. By far the most common type of aid is the college loan. The financial aid process and college loans are discussed in Chapter 26, "Studying Up on Student Loans."

Working His Way Through College

Working and going to school at the same time as an alternative or supplement to borrowing makes good financial and practical sense. Your child avoids or minimizes the debt he'll have to repay after he graduates, and he gains valuable work experience that can translate into a higher starting salary after graduation.

Of course, night school is the ultimate work–study arrangement if your child holds a day job. But if he wants to get his degree faster than he could going to school only at night, he should consider finding a school that offers a work–study program. This type of arrangement means that he'll go to school for a semester or two and then work for an outside employer the following semester. Some schools offer work–study programs that will allow him to work at two or three companies before he graduates.

There are important benefits to work–study programs:

➤ *He gets paid for his work.* This will help him pay for the time he's in school.

➤ *He'll earn valuable experience on the job.* This can mean that he'll get a higher-paying job after earning his degree than those straight out of college with no experience.

The main downside to work–study is time. It may take your child a little longer to graduate than if he had simply attended classes for four years. However, some work–study programs are year-round, allowing your child to get his work (and money-earning) experience without delaying his degree.

He might also consider serving his country as a way to work his way through college.

➤ *Join ROTC to earn additional money.* Make sure your child understands the time commitment while he's in school and knows his military service obligation once he's finished.

➤ *Join the military.* While she's in the armed services, your child can earn education money. Once she has completed her term of service, she can use that money for her education. The added benefit of this type of service is that she may gain work experience and maturity that will help her not only while she's in college, but also when she gets out into the real world.

Financial Building Blocks

According to the National Center for Education Statistics, today, 8 out of 10 full-time students are working while they're in school—that's more students than ever. These students also are working more than just a few hours a week: About 50 percent of full-time students work at least 21 hours a week (only 14 percent worked this much back in 1970).

Work-study programs aren't the only way your child may have a work obligation during college. Her financial aid package may require her to work a certain number of hours at an on-campus job—as a dorm counselor, librarian, or in the cafeteria. These jobs may not provide any important work experience, but they cut down on the amount of loans that will have to be repaid.

Of course, your child may work during summer break or at other times at off-campus jobs as well. The money earned from these jobs can be used toward tuition, books, or spending money—whatever's needed.

Facing Up to Problems

Many a responsible adult has been known to have stolen bubble gum as a young child. But others who have followed similar behavior have wound up in Sing Sing or Soledad. It's not uncommon for kids to steal or shoplift when they're young: The key to whether it becomes a lifelong endeavor is up to you.

Watch Your Step

Shoplifting may be a warning sign of emotional problems. Don't ignore this possibility, and get help.

Kids shoplift for different reasons. Sometimes they're acting on a dare from friends, just to see if they can get away with it. Sometimes they're doing it because it's the only way they know to get what they want. And sometimes they do it because they don't think it's wrong. You should address the specific cause of the problem so that you can find a solution.

➤ If your child has stolen because of a dare or to fit in with a group of kids, it's important for you to deal with the issue of peer pressure. Parenting resources are listed in Chapter 1, "Money (and How It's Handled) Matters."

➤ If your child has stolen because it's the only way she knows to get what she wants, the cause of the behavior may be partly economic. You may be able to address this by increasing her allowance, by encouraging your child to work, or by buying the things she needs yourself.

➤ A core value in Judeo-Christian ethics is "Thou shalt not steal." This value has been codified in our law, and your child needs to know in no uncertain terms that this behavior is morally wrong. What's more, it's illegal. He could face legal problems that can seriously injure his entire future. Stealing is taking something that doesn't belong to him, and it's harmful to the person he's taking it from. Whatever means of explanation and discipline you use, make sure that you convey the severity of the problem and ensure that it won't happen again.

The Least You Need to Know

➤ Shifting spending responsibility to your child builds self-reliance.

➤ You, and not your child, decide who pays for what during a discussion of this arrangement.

➤ Shopping for clothes teaches your child to budget money and shop for values.

➤ Owning a car is a costly undertaking for a child.

➤ Paying for college in most families is largely a child's responsibility.

➤ Stealing and shoplifting are behaviors that must be dealt with in no uncertain terms.

Chapter 13

So Many Choices (So Little Money)

> **In This Chapter**
>
> ➤ Exploring spending options
>
> ➤ Establishing priorities
>
> ➤ Shopping for things

When your child comes into money—with an allowance, through working, or by gifts—she may feel flush with power. She doesn't have to ask you for a candy bar or a comic book. She's more or less free to use the money as she wishes. Here's where you as a parent come in: It's an important money-management skill that your child learn to plan ahead when it comes to spending money. This will allow her to gain financial discipline, a skill that will serve her well throughout her life.

In this chapter, you'll learn how to guide your child on her spending choices. You'll see how to set priorities and help your child learn the value in postponing purchases. You'll also find out how to explain the importance of being a good shopper for the things she wants and needs. In the next chapter, you'll see how your child can make a budget to structure her spending (and saving) activities.

Options for Using Money

Let's say that your child has a fistful of dollars and is raring to go to the mall for the afternoon. Do you let him do as he pleases with that money? The answer depends on his age and what he has been taught about how to handle the money.

When you start to dispense an allowance, you should couple that activity with guidance on how to use the money. If you don't, your child may waste money on frivolous things and be short on cash for the things he needs. More importantly, he will develop poor spending habits that will be hard to break as he grows older. One kid used to immediately spend all the money that came into his possession on whatever he wanted at the time—usually comic books and trading cards. Today, that kid is a highly successful professional who still spends his money without any restraint—now on antiques and motorcycles. He's constantly short of cash for the things he needs, and he even had to borrow money from his mother to pay his taxes.

This person needs to learn to gain control over his money. He needs to know how to save for the future while spending the balance wisely now. As with bad habits, good spending habits also last a lifetime.

Another kid had only a tightly limited allowance and learned to spend it very carefully. As an adult, she was able to use her good purchasing skills in developing a successful retail business. By buying smart for her inventory, she could offer customers lower prices to attract sales.

Schools generally do a poor job in teaching about money, so it's primarily up to you as a parent to educate your child in this area.

Financial Building Blocks

You can improve the teaching of money management to your child by bringing the School Financial Planning Program of the National Endowment for Financial Education to your child's school, Boys and Girls Clubs, or other places near you (click on www.nefe.org). This program is designed to bring financial literacy to America's youth.

Planning for the Future

The future to a young child may mean the arrival of summer at the end of the school year; it's impossible to think about growing up, going off to college, and even moving out on her own. Still, the future is closer than she thinks. As adults, time seems to go more quickly than it did as a child—what seemed like years away now passes in the blink of an eye.

Your child needs to learn the importance of saving for the future, including these issues:

➤ What she's saving for

➤ What she has to put away to get there

➤ How long it will take her to reach her savings goal

For example, if your 11-year-old wants a Discman that costs $100, he should know that if he puts $5 a week toward this wish, it will take him 20 weeks (or about five months) to reach his goal. He can probably handle the math himself, but you'll have to encourage him to do it.

If your child sets a goal that would realistically take her years to reach, there's nothing wrong with agreeing to match her savings or contributing to her savings fund. After all, if your employer offers you a 401(k) plan, he probably matches (on some basis) what you put into the plan. For example, if your 10-year-old wants to save up for a video game that's going to cost $30, you might suggest that she save $2 each week for two months (eight weeks). She then will have saved $16, and you can pay the difference, which is roughly half the cost of the game.

Setting savings goals is explored in more detail in Chapter 16, "Setting Savings Goals That Work." The important thing to note here is that your child should get the idea that saving is a part of being grown up enough to have money.

Spending It Now

Whatever isn't set aside for saving can be used toward other things, such as buying magazines or going to the video arcade. If your child decides that he's going to spend his money, he needs to make informed shopping decisions. He shouldn't rush out to buy that CD on a Tuesday if there's going to be a sale on CDs the following day. Tips on spending wisely are discussed later in this chapter.

Kids may not readily see the need to become a good shopper, so it's up to you to explain that finding bargains is a way for your child to stretch her spending dollars. Instead of buying one sweater, a particular sale may allow her to buy two for the same price as one. She's getting more for her money in this instance.

Piggybank on It

If your teenager is saving for a big-ticket item, such as a car or college, savings shouldn't be made by putting dollars bills in his sock drawer. The money should be invested so that he'll be able to reach his savings goal quicker. Saving and investing money are discussed in Parts 5 and 6 of this book.

Piggybank on It

Matching or contributing to a child's purchase doesn't undermine her savings discipline. On the contrary, it serves as added incentive for her to stick with her savings plan.

Your child also might not be familiar with certain money terms. However, developing an understanding these terms is important for him to become a wise spender. Here are some things you may need to explain to younger kids:

➤ *Bargains*. Just because something is on sale doesn't mean it's a bargain; it's only a good deal if it's something that needs to be bought (something allocated in his budget). And it's only a good deal if it really represents a cost savings when compared with a similar purchase that's not labeled a "bargain."

Financial Building Blocks

Ogden Nash wrote: "O money, money, money, I am not necessarily one of those who think thee holy, but I often stop to wonder how thou canst go out so fast when thou comest in so slowly."

➤ *Brand names.* Kids are bombarded with ads on TV and even at school. They can recognize that the golden arches mean McDonalds and that the swoosh means Nike. Brand names are used by companies to capture consumer loyalty, and it's fine for your child to want to buy a quality item that also is a brand-name item. But it's not always a brand name that is the best buy. Store-brand socks purchased at Kmart, for instance, may be of equal quality to those with the Footlocker label on the side. Prove it to your child by buying a pair of each socks and then seeing how well they wear over time.

Watch Your Step

Testing for a bargain of an item that you want to purchase can be tricky. Do the math. My daughter once added up the components in the Burger King kid's meal and found that the burger, fries, and soda purchased separately were cheaper than the one-price meal. She wasn't interested in the toy included with the meal, so the separate purchases were the true bargain for her.

➤ *Expensive.* Young kids have no idea what things cost. They may know that $50 is more than $25, but what does $50 really mean? One way you can show your child what the value of that money means is to compare it with another item of equal cost. For example, if he wants to buy *Next Generation,* a monthly magazine on video games that costs $5.99, explain that the same money can buy a ticket to the movies (except in cities where ticket prices have soared).

How can you get your child to become a bargain-hunter? Get her involved in the hunt! If your teenage daughter is looking for a new pair of shoes, try several different approaches on how to comparison-shop. Use your local newspaper as a reference material to search for advertised sales (typically Wednesdays' ads are heavy in sales). Or, make a shopping trip a learning experience by accompanying her to the stores. Point out prices and note how they compare to prices in other stores for similar shoes. Or, use alternative shopping places to find bargains. Teenage girls love to shop in thrift shops to find retro clothes and other bargains. Likewise, kids of all ages may enjoy garage sales and flea markets for the many bargains they can offer.

You can teach your elementary school child the power of bargain-hunting by making a game of it. Challenge your 10-year-old to put together a weekly grocery list for the family using a set dollar amount. For example, say that you allot $100 for weekly groceries for purposes of this game. See what your child puts on the shopping list. Remind him that he must include not only Oreos and Coca Cola, but also milk, orange juice, and lettuce. Be sure to discuss when it's advisable to substitute store brands for brand labels as a way of saving money without sacrificing flavor, quality, and so on. Also critique his list—the good and the bad—by pointing out what bargains he has found or what he has left off the list that should have been included.

Variations on this game include these:

➤ Give your child the menus for the day, and tell him how much he has to spend for your family's food (for example $20 or $25). Then let him look through local newspapers to find the best prices for the items on the menus.

➤ Give your child the dollar amount he can spend on meals for the day. Let him put together the menus for that day, based on the bargains he finds in the newspapers.

Money ABCs

Priorities are an ordering of things in terms of importance. The most important things come first, and less important things can follow.

Setting Priorities

As adults, we know that paying for the essentials— housing, food, clothing, and medical care—come first. Everything else is nice but nonessential. Knowing what's necessary versus what we'd like to have is just another way of saying that we know what are priorities are.

Kids need to find their priorities, too. They need to know what they must have versus what they'd like to have. It's essential to distinguish between the two so that they'll use their money responsibly to take care of essentials first. However, it's also essential to know the difference so that kids can formulate a budget. In that budget, essentials must be included, and nonessentials can be included if there's room (or can be made part of a savings component within the budget). Chapter 14, "Buying on a Budget," covers this topic in more detail.

Money ABCs

Delayed gratification is a psychological term that means postponing enjoyment of something until a later time. But this term also applies to money matters, such as putting off buying something until you have the money to pay for it so that you won't go into debt or be unable to meet other financial responsibilities.

Delaying Gratification

Adults know that putting off getting something you want only makes it sweeter when you get it. For instance, anticipating an upcoming vacation is part of the enjoyment of the vacation itself.

Postponing a purchase may result in that purchase never being made. Maybe your child can't wait to get the latest type of boots. Waiting a while can mean that a newer type comes along that's hotter than the last. Postponing a buy can mean that your child will pass up a purchase that would only have been used or enjoyed for a short time. Of course, this is your experience talking. All you can do is point out what postponing a purchase can do and then let your child make the spending decision.

Piggybank on It

Did your child include an entry for savings in the Things Your Child Needs column? If not, then it's up to you to explain the place of savings in her list of priorities.

Figuring Out Priorities

To get an idea of what your child views as essential versus nonessential, have her write down what she thinks she needs in the first column and then what she wants in the next column. At this point, don't be concerned with the cost of the item. That's something that can be worked out when it's budget-making time. The point here is to identify what she thinks she must have.

Things Your Child Needs	Things Your Child Wants

Now review her lists with her. Discuss items that she has listed in the Must Have column that you think are not essential. Maybe she has entered weekly movies and you think this is a little excessive. If you require her to pay for certain things and she has omitted them from the essentials column, then you'd better have another talk about her spending responsibilities.

Savvy Shopping Strategies

Kids are going to be shoppers for their entire lives, and they can learn how to be *effective* shoppers if you teach them. In this way, they'll get the biggest bang for their spending buck.

Financial Building Blocks

According to recent studies noted by the National Endowment for Financial Education, teenagers in the United States spend an average of $3,500 each year. Total teenage spending is more than $100 billion annually. How well children use their spending dollars depends in part on what they've been taught.

Here are some actions that well-informed consumers typically use.

➤ *Make a shopping list.* Have your child put down on paper the things he's looking for on a shopping outing. By listing purchasing targets, he's more likely to avoid spending money on nonessential (or non-budgeted) things and won't short on cash for the things he needs.

➤ *Become an informed consumer.* Your child should learn about the things she's going to buy. For example, are the skates she's eyeing well-built? Have there been safety problems with that brand? Check out *Zillions*, the kid's magazine from *Consumer Reports*. Encourage your child to ask questions. Sales help in many stores aren't helpful at all and may even be rude to young customers, but as long as your child is well-behaved, she's entitled to help as much as any other customer. Don't let your child be intimidated into not asking for help with anything she wants to know about the merchandise in the store.

Piggybank on It

Making a list can also save time. The old expression "Time is money" means that saving time is a thing of value. This becomes truer as your child gets older and can use his precious time for better things than shopping.

➤ *Do your homework for shopping.* As with preparing for the next day's lessons in school, it's important to do prep work before going on a shopping expedition. Having a shopping list is only the starting point. Check out advertised sales for the items on the list. Compare the advertised prices to see which store offers the

Watch Your Step

According to *Consumer Reports,* kids online are being enticed by questionable sales practices to buy products through their home computers. If you're concerned about your young child's sales resistance, consider using software packages that block your child from objectionable sites.

Piggybank on It

In *Breakfast at Tiffany's,* Holly Golightly used to window-shop the diamonds at that famous store. It doesn't cost anything to window-shop; it only costs money to buy something. Like Holly, kids who enjoy the shopping experience can indulge themselves without breaking their pocketbooks.

better deal. It's not uncommon for stores to put the same items on sale in the same week. During a sale, that pair of running shoes may be cheaper at Macy's than at the Footlocker, or they may be even cheaper still at Kmart.

➤ *Be a bargain hunter.* Saving money by buying sale items, using coupons, or shopping at outlet stores means that your child's dollar will go farther. If he goes to a movie matinee when tickets are half-price, he'll be able to go twice as often for the same cost. You can get a young child started on being bargain-hunter by involving him in supermarket coupons. Have him clip coupons from newspapers and ads. Have him select coupons that match items you've put on your shopping list. Bring him to the store and let him hunt for items that match the coupons he has put aside. Then show him the cash register tape displaying how much savings those coupons produced. In my A&P, the tape even shows a percentage of the total purchase. For example, if the total (before coupons) came to $100 and coupons amounted to $10, using coupons resulted in a 10 percent savings.

➤ *Save receipts.* When your child buys something, she should learn to save the cash register receipt. There are two good reasons for doing so: It's necessary to have the receipt if she wants to return or exchange the item she's bought, and receipts serve as a record-keeping device. By adding up what's on the receipts she has collected for a month, your child can see how much she has spent in that time.

The Least You Need to Know

➤ Gaining control over using money is a vital skill of money management.

➤ Kids need to plan for their future, even if that time seems far off to them.

➤ Setting priorities is the first step in making a budget.

➤ Delaying gratification can enhance your child's enjoyment of the things he'll eventually get.

➤ Kids need to be taught how to be good shoppers.

MAC & CHEESE, RAMEN NOODLES, PEANUT BUTTER AND JELLY...

Chapter 14

Buying on a Budget

In This Chapter

➤ Getting value from making a budget

➤ Designing a money-spending and saving blueprint

➤ Living with a budget

You've heard the expression of how money burns a hole in the pocket of some individuals. As soon as they come into cash, these people feel compelled to spend it. This behavior is the opposite of sound money management, though. One explanation for this behavior is their personality, and these people may display this behavior from an early age. Another explanation for that spend-all mentality, however, is that their parents never showed them how to manage their money effectively.

In this chapter, you'll learn why it's important for your child to make a plan for the use of his money. You'll see how your child can design a budget to meet his present and future needs—such a budget, of course, differs considerably with the age of your child. You'll also get some ideas about how to help your child live according to his money plans.

The Meaning of a Money Plan

If your child has a part-time job and gets a paycheck on Friday afternoon but spends it all at the mall on Friday night, she's shortchanging herself. The same is true of a child who blows his weekly allowance all on one video game and can't join his friends at the movies.

Money ABCs

A **budget** is a plan that's made to tell a person how he's going to spend or use your money during a certain period (such as each month or from paycheck to paycheck or allowance to allowance).

➤ Your child is depriving herself of having the money she needs to meet expenses that may not arise until her next paycheck or allowance.

➤ Your child is not putting anything away toward his future because he's not saving money to invest.

➤ Your child is getting into bad money habits that will be hard to break as she gets older.

So how does your child gain the discipline he needs to spend and use his money wisely? The answer is simple: Set up a budget.

Instead of calling the plan a budget, you can refer to it as a money plan. To some people, a *budget* sounds like something very restrictive. A *money plan* sounds more like mere guidelines for the use of money that your child can follow but adapt along the way.

Obviously, a budget for a young child will be looser and less defined than for a teenager who has substantial money responsibilities. As a result, the budget will have to be reviewed and amended periodically as a child ages, as the amount of money coming in changes, or as other factors are altered (all of which are discussed later in this chapter).

When to Begin a Budget

As with just about any other money lesson, it's never too early—or too late—to start. The concept of making a budget can be broached as soon as a child comes into money—from a tooth fairy, a birthday gift, or an allowance.

Start simple if your child is in the early years of elementary school. Keep the idea of a budget to making some plans on how to use the money. Get your child to think about what she wants to do with the money and how much that plan costs. Be sure to include suggestions at this time about saving money. She may not yet know what she wants to do with her money or what she'll need in the future, but by saving up, it will be there for her.

If your child is older and is already receiving a substantial allowance, it's high time to educate her about making a budget. She's old enough to understand more about how planning will let her stretch her dollars and ensure that she'll have what she wants down the road.

If your child is in high school and you've let her spend without making a budget up to now, it's not too late to begin the budget-making process. Without learning about budgeting from you, your child might easily develop the hand-to-mouth approach to handling money that many adults unfortunately follow.

Budget Preliminaries

Before you run a race, you do some things first: You train, you eat properly the morning of the race, and you do warm-up exercises. These preliminary steps help you perform the best you can. It's the same with making a budget. You and your child need to get some things straight before a budget can actually be made. The first step in making a budget is to know three key things:

➤ *How much money is coming in.* This is the easy part. Your child knows how much he's taking in through his an allowance, earnings from a job, or a combination of both.

➤ *What types of things the money will be used for.* Have your child make a list of the items he must pay for if he wants to have them. Use the following list to give you both some idea of the types of things he may be required to pay for. (Obviously, some of the items apply only to older kids.) Be sure to have him add his own items on the blank lines at the end of the column. Refer to Chapter 12, "Picking Up the Tab," in which you decided what expenditures your child is responsible for.

Things Your Child Must Pay For (If He Wants Them)

Item	Yes	No
Car	_____	_____
Car insurance	_____	_____
CDs, cassettes, records	_____	_____
Clothing	_____	_____
College	_____	_____
Computer	_____	_____
Dating costs	_____	_____
Gas for car	_____	_____
Movies and concerts	_____	_____
Personal telephone line	_____	_____
School lunches	_____	_____
Snacks and candy	_____	_____
Sports	_____	_____
Toys and games	_____	_____
_____	_____	_____
_____	_____	_____
_____	_____	_____
_____	_____	_____
_____	_____	_____
_____	_____	_____
_____	_____	_____

➤ *What portion of his money will be set aside for something other than spending.* This is the part that goes into savings and can be invested for his future. Some of the money that's not spent on his current wants and needs can also be given away to charity (as discussed in detail in Chapter 15, "Giving It Away").

Parsing a Budget

Just as grammarians parse a sentence by breaking it down into parts, your child needs to fragment her budget into separate shares for spending and saving. This apportionment will differ with your child's age, how much money she's taking in, and how much she's responsible for buying on her own.

Money ABCs

Short-term goals are those that can be reached in a short time. Maybe this involves having enough cash to buy holiday gifts for the family. **Long-term goals** are those that can be months or years ahead, such as buying a car, going to college, or having enough money to move out of the house.

Financial experts advise adults to save 10 percent of their income. Unfortunately, Americans on average fall far short of this recommended savings target. Still, you can help your child learn about savings by building it into her budget.

To determine how much should be saved on a regular basis, your child needs to set up savings goals. Setting goals will allow her to meet short-term and long-term financial objectives. When a child is young, she can't be expected to think too far ahead: What's college to a kid who's just started elementary school? In helping a small child set goals, make them ones that she can realistically reach in a few weeks or a month or two. In effect, a small child's goals aren't separated into short-term and long-term; they all seem far away to her. As a child gets older, however, she can set goals that stretch farther into the future.

Financial Building Blocks

Of all the industrial countries throughout the world, Americans have the lowest savings rate. According to the U.S. Commerce Department, Americans save less than 5 percent of their income each year. Canadians save about 8 percent of their income annually. In contrast, the Japanese save about 13 percent.

The big question for most people is how much to allocate to saving and how much to charity. There's no quick answer, and the question is discussed in detail in the next chapter. However, it's a good idea to build charitable giving into the budget.

Beginner's Budget

The purpose of having a budget is to set up guidelines for your child to follow in spending (and saving) his money. The budget isn't binding or fixed in stone; no alarms will go off and no police will arrest him if he overspends from the allotted amount from one category and underspends from another. But, the better he sticks to the plan, the better able he'll be to pay for the things he wants and needs.

Now that your child knows the information he needs to make a budget, he can begin the process. Assemble paper and pencil (and a calculator) and begin.

Watch Your Step

Don't set up a budget for your child; let her work through this task herself. The budget process is an invaluable experience. If you *tell* her what she's got to spend on this or that, she'll never learn how to make smart money decisions on her own.

Budget Period and Categories

The federal government sets an annual budget that begins on October 1 of every year. Grown-ups typically use a monthly budget because many expenses—rent or the mortgage, the phone and electric company bills—come once a month.

Your child's budget can span any length of time.

➤ Younger children may be able to focus only on smaller units of time. They may be better off using a weekly time frame that runs from the start of the school week through the weekend.

➤ Teenagers can probably handle whatever time frame they want to select. They may want to use a monthly budget like you, or a budget that runs from allowance to allowance or from paycheck to paycheck (for example, you're paid twice a month, or weekly). So, they can have a budget that runs 15 days or 7 days. Whatever helps them to manage their money best will work. For the purposes of this chapter, we'll call this their *budget period*.

Watch Your Step

The total dollars your child has budgeted for a certain amount of time *must* equal the dollars he has available during that time. For example, if his allowance is $15 a week, his budget for a one-week period should total $15—not a penny more or less.

Review the list of items your child has to pay for. Now jot down what she thinks it's going to cost her to pay for them during each budget period. If she pays for an item once a year, such as a magazine subscription, but her budget period is monthly, be sure to divide the cost of the item by 12 and enter only $1/12$ of the cost in her monthly budget. If the budget period is weekly, divide by 52.

Piggybank on It

The amount of the fixed expense may not be identical each month, but the budgeted amount is. For example, a telephone bill may run $20 one month and $30 the next, but the monthly budgeted amount of $25 remains constant from month to month.

Each item she must pay for or set aside is called an *expense*. Every budget has two types of expenses: fixed expenses and variable expenses. Fixed expenses occur each week, and the amount of these expenses generally remains constant from week to week. Fixed expenses that your child might have include these:

➤ Savings allocation

➤ Donations to charity

➤ Telephone bill (arising on a monthly basis)

➤ Transportation costs (bus fare, gas for the family car)

Variable expenses are the opposite of fixed expenses. These are also referred to as *flexible expenses* because they aren't rigid. In some weeks, variable expenses may not even be there. Examples of variable expenses your child might have include these:

➤ Entertainment costs

➤ Clothing

➤ Gifts for relatives

Money ABCs

Things that are more or less stable in amount from month to month—for example, donations for charity—are called **fixed expenses**. Items whose cost changes from month to month, such as entertainment costs, are called **variable expenses**.

In making a budget, fixed expenses are listed exactly as they'll be paid or are expected to be paid. For variable expenses, make an estimate of what they might be. Even though they may not be the same each month, it's a good idea to provide a certain amount for them on a regular basis. Then, if they don't arise in a certain month, that money can be set aside. These set-asides will accumulate and be used later when the variable expense comes along.

Setting Up a Personal Spending Plan

Now that your child knows all the components in his budget, it's time to put things down in writing. Use the following chart to fill in his personal budget. Some common budget items are already listed. Make sure that he includes his own items from the list he completed earlier in this chapter.

Your Child's Personal Budget for His Budget Period

Expense	Amount
Car expenses	$_____
Clothing	$_____
Donations to charity	$_____
Entertainment	$_____
Savings	$_____
Sports	$_____
Toys and games	$_____
Transportation	$_____
_____	$_____
_____	$_____
_____	$_____
_____	$_____
_____	$_____
_____	$_____
TOTAL	$_____

Your child can test out his budget at an interactive Web site that lets him enter his income and expenses and then displays the amount he's short (or over) each month (www.mastercard.com/cgi-bin/budget_worksheet). He can then adjust the income or expense sides to balance his budget.

Remaking a Budget

A budget isn't carved in marble. It's something that can be adjusted when needed, as discussed later in this chapter. In fact, the budget should be completely made over at certain times.

➤ *When income increases.* If your child gets a bigger allowance or starts to work part-time, she'll have more money to plan for.

➤ *When expenses increase.* As spending responsibilities are shifted to your child, she'll have to budget for them accordingly. For example, if she's the one to pay for after-school activities, then she'll have to manage her money by putting these items into her budget. Spending responsibilities typically increase with your child's age, but they can also increase if your

Piggybank on It

The savings portion should be treated as a payment to your child (list it like any other expense). Don't let your child get into the bad habit that so many adults have of putting into savings only what's left over at the end of the budget period—in this case, there's typically nothing left over.

child's wants start to exceed your ability to provide. For example, if your child wants a car and you're not going to buy her one, she'll have to adjust her budget to expand her savings so that she can buy the car on her own.

Living with a Budget

Once a budget is set, it should be followed. For some, this is easier said than done, but if your child has a system in place to put the budget into action, things will go easier.

For young kids, it's helpful to keep the money that they're going to spend and save close at hand. You can use an envelope system to hold money for the different items on the budget. You can use an old-fashioned piggybank, a newfangled coin bank, or just a simple jar to hold the child's savings. Even though my daughter is older now, she still keeps a jar on her desk to accumulate the money she plans to donate to charity.

Piggybank on It

At a minimum, it's probably a good idea for your child to make a fresh budget at the start of each school year. This time of year seems to mark changes in a child's life—changes that may need to be reflected in a budget.

When a child is a little older, she may not need to separate the money for each item in the budget. She can hold the money that she's planning to spend for the budget period in her wallet. But savings should be put in a different place so that they're not inadvertently spent. Where to put savings is the subject of the next part of this book.

Once a child starts earning a paycheck, money should be put into a bank account. Then money can be withdrawn as needed to meet expenses. Again, savings can be separated from money used to meet ongoing expenses. For example, expense money can be deposited in a checking account, while savings can be invested elsewhere.

Keeping Track of Things

A budget is a money allocation plan you put in writing. But what good is a budget if it isn't followed? The only way to know if it's being followed is to keep track of things.

Many financial experts suggest that a person keep track of all his expenses, and this advice goes for adults as well as children. Following this advice, some people write down everything they spend, down to the last penny. The cup of coffee, the tip to the cab driver, and the subway token all get listed in their little money book. Their entries may look something like this:

Date	Type of Expense	Amount
1/14	Newspaper	$.50
1/14	Lunch with Jimmy	$4.55
1/15	Newspaper	$.50
1/16	Newspaper	$.50

Date	Type of Expense	Amount
1/16	Coffee at Starbucks	$1.35
1/17	Newspaper	$.50
1/17	Movies	$7.50

Today's computer-savvy kids may want to use software designed for personal record-keeping. Programs such as Quicken allow a child to set up accounts—for entertainment, clothing, savings, and so on—to track where his money goes.

Is it necessary to go to this extreme? That depends. It's a good idea to write down everything if your child doesn't know where his money went. If he's always short of cash, he probably doesn't realize what he's spending his money on and should track his expenses pretty closely. (Many adults who earn impressive salaries are always surprised at the end of the year when they can't say where all that money went!)

Keeping track of things takes time, especially in the beginning when the habit is just forming. It may be helpful for you to suggest a specific time your child should review his budget and tend to his record-keeping. For example, if you give him a weekly allowance, you might want to sit down with him while he makes his weekly budget. Or, if you make your own monthly budget at a certain time, you can ask your child to join in the activity by making his budget at the same time.

Once your child gets used to living by a budget, it may become less important to write down everything he spends. However, it may be helpful for him to continue doing it for some time so that he gets a clear picture of where his money is going. He may even be shocked by what he's wasting money on. It may not seem like much to buy a soda for $1 at the vending machine, but when he sees that he has bought 10 sodas in one week for a total of $10, he might want to forgo this type of purchase and use the $10 for something else.

You can get a kit designed for children up to the age 12 to use in keeping track of their money from Finity Corporation at www.finitycorp.com/hazam.htm. This kit contains a parent's guide, as well as a money folder to hold records about your child's money and envelopes for storing the money.

Piggybank on It

If your child keeps track of all his spending, he should use a small notebook that he can easily carry around. Make the spending entry at the time of or shortly after purchase so the expense won't be forgotten.

Making Adjustments

When you gain weight, you have to let out the waistline in your pants. When you lose it, you can take it in again. As with adjusting your clothes when your size changes, your child should be flexible about her budget without becoming irresponsible. If she needs something special one month (for example, buying Christmas presents for family and friends), she'll just have cut back on something else. Asking for an advance on an allowance is discussed in Chapter 25, "Borrowing from Family and Friends."

Some things can be trimmed; others cannot. Your child can always forgo buying that CD this month if she wants to spend that extra money on something else; she can't just decide not to pay her phone bill if she's responsible for it because she'd rather put the money elsewhere. When living within a budget, it's the variable expenses that will have to be adjusted as needed. Be sure to treat regular savings as a fixed item, too, so that they're not neglected.

Adjusting the budget is one way to live within it. Another is to find better ways to pay for things. For example, become a better shopper, look for bargains, and stay alert for sales.

Another way to make a realistic budget is to build in a cushion by adding a Miscellaneous Expense category. This catchall category covers the unknown expenses that might (and usually do) arise. If at the end of the budget period you haven't spent this extra amount, you can save it or apply it to a future expense. More likely than not, however, something always arises to eat up that miscellaneous amount.

Instead of using a miscellaneous category to cover the unexpected, you child might consider building up a savings fund. The bigger the cushion he creates to anticipate future expenses—such as a Mother's or Father's day gift—the easier it will be to fit those expenses in without having to make cost-cutting adjustments later.

Finally, another way to live within a budget is to increase the income side of it. If your child can't live on the allowance you're giving her, maybe it's time for her to get a job. Or, maybe it's realistic to adjust the allowance. The income side of the budget should be revisited especially if your child is sticking to the budget but still can't afford the things she needs.

The Least You Need to Know

➤ A budget helps your child to have the money he needs for the things he wants.

➤ To set up a budget, your child needs to know how much money she has coming in and what she has to use that money for.

➤ Fixing financial goals can help your child structure his spending (and savings) plan.

➤ A budget should run for a set period of time, typically from allowance to allowance, paycheck to paycheck, or month to month.

➤ A savings plan should be built into a budget.

➤ Review a budget periodically, as new money comes in or as expenses change, and make revisions accordingly.

Chapter 15

Giving It Away

In This Chapter

➤ Being a generous person

➤ Making gifts

➤ Donating to charity

Maybe your child must spend her money on herself because her expenses are high and because she needs to pay for college or for some necessity. But more likely than not, demands on her money are nominal—especially when she's young. She's probably dreaming of buying a new video game, going to a theme park, or otherwise spending it on herself. It's a good idea, and the start of a lifelong habit, to encourage her to allocate some money to others.

In this chapter, you'll learn how to encourage her to think about helping charities. You'll find out about letting your child use her money to make gifts to family and friends, and if she decides she wants to give to charity, you'll see how you can guide her in making her contributions.

Generosity Can Be Taught

When you look at a group of preschoolers, it's easy to spot the ones who are good at sharing: They readily offer the use of their things to others. But some are more reluctant than others to part with anything. They horde their snacks and stand guard over their toys so that no one else can get at them.

The ability to share is what's needed to be a generous person—and being a generous person will allow your child to give a portion of his money to others. Sharing can take two main forms:

➤ Making gifts to family and friends

➤ Making donations to charitable organizations

School-age kids are old enough to understand that other people may be in need. They see people in trouble all the time on TV, in movies, and even in their own neighborhood. Older kids certainly should know about the need to support charitable causes. If your child doesn't, it's not too late to fix the situation. For starters, encourage your son to visit a soup kitchen or your daughter to visit a women's shelter. This simple reality check may be all that's needed to bring your child up to speed on the need to help the less fortunate.

Many kids don't need to be taught to help people in need: It just comes naturally to them. However, elementary school children with a generous and sympathetic nature need to be educated about the difference between people in obvious need—such as panhandlers on the street—and legitimate charities that provide assistance to such people. Young kids may be more than willing to hand over all the money in their pockets to beggars, not realizing that the money may only go toward the purchase of drugs or alcohol. Explain to them the difference between having sympathy for those with obvious problems and providing monetary help to them.

Piggybank on It

Kids learn generosity by example. If you're a regular contributor to Cancer Care or Comic Relief, your child will learn to be a giver, too. He may not choose the same causes you do, but he'll learn to share.

Giving Gifts to Family and Friends

There's hardly a mother around who hasn't received a macaroni necklace from her preschooler. But as your child gets older, he'll reach a point where he stops making presents and starts buying them.

To have the money available to buy presents for you and others in the family, your child will have to forgo spending that money on himself. This means building into his money plan a set aside amount for buying gifts in the future.

After doing so, he should spend only what he has saved for this purpose. Adults frequently say that they've overspent at Christmas and regret it in the months that follow. Your child shouldn't fall into this overspending trap.

When kids get to elementary school, they may be invited to numerous birthday parties by classmates and neighbors. Buying gifts for all these parties usually falls on you, and at times it may seem that you'll go bankrupt just buying birthday gifts for 8-year-olds.

As your child gets older, however, he may take on more of the gift-buying responsibilities or you may decide to share the cost. For example, you might say that you'll pay $10 toward a gift and let your child pay any additional amount if he wants to get a more expensive present.

Should you put limits on how much your child should spend on a gift for you or his friends? While you shouldn't enforce a dollar limit, it's a good idea to provide guidance on how much is appropriate to spend on various occasions, especially for younger children who don't yet have a good sense of what things cost. You may want to point out that excessive gifts can be embarrassing to the recipient. You might suggest a dollar amount for a Mother's or Father's day gift (your child may have no clue as to what he should spend on you). As he gets older and has more of his own money to spend, he'll make his own decisions on how much of it to use on gifts.

How do you handle the generous child who lacks the funds to buy the presents he wants to give? In some neighborhoods, high-schoolers exchange Christmas presents with all their close friends, which many number into double digits. While some teenagers can afford to give CDs to each of these friends, others may be strapped for cash. This situation can create embarrassment for those who can't give gifts of equal value. There's no easy answer for what to tell a child who lacks the resources to give similar gifts. As with any other money issue, this is just another example of trying to keep up with the Joneses. Suggest another tack, such as providing non-monetary gifts (such as a free car wash by your child) that are sure to be appreciated.

Doling Out Dollars to Charity

Andrew Carnegie spent the first half of his life making a fortune and the second half giving it away. He set up libraries across the country and benefited numerous charitable organizations. But your child doesn't have to be a Carnegie, a Ford, or a Rockefeller, to become a philanthropist.

However modest her donations, getting into the giving habit is a sound financial management principal for your child. She'll get into the positive habit of giving and will learn to build it into her spending plans. When she gets older, she'll be rewarded for her giving by being able to claim a tax deduction for her contributions. For now, though, she'll be rewarded in other ways—satisfaction in helping others and learning to put off her own needs in favor of someone else.

Piggybank on It

If the dollar amount that's appropriate for your child to spend seems too little to buy what he might consider to be a decent present, suggest that your child pool his funds with a sibling (when it's a gift for you) or a friend (when it's a gift for another friend). Just make sure that the joint gift-givers agree on what the present should be.

Money ABCs

Philanthropy is a fancy word for giving. A **philanthropist** is someone who gives to charity.

Guidelines for Donations

How much should your child give to charity? There's no magic percentage or dollar amount. Obviously, he can't give it all because then he wouldn't have money for the things he needs. But in just about every person's budget, there's room for some charitable giving.

Adults can get some idea of what people in their income bracket are giving by looking at annual IRS statistics on charitable contribution deductions that are published in the IRS Statistics of Income Bulletin (find the SOI bulletin at www.irs.ustreas.gov/prod/tax_stats/index.html). For example, taxpayers with incomes between $15,000 and $30,000 gave on average in 1996 (the latest year for which statistics are available) of $1,337 to charities. These statistics don't dictate what they should give, but they do show adults what others are doing. Obviously, kids don't make contributions with tax write-offs in mind, so they need to be guided by their generous nature and the size of their pocketbook.

Religious precepts may be useful in guiding your child on what to set aside for donations. For example, in Judaism, "tzedakah" (the Hebrew word for "charitable giving") to the poor is an obligation. According to Jewish law, Jews should give one-tenth of their income to help the poor. But it's also part of Jewish law that those without the means aren't required to give that amount. Tithing (giving one-tenth of one's income to charity) is part of many Christian faiths as well. By this thinking, if a child gets $10 a week as an allowance, he should be giving $1 to charity. Still, he may be able to give more (or might only afford less) based on individual circumstances.

Financial Building Blocks

If your child can't give the kind of cash he'd like, he can give of himself. He can volunteer his time to local charities, or elementary school kids can collect for UNICEF when going door to door on Halloween. Many high schools are now requiring volunteerism as a condition for graduation. Local volunteer ambulance corps and fire companies also are always looking for new recruits—usually 16 and older—to lend a hand. For more information about volunteering and making a match with the right organization, your child should check with his school or click on www.impactonline.org.

Some experts advise that the amount given to charity shouldn't be limited to a percentage of income. Rather, it should be based on excess income. In other words, wealthy people have more excess (or discretionary) income after meeting their housing, food, and other basic requirements. Wealthy people should be giving to charity more generously than moderate income people as well. The same might be said of kids: Those with generous allowances and parents who pay for almost everything are in a position to do so more than kids, who have to use their money to meet their basic needs.

Ideas on Where to Give Money

From the time your child is in elementary school, she's probably already involved in charity work, even if she doesn't know it. She may be selling candy bars for the school baseball team, or she may be selling cookies for Girl Scouts. At Halloween, your child may collect money for UNICEF. These are all charities that your child's efforts are supporting.

Watch Your Step

Tax deductions for charitable contributions can be claimed only by someone who itemizes her deductions. Because the standard deduction in 1999 for a dependent child with earned income is $4,300, even a working child probably won't be itemizing deductions and won't get any tax benefit from her charitable contributions.

If your child decides she wants to donate a portion of her allowance, earnings, or money she has received as a gift to charity, you'll have to help her identify the one or two places where she'll give her money. No matter how big her heart may be, it's not practical for her to give to everyone. She'll have to decide what's important to her and find the charities that address her objective.

1. *Discuss your child's concerns about the world.* Does he want to help cure disease (and which particular one)? Support the arts? Support education? Feed the hungry? House the homeless? Support your church or other religious organization? This type of discussion will help your child identify the area or areas that he'd like to help.

2. *Find the charity that's trying to fix the problems your child is concerned about.* Maybe a well-known charity comes to mind. For example, a child whose grandfather died of heart disease may want to give to the American Heart Association (www.americanheart.org). Or, maybe your child wants to help kids with terminal or life-threatening illnesses have a special experience. He can give to the Make-A-Wish Foundation of America (www.wish.org) or The Wishing Star Foundation (www.wishingstar.org). Or, maybe he wants to help an inner-city kid attend summer camp by giving to the Fresh Air Fund (www.freshair.org).

Watch Your Step

Make sure that the organization your child wants to support is a legitimate one whose funds are used for charitable purposes (rather than mostly for staff and other administrative expenses).

If you're not sure which organization is best, the two of you can do a little digging. Your community may have various programs that might fit your child's charitable goals. Just by looking around, you may see local organizations asking for help. For a listing of more than 600,000 organizations nationwide, click on www.guidestar.org or check out resources available at your local library on charitable organizations.

How your child actually makes a contribution depends a little on age. Older kids can save up their contribution dollars for some time (maybe even year by year). If they have their own checking accounts, they then can write out a check and send it off to their favorite charity.

Piggybank on It

With your okay, your child can make a charitable contribution or pledge of a contribution online to his favorite charity—he'll need the use of a credit card to do so. Click on www.giveonline.org for details.

Younger kids don't necessarily see that same direct connection of their money going to charity, unless they actually place their cash in the church collection plate each week or in the Salvation Army kettle at Christmas time. Instead, they can save up their money in a special jar dedicated for this purpose. Label the jar "My contribution money" or something else to reinforce the idea that the money in the jar is for a special purpose. When the money reaches a certain amount (say, $10 or $25 dollars) or when you reach a set time interval (such as the end of each school year), the money can be sent to the charity your child has selected. You will probably have to change her money into the form of a check to send the contribution through the mail.

The Least You Need to Know

➤ Kids may be generous by nature or can learn from you.

➤ Making gifts to family, friends, or charity means having to forgo using money for personal purchases.

➤ A child of any age can become a philanthropist.

➤ There's no rule of thumb on how much of an allowance or earnings a child should give to charity, but religious practices may provide some guidance.

➤ When making donations, decide on the type of cause your child wants to help, and then find the charity that serves this purpose.

Part 5
Rainy Day Precautions

In the 18th century, writer Henry Fielding said that "a penny saved is a penny got." In other words, saving money means having it later on when it's needed. Another old adage refers to saving for a rainy day, which was correct, too, but limited. It's not only for bad times that we save; it's also for the good things we want to get in the future.

Saving involves a two-step approach: setting aside funds today (which means going without for now) and putting that money somewhere (hopefully where it will build up a savings fund).

In this part of the book you'll learn how to help your child set savings goals so that he'll want to put money aside. You'll see where he can put money, depending on how much money is involved and whether he's a young child or a teenager. You'll even learn about getting your child to focus on the idea of saving for his own retirement.

Chapter 16

Setting Savings Goals That Work

In This Chapter

➤ Making wish lists

➤ Projecting what your child needs to save for college

➤ Making special college savings

Saving money isn't easy—it means a measure of sacrifice now so that the money will be there in the future. But saving is a necessary financial management skill. The earlier it's learned, the easier it is to maintain throughout one's life.

Savings can take two forms: savings for the little things, such as going to the prom; and savings for the big things, such as going to college. Saving for college requires special attention because unique savings programs exist just for this purpose.

In this chapter, you'll learn about helping your child set savings goals; he needs to know why it's important to save and the benefit he'll get by doing it. You'll also find out how you can project what money your child will need to complete his education. Finally, you'll focus on special savings plans for your child's college education that you and your child should consider.

Wishing on a Star

Did you ever dream about owning a Ferrari? Did you ever want to put a pool in your backyard (or even have a backyard to put one in)? An adult's financial goals generally require a heavy savings commitment to reach them. Grown-ups save to buy a home, start a family, maybe start a business, and have a comfortable retirement. Those who are successful in meeting their goals generally are the ones who are experienced in saving. These people learned about saving early on.

You can help your child get the things she wants in life by learning to save up. Unless your child was born with a miser gene, she'd probably prefer to spend, spend, spend. But there's just as much satisfaction to be gained from saving as from spending, if she knows what the payoff will be. She needs to understand that she'll never have financial maturity if she doesn't have good savings habits.

To help your child become a good saver, you need to help her understand what saving is all about, and you need to help her decide what she's saving for. You'll find tactics for both, and later in this chapter you'll find some saving strategies for college costs. In the chapters that follow, you find out about other saving ideas as well.

Watch Your Step

Don't undermine your child's savings resolve by leaping in to buy the thing he's saving for. You may satisfy his desires today, but you're teaching him that he doesn't have to save to get the things he wants.

There's Nothing Wrong in Wishing

Does it always seem that your child is asking for this or that? As a parent, demands are constantly being made of you by your child—for attention, affection, and acquisitions. When it comes to wanting material things, there's nothing inherently wrong in the wanting. Having a goal serves as incentive for achieving it.

So let your child dream, as long as he understands that it's up to him to make his dreams come true.

Making a Wish List

A wish list is just another way of putting down financial goals on paper. According to one survey, teenage boys typically save up for a car, teenage girls for college, while younger children have no particular savings goals. Your child can learn to become a more determined saver by deciding what he's saving for.

Piggybank on It

When estimating costs of the things your child wants, it's always better to err on the high side. The worst that will happen is that she'll reach her goal sooner. If the target savings is too low, she won't save enough to reach her goal.

Use the following worksheet to list your child's goals. You'll see that there are two columns: short-term and long-term. Short-term goals are ones that can be reached in a matter of weeks or a couple of months. Long-term goals can take months or even years to attain (a few suggestions have been entered in this column for you). When a child is young, he'll probably only have short-term goals; he can't be expected to think in terms of months or years. That's okay. Just having short-term goals is enough to get him started on the road to saving success. For example, an elementary school child might want to set a savings goal that can be reached within a few weeks or a month because this time frame is easily understood. The important thing is to have some sort of goal so that he can develop the savings habit.

Short-term goals	Long-term goals
_____	Prom
_____	Car
_____	College
_____	Senior class ring
_____	_____
_____	_____
_____	_____
_____	_____

Now that your child knows what he wants, you'll have to help him put a price tag on what he's saving for. For example, if he wants to save up for the prom, make sure that he tallies all the expenses involved (tickets, tuxedo rental, corsage, limo, after-prom party, and so on).

Making Wishes Come True

Having a savings goal is only half the battle; your child must know how much she needs to save to reach her goal. There are different ways to figure what's necessary to put aside.

➤ *Use a regular savings plan.* Decide how much of each allowance or paycheck will be set aside, regardless of the savings goals. Then the item can be purchased when the goal is met. When my girls started baby-sitting, I suggested that they put half of everything aside for long-term goals. They could save up or spend the rest. This one-half rule worked so well that they had a nice bank account when they went to college.

➤ *Save as much as possible.* Supplement a regular savings plan with additional savings. This way, your child will reach his goal when he has saved what's needed to buy or do the thing he's aiming at. For example, if something costs $100 and his regular savings amount is $5 a week, then it would take him 20 weeks (or about five months) to reach his goal. But if he gets an extra $5 here or $10 there, he can cut his saving time considerably.

➤ *Back into a target savings amount.* If your child knows how long she has to save for something, she can divide the dollars she needs by the time she has. For example, if it's going to cost her $500 to go to the prom and it's August before her senior year, she'll have 10 months in which to save up for this big expense. That means she'll need to put $50 aside each month ($500 ÷ 10) to pay for prom expenses.

Targeting a savings amount is most effective for the big ticket items she's saving for. You'll see that in a minute when it comes to saving for college.

Setting Savings Goals for College

From the day your child was born, you may have dreamed he'd go off to Harvard or Yale one day. For your elementary school child, that dream seems a long way off, but the high cost of college today means that you'll want to start saving for it as soon as you can.

Financial Building Blocks

What's it going to cost when your kid is ready to start college? No one knows for sure because no one knows how much costs will escalate in coming years. Here's a projection of what it might cost your child for a four-year degree (assuming that costs will rise at 6 percent annually):

Year	Public college	Private college	Top private college
2000	$60,000	$120,000	$140,000
2005	$80,294	$160,587	$187,352
2010	$107,451	$214,902	$250,719
2015	$143,793	$287,587	$335,518

How much should you save and how much should your child save? Given the high cost of college, it's probably a good idea for both of you to start saving now if you haven't already begun to do so.

Here's what you and your child together would need to save monthly to have the targeted funds on hand when your child heads off to college. You'll see that the amount that must be saved increases with the age of your child. The younger your child, the longer you have to save, and thus the smaller your monthly savings will have to be. Of course, the required savings also varies with the kind of investment return you can receive. Let's assume that you target $100,000 as what you think will be needed for college for your child. You put a fixed amount of money into savings on the first of each month and earn 8 percent on your money (compounded monthly) every year. In this case, your savings each month should be the following:

Your Child's Age	Monthly Savings Amount
1	$208
2	$232
3	$259
4	$289

Your Child's Age	Monthly Savings Amount
5	$375
6	$367
7	$416
8	$475
9	$547
10	$635
11	$747
12	$892
13	$1,087
14	$1,361

When your child is within four years of college, the monthly savings amount gets to be a very large number because there's only a short time left to save. Also keep in mind that this savings model doesn't take taxes into account. If the earnings are reduced by taxes (the savings is in a taxable vehicle), then even more must be saved to offset the tax cost.

Financial Building Blocks

You can make more specific projections for your own situation. You can change the variables—years to college, cost of the school, rate of return, and even the projected rate of inflation for college costs. Use one of several college calculators available online. Here are two good ones:

From T. Rowe Price: www.troweprice.com/college/trowecollegeFundHome.html

From Fidelity: personal431.fidelity.com/planning/college_toc.html

Special Saving Strategies for College

In saving for college, you'll have to decide how much responsibility you want to take and how much to put on your child. After all, it's her education. In wealthy families, it's usually parents or even grandparents who save for the child's education. In less wealthy families, it's a combination of all concerned.

Watch Your Step

Some financial experts advise parents *not* to save for their child's education at the expense of their own retirement savings. In other words, make planned retirement savings first and contributions to a child's college fund second.

Money ABCs

Tax-deferred means that you're postponing the time when income will be subject to tax. You don't avoid tax entirely; you only delay when it happens. **Tax-free** means that income will never be taxed.

Some financial advisers suggest that you put money only in a parent's name because savings in the child's name counts more heavily against him if he applies for financial aid. However, there are several points to consider. First, you don't know now whether she'll need any aid in the future. Second, the aid formula could change. There has already been a proposal in Congress to base the financial aid formula on the family as a whole (rather than parent and child separately).

Tax-Advantaged Plans

Congress has sanctioned various savings plans designed to encourage people to save for a college education. These plans have tax incentives to make your saving chore a little easier. Three main savings plans are now found in the tax laws:

➤ State-qualified tuition programs

➤ Education IRAs

➤ U.S. savings bonds

None of these plans allows for an income tax deduction on your federal income tax return for contributions you make. The tax incentive that's built in is the opportunity for tax-deferred or tax-free income.

You have to make a choice of which type of plan to use. You can't contribute money to two plans in the same year. Doing so can result in a 6 percent penalty.

You can learn about federal tax incentives for college savings by clicking on the IRS Web site at www.irs.ustreas.gov. In particular, you can view or download IRS Publication 970, Tax Benefits for Higher Education. Or call for a copy at 800-TAX-FORMS.

Special State-Sponsored Tuition Programs

At present, almost every state has adopted some form of a qualified tuition program. The types of plans vary considerably from state to state. For example, the dollar limit on what you can put in each year or in total for your child changes in different states. Qualified state tuition programs allow you, grandparents, or anyone else to put money toward your child's college education.

Two types of qualified state tuition plans may be open to you in your state. The first and most common is a *prepaid tuition program*. If you put in a certain amount of money, all your child's tuition and fees are guaranteed to be covered. If you make the required payments, the tuition is covered even if it rises more than was expected. With most prepaid tuition plans, your child must attend a college within your state (although some pay for out-of-state schools). If your child doesn't attend college or attends one out of state that's not covered, a certain amount of money is refunded to him (at least contributions minus an administrative fee, but sometimes earnings as well).

The second type of plan is a *savings plan* and it's now offered in 18 states. You may see it called a 529 plan because this is the section in the Internal Revenue Code that allows it. In a savings-type plan, contributions are made to an IRA-like account for the benefit of your child. The money is invested in stock funds, bonds, or other savings vehicles by Fidelity or other managers selected by the state. You're prohibited by law from having any say in how the money's invested for your child. Earnings on the account accumulate on a tax-deferred basis.

Earnings on the savings plan are taxed when your child uses the money to pay for tuition, fees, room and board, and other college-related expenses. Of course, distributions for college expenses aren't all income. Part of the money is just a return of your own savings; it's only the other part that's taxable. If, by some miracle, all the money isn't used up, the funds must be distributed by the time your child reaches the age of 30. Alternatively, they can be rolled over to a younger brother or sister and used for his or her education.

State programs aren't all good news, though. In savings plans, you can't control investments and have no guarantees about investment returns. You may be able to save more outside the program than could be accumulated within it. In prepaid tuition programs, if your child goes out of state or doesn't go to school, your return may be much smaller than you could have saved privately.

To find out about a program in your state, don't ask your local banker; the banks have nothing to do with state programs. Instead, contact the state education department in your state capital or the agency that's administering the program in your state.

Piggybank on It

Your state may let you deduct contributions on your state income tax return. To the extent that your contributions are deductible, the state is essentially subsidizing your contribution. For example, if your state tax rate is 5 percent and you make a $1,000 contribution, it's really only costing you $950 because you're saving $50 in taxes).

Piggybank on It

Contributions to qualified state tuition programs are gifts to your child, but they don't usually trigger gift tax because of the annual gift tax exclusion (currently $10,000 per recipient). Larger contributions also can be treated as having been made over a five-year period. Thus, even a $50,000 contribution wouldn't result in any gift tax.

Educating Yourself About Education IRAs

You probably know all about IRAs for retirement savings. Well, there's a special savings vehicle for college costs called an education IRA. Aside from the name, the two types of savings plans don't have too much in common. For example, you must make annual contributions to an education IRA no later than December 31, while you have until the following April 15 to fund a retirement IRA.

You can put up to $500 each year into an education IRA for your child until the year in which she reaches 18. An education IRA is really just a fancy custodial or trust account set up in your child's name: She's the beneficiary of the account you set up at a bank, brokerage firm, or mutual fund. Anyone—even your child—can contribute to this account if eligible to do so, but the total amount for the year can't be more than $500. Contributions can be made to more than one education IRA as long as the total is no more than $500 each year.

Who's eligible to make a contribution? Anyone who has a modified adjusted gross income (MAGI) below a threshold amount fixed by law can do so. This threshold is $150,000 for people filing joint returns and $95,000 for single individuals.

A partial contribution is allowed for joint return filers with MAGI between $150,000 and $160,000; for single people, it's MAGI between $95,000 and $110,000.

The incentive for contributing to an education IRA is that the earnings on your contributions will never be taxed if the money is used for a qualified purpose. This includes most college expenses—tuition, fees, books, supplies, and room and board for a child who's at least a half-time student (there are further limits on treating room and board as qualified expenses).

Withdrawals for nonqualified purposes are taxed and can even be subject to a 10 percent penalty on top of the tax.

Watch Your Step

There have already been attempts in Congress to increase substantially the annual contribution limit to education IRAs. Stay alert to possible law changes that can make this type of education savings plan more attractive.

Money ABCs

Modified adjusted gross income (MAGI) means adjusted gross income without regard to any foreign income that you're allowed to exclude. This means your income before subtracting your itemized or standard deductions and your exemptions.

Education IRAs have received a great deal of hype from the media, but serious financial advisers aren't so keen on them. They don't allow for much savings (the top investment for each child is only $500 × 18 years if the account is started when the child is born). So if you do make education IRA contributions, don't rely too heavily on them to pay for your child's college. You may not even want to get started with them, because the restrictions may be more trouble than they're worth. But you can't stop Grandma from making contributions to your child's account.

Special Use for Savings Bonds

You're probably familiar with U.S. savings bonds. Today you can buy Series EE or Series I bonds at your local bank, or you may even be able to do so through a payroll savings plan. But did you know that if you use the bonds to pay for higher education for your child (or even yourself or your spouse), the interest may be entirely tax-free?

Tax-free treatment applies if all the following conditions are met:

➤ You buy the bonds (and you're over age 24).

➤ You redeem the bonds to pay for college tuition and educational fees for your child. However, education expenses taken into account don't include amounts covered by scholarships or used for purposes of education tax credits (explained later in this chapter).

➤ Your income is below a threshold amount that's adjusted annually for inflation. For example, in 1999, a full exclusion applies if your adjusted gross income is below $79,650 on a joint return, or below $53,100 if you're a single parent.

Watch Your Step

Tax-free treatment doesn't apply to grandparents who redeem their bonds to help with their grand-children's education. It also doesn't apply to bonds issued in the child's own name.

Each year, you can buy up to $30,000 worth of bonds (for EE bonds, this means a $15,000 invest-ment). But bonds come in a variety of small denominations. Savings bonds certainly have yielded less return than stock market investments, but they're entirely safe because they're backed by the full faith and credit of the federal government. If you don't use the bonds for your child (say, he gets a full scholarship), you can always use them for yourself, perhaps to supplement your retire-ment income. Bonds continue to earn interest for up to 30 years.

To learn more about savings bonds, you can get information from the U.S. Treasury at www.savings-bonds.gov and www.ustreas.gov/opc/opc0035.html.

Watch Your Step

If you have only a short time until your child starts college and you know he's going to rely partially on financial aid to supplement savings, be aware that under the current federal financial aid formula, you're expected to contribute only 5.65 percent of your savings to his college. Your child, however, is expected to contribute 35 percent of his savings.

Plans That Aren't Tax-Advantaged

Whether or not you use one of the tax-sanctioned savings programs, you and your child can save in the regular way. Here, you have a number of important decisions to make along the way.

Piggybank on It

While growth mutual funds offer the opportunity for the largest increase in a savings fund, they're riskier than fixed-income investments, such as CDs. Some financial experts advise that mutual funds are fine when a child is young, but once he's within three years or so of starting college, money should be primarily in wholly safe investments so that you'll know the money will be there however the stock market performs.

➤ *In whose name will the savings be held?* You can put money in your name, your child's name, or both. If you put it in your child's name, you'll have to use custodial accounts or trusts to hold the money. You can manage the savings for your child, but once the money is put into the child's name, you cannot recoup it; the money belongs to the child.

➤ *What type of investments will you make?* This depends on many factors—how many years remain until your child will start college, how much risk are you comfortable taking, how much money you have to invest. The longer your savings horizon, the greater risk you should try to take. Generally, you'll want to invest for the greatest growth on your money, the kind you can get from stock mutual funds (mutual fund investing is discussed in Part 6 of this book). If you have only a year or two left to save, you may want to choose investments whose returns are guaranteed.

Falling Short of Education Savings Goals

If your child saves for college but falls short of his savings goal, don't despair. There are plenty of other ways to pay for college besides or in addition to savings. These alternatives shouldn't be used to dispense with the need to save, however. Instead, they should be used to supplement his savings efforts. After all, college is costly and most people aren't able to save up for the full amount.

Money ABCs

A **tax credit** is a dollar-for-dollar reduction of the tax you'd otherwise have to pay. For example, if your credit is $1,000, you'll save $1,000 in taxes you'd otherwise send to the government.

➤ *Financial aid.* Getting scholarships to pay for school is discussed in Chapter 11, "Getting Money Out of the Blue." Taking out student loans is discussed in Chapter 26, "Studying Up on Student Loans."

➤ *Tax incentives.* The federal government allows parents to claim special tax credits for sending their kids to college. There's the Hope scholarship credit that saves up to $1,500 of taxes, based on the cost of attending the first two years of college. The credit is valid for 100 percent of the first $1,000 of expenses, plus 50 percent of the next $1,000 of expenses (for example, if you pay $2,000 in expenses, you'll get the full $1,500 credit).

A lifetime learning credit is valid for 20 percent of up to $5,000 of higher education costs. This will increase to 20 percent of up to $10,000 of such costs starting in 2003. However, these credits can be claimed only if your income is less than a set amount.

➤ *Working.* About two-thirds of college kids work to supplement their college money. For most, working doesn't hurt their academic performance—it may even help them manage their time better.

The Least You Need to Know

➤ Setting savings goals serves as incentive for achieving them.

➤ Use a regular savings plan, with modifications, to reach savings goals.

➤ Start as early as possible on a college savings program.

➤ Use tax-advantaged savings plans to build up college funds.

➤ Use ordinary savings strategies to amass money for college.

➤ If your child falls short of his college savings goal, supplement it with financial aid, tax incentives, and other means.

THAT'S ME.

Chapter 17

Piggybanking It

> **In This Chapter**
>
> ➤ Stuffing the piggybank
>
> ➤ Using a savings account
>
> ➤ Having bigger and better savings
>
> ➤ Buying savings bonds

For most kids, having money in hand is a great temptation to spending it. But learning to save means that the money will be there later when your child needs it. In fact, it may even grow so that there's more available to spend in the future.

In Part 4 of this book, you learned how to determine how much of your child's money should be devoted to savings. In this chapter, you'll learn about different ways your child can save her money. There's a simple way for the youngest child, and as your child gets older, she can use more sophisticated savings arrangements. Here you'll learn about bank savings accounts, CDs, money market funds, and savings bonds. In the next chapter, you'll learn about other places your child can put her savings to grow it for the future.

Keeping It Under the Mattress

The local hospital in my town used to provide each child born there with a ceramic piggybank decorated in gold paint with his date of birth. These banks served as the first savings vehicle for many kids. Children were encouraged to stuff their coins into the top of the bank and were discouraged from pulling the rubber plug at the bottom to release the coins.

Piggybanks aren't a new idea: Even mechanical savings banks were around more than a century ago. A windup or other device let a metal figure snatch a coin and deposit it within the body of the bank.

Financial Building Blocks

Antique mechanical banks aren't kid stuff anymore—they can go for several hundred dollars apiece. One man's collection had three antique mechanical banks that sold at auction for $500,000 each—one from the late 1800s fetched as much as $750,000!

Your child doesn't need a fancy bank or even an official piggybank in which to keep his coins; any mayonnaise jar with a slit cut in the lid can serve the purpose. The idea is to find one place where your child will go to put his pennies.

For a very young kid—5 or 6—this is probably all he'll need to learn the rudiments of savings. When he goes to take the money out of the piggybank to make a purchase, he'll quickly come to understand that he'll never be able to take out more than what he puts into it. If he saves every penny of his $5 weekly allowance, he'll only have $20 at the end of a month. At this stage in his life, he'll want to learn about better ways to save.

Visiting Your Neighborhood Bank

When I was in elementary school in New York City, we used to be able to bring in coins each week that we privately put into small brown envelopes with our names on it. The school kept track of our savings (the funds were actually deposited in a passbook savings account at a local bank and earned the going rate of interest). When I moved on to junior high, I was able to take several hundred dollars with me. This was the first banking experience that many of us enjoyed.

Money ABCs

A **deposit** is an addition of money to your child's account. It's the opposite of a **withdrawal**.

Today, that option no longer exists, but you can help your child experience the savings process by setting up a savings account at a local bank.

Having a savings account at a local bank will show your child two important things:

➤ *Where money is kept.* While most of the bank's money isn't physically all at your local branch (it's reinvested in other assets, such as loans to customers), the bank is still the place where deposits are made.

Financial Building Blocks

The American Bankers Association Education Foundation has designated April 17 as National Teach Children to Save Day. Bankers on that day visit local elementary schools to explain and tout the virtues of saving in their banks. For information, call 800-338-0626.

➤ *What interest is all about.* Interest is income earned on your money. When a deposit is made in a bank, you essentially are giving the bank the use of your money. The bank lends it out as mortgage money or for other loans and then charges the borrowers interest. For the use of your money, you earn interest.

Bank savings accounts show your child some very important money management elements. These concepts underlie any type of investment decision's she'll make throughout her life.

➤ *Making deposits and withdrawals.* You can show your child deposit and withdrawal slips used for these transactions and how to fill them in.

➤ *Safety.* When we think of safety, we picture avoiding accidents and getting injured. Well, it's really the same thing with money. Safety means that your child won't get injured *financially* by putting his money in a bank. The investment is safe, and he can count on being able to take out what he has put in (and then some). Money in most banks today is FDIC-insured up to $100,000. (Make sure that your child's bank has this protection by looking for an FDIC sign in the window or by asking someone there.) FDIC is a quasi-federal agency that promises to pay what's in each account—up to that dollar limit—if the bank should experience financial difficulties and fold. It's a form of insurance.

➤ *Liquidity.* This doesn't mean that the money turns into liquid gold—it refers to access to money. Your child can take the money out of

Watch Your Step

With the success of the stock market in recent years compared with the low interest rates paid by the banks, some investment advisers have been dissuading youngsters from putting their hard-earned pennies into the local bank in favor of riskier stocks. But if there's an economic downturn and the stock market takes a dive, those kids with savings accounts can rest easy. The bottom line is to include both types of investments in a savings program.

the savings account at any time, and there are no penalties for doing so.

While savings accounts offer safety and liquidity, there's a price for these benefits: a low return on the money. As your child becomes willing to sacrifice some safety or some liquidity, she'll be able to get a better return. Some alternatives are explained later in this chapter; other types of investments are explained in the following chapter.

Starting a Savings Account of His Own

If your child has been to town, he knows the whereabouts of a bank or two. But what he doesn't know is what type of account he'll be opening and how to go about doing it.

Two types of bank savings accounts exist: statement accounts and passbook accounts.

➤ *Statement accounts* provide your child with a monthly report of what has happened to the account. It shows money that has been deposited, withdrawals that have been made, interest that has been credited, and any fees charged against the account.

➤ *Passbook accounts* give your child a little booklet that every transaction is entered into. Whenever money is put in, the deposit must be posted in the passbook.

Some checking accounts pay interest (these may be called NOW accounts.) However, these accounts aren't designed for savings; they're used to write checks to pay bills, and the interest is only an extra feature of the account. Using checks is discussed in Chapter 5, "What's Money?"

If your child is under the age of 18, he may not be able to open a savings account without your help. Even if your child earned the money himself, the bank may insist that the account be opened as a custodial account under the Uniform Gifts to Minors Act (UGMA) or the Uniform Transfers to Minors Act (UTMA). The type of custodial account depends on which act has been adopted in your state; most now use UTMA.

You'll have to sign as custodian to open the account, the title of which will read: Account of [YOUR NAME], as custodian for [YOUR CHILD'S NAME]. The account will be listed under your child's Social Security number, and all interest belongs to and is taxed to him.

When your child reaches 18 (or 21, if state law imposes that age requirement), the title of the account can be changed to eliminate the custodianship.

Having a custodial account is a great way for a child under age 18 to save money. She can look at her monthly statement or passbook to see how her money is growing. But the problem with a custodial account is that you, not she, have the power of the pen over the account. She must wait for you to put the money in or take the money out.

Some banks don't enforce the formality of a custodial account. They'll allow your child to open her own account as long as she can sign (not just print) her name. In this way, she can physically make her own deposits and withdrawals.

Some banks even go out of their way to attract kids as customers. For example, one bank in California offers a Looney Tunes Savings Club that features Looney Tunes characters on deposit and with-drawal slips (www.downeysavings.com/checkingsavings/savings/looneytunes/index.asp). There's also the State Street Bank Kids' Club that gives stickers with each $5 deposit, requires no minimum deposit and offers other special activities for kids at www.peoplesonline.com/kids.htm. The Washington School Employees Credit Union offers several Youth Clubs for savers of any age. For example, those 12 and younger can join Savvy Savers to set up a savings account. This entitles a child to a birthday card and semiannual newsletter (see www.wsecu.org/html/club.html for more information). Another site to check for kids' accounts is Commonwealth Bank, at www.commonwealthbank.com/kids/html.

Your local bank isn't the only place for a savings account. Credit unions may also offer savings accounts to the children of credit union members. Some offer special accounts just for kids.

Some savings banks even let your children mail in deposits. For example, Young Americans Bank in Denver boasts savers from every state and has no minimum deposit requirements (call 303-321-2265, or check out their Web site at www.theyoungamericans.org).

Watch Your Step

Changing the title to a custodial account isn't automatic. Even though bank records may show your child's age, the bank doesn't pay attention to his birthday. If you don't change the title, it may remain a custodial account indefinitely.

Watch Your Step

Check for any minimum deposit or account balance requirements. Some banks restrict the size of accounts, and others may charge fees for account balances below certain amounts. Also ask whether there are any special breaks for young depositors; there often are.

Deposits in savings banks can be made whenever your child has the money to do so; there's no restriction on how often he can put money into the account. You'll want to encourage regular deposits, but your child can make them more or less frequently. There may be some restrictions on how often withdrawals can be made, however, and if deposits are made by check (for example, a gift your child received from his aunt across the country), he'll have to wait several days for the check to clear before withdrawing those funds.

Getting Interest

There's something very interesting about interest: It's a way to make money on money. Once your child gets the ball rolling by putting money into an interest-bearing account, it takes on a life of its own. This is because most types of savings accounts pay compound interest.

You may recall the old riddle you faced in elementary school. Would you rather receive $100 a day each day for a month, or start with a penny on day one and receive double the amount each day? The first alternative is tempting, and after a month you'd have more than $3,000. But with the second alternative, you'd be a millionaire in just a month even though you started with a penny. This is because of what's often referred to as the magic of compounding. In this example, we're talking about 100 percent interest each day, but most savings accounts today pay less than 3 percent annually (not 100 percent each day). The principal is the same, though. Here's an example to explain how compound interest works.

Money ABCs

Compound interest is interest that's figured on all the money in the account, including any prior interest that has been earned. **Simple interest** is figured only on the money you've put in (not on the interest that has already been earned).

Financial Building Blocks

There's a handy way to see how long it will take for money to double. This is called the **rule of 72**. Divide the number 72 by the rate of interest the savings account pays to find the years it will take to double the money that has been deposited in it. For example, if your child earns 5 percent, it will take 14.4 years to double his money. If he earns 10 percent, it's just 7.2 years.

Say your child saves $100 at 5 percent interest. At the end of the first year, she'd have $105 ($100 investment plus 5 percent interest). At the end of year two, she'd have

$110.25 ($105, plus 5 percent interest). At the end of the third year, she'd have $115.76 ($110.25, plus 5 percent interest). As you can see, as the size of the account grows, the amount of interest earned each year also increases because the interest rate is being applied to an ever-increasing pot.

The following chart shows how every dollar your child invests will grow over the years, depending on the rate of interest received (assuming annual compounding). As you both can see, if she saves $50 at 7.5 percent interest, she'll have $72 after five years ($50 × $1.44 shown in the chart).

To see how much your child must invest on a regular basis to reach a savings goal, or how much she'll have at the end of a set time if she has a particular amount to invest regularly, use a savings calculator that can be found at www.aba.com/aba/ConsumerConnection/persfin.asp or www.national-city.com/natcity/personal/savings/savcal. You just enter the requested information, and the computer will do the rest. You can, of course, vary the information (for example, change your child's savings goal) and recalculate the results.

Piggybank on It

The faster the period of compounding, the greater the return. Unless otherwise noted, compounding is done on an annual basis. However, on some savings accounts there may be monthly, quarterly, or semiannual compounding. Because compounding means that interest is figured on interest, the more often compounding is figured, the faster the money will grow.

How Interest Makes Your Money Grow

Year	5 percent	6 percent	7.5 percent	10 percent
1	$1.05	$1.06	$1.08	$1.10
2	$1.10	$1.12	$1.16	$1.21
3	$1.16	$1.19	$1.22	$1.33
4	$1.22	$1.26	$1.34	$1.46
5	$1.28	$1.34	$1.44	$1.61
6	$1.34	$1.42	$1.54	$1.77
7	$1.41	$1.50	$1.61	$1.95
8	$1.48	$1.59	$1.72	$2.14
9	$1.55	$1.69	$1.92	$2.36
10	$1.63	$1.69	$2.06	$2.59
15	$2.08	$2.40	$2.96	$4.18
20	$2.65	$3.21	$4.25	$6.73
25	$3.39	$4.29	$6.10	$10.83

Source: CCH Financial and Estate Planning Guide

Joining the Big (Savings) Leagues

Savings accounts are Mickey Mouse investments: In today's low interest environment, they pay only a very modest rate of interest. You can consider several alternative investments that pay interest as well. These may not be as safe or liquid, but they'll give your child more interest over the long run.

Here are some of the other types of investments that may pay a higher interest rate:

➤ Certificates of deposit

➤ Bank money market funds

➤ U.S. savings bonds

Financial Building Blocks

Other interest-bearing investments, such as Treasury bills and bonds, corporate bonds, municipal bonds, zero coupon bonds, bond mutual funds, and bond unit investment trusts exist. These investments are more sophisticated and may require a relatively large initial investment that's probably beyond your child's means. Still, as part of your child's financial vocabulary, these investments are explained in the next chapter.

CDs Aren't Just Musical Recordings

Certificates of deposit (CDs) aren't only things your child plays on a stereo or computer. They're also a type of investment that works like a savings account. The CD pays compound interest, and CDs have the same FDIC insurance protection as savings accounts.

Piggybank on It

Your child can start saving in a savings account. Then when the balance is a $1,000 or more (or whatever's required for a CD), that money can be shifted into a CD.

The difference between a savings account and a CD, however, is making a commitment. Your child agrees to put a fixed amount of funds for a set time—for example, six months, one year, or five years—and receives a fixed amount of interest. Your child knows from the day he puts in his money what he'll have when the CD comes due.

The bad thing about CDs is that today interest rates are very modest compared with stock market returns, so the money won't grow as fast as it could with other types of investments.

CDs are called just that because a certificate is issued when the investment is made. The certificate is a statement that shows the following:

➤ *What's being deposited.* Usually certain minimum deposit requirements exist. The higher the requirement, the greater the interest that will be paid. CDs usually require a deposit of $1,000 or more.

➤ *What rate of interest is being paid.* You'll see two rates of interest quoted. One is the stated rate of interest that's being paid. For example, it may be 5 percent annual interest. The second rate quoted is the APR, or annual percentage rate. This rate takes into account the impact of compounding, so the APR will always be higher than the stated rate of interest.

➤ *How long the money must remain in the account.* This is called the *term* of the CD, and it's usually three months, six months, one year, or longer. Usually the term is expressed in terms of years. If it's less than a year, it may be expressed in terms of months (typically three, six, or nine months). Sometimes the term can be set at just about any date you want.

Watch Your Step

The bank can't prevent your child from taking his money out before the end of end of the term, but he'll face a penalty. The extent of the penalty depends on the term of the CD and how much prior to maturity the money is being withdrawn.

Piggybank on It

Interest rates paid by banks can vary quite a lot, so shop around. The bank across the street may pay 1 percent more for the same term CD.

It's a simple rule to remember: The longer the CD, the higher the interest. Here's a sample of what interest rates were available at one local bank (rates change on a daily basis):

Term of the CD	Interest Rate
6 months	4.10 percent
1 year	4.27 percent
2-1/5 years	4.36 percent
5 years	4.54 percent

Bank Money Market Funds

Banks may offer investors a special kind of savings account, called a money market fund. With a minimum investment of $1,000, $2,500, or $5,000 (depending on bank requirements), money can earn interest for any period of time the money is left in the account. There's no minimum investment period, and there's no fixed interest. Your child will know what the fund is paying on the day he goes in, but the rate floats with

Piggybank on It

Mutual fund companies also offer money market funds. These funds pay dividends, not interest, even though the funds themselves earn their money by collecting interest. Money market funds with mutual fund companies generally pay a little more than bank funds.

the prevailing interest rates and thus can go up or down. Currently, bank money market accounts are paying only between 2 percent and 3 percent annually.

Again, bank money market funds aren't for the very young saver who has only a few dollars to start with. But once a savings account has accumulated the money market fund minimum, it may be a good idea to switch some money to this type of investment.

Saving It in Savings Bonds

Savings bonds used to be a way for the federal government to raise money to pay for the war effort. Savings bonds were big in World War I and World War II, and they continued to be issued long after the war ended. Savings bonds are really loans used to finance the government.

Financial Building Blocks

Savings bonds are still popular investments with the populace: There's a bondholder in more than one of every three American households today. Total holdings are more than $185 billion, and 15 million people continue to buy savings bonds each year.

Watch Your Step

Interest on savings bonds bought in your child's name isn't tax-free, even if the bonds are used to pay for her education. The special income tax exclusion for interest on savings bonds used for higher education purposes applies only to bonds bought by someone age 24 or older.

Today, savings bonds are still going strong. Many adults commonly buy savings bonds through payroll deduction programs, and kids can buy bonds, too. There's no minimum age requirement for buying savings bonds.

Today, you can choose from two types of U.S. savings bonds: EE bonds and I bonds, as explained here. Both types of savings bonds have certain things in common.

➤ *They pay interest.* How interest is figured depends on the type of bond involved.

➤ *Interest is subject to federal income tax but not to state income tax.* This interest may be deferred until the bond matures or is cashed in. This means that there's no current income tax to pay on the interest. However, your child can choose to pay interest annually. This may make sense because your child will pay little or no tax on the interest until he starts earning a respectable income. If you buy savings bonds and redeem them to pay for your child's education, you may be able to exclude some or all of the interest on your own tax return (see Chapter 16, "Setting Savings Goals That Work").

➤ *Interest is assured.* A savings bond (like other Treasury securities) is the safest investment possible because it's backed by the full faith and credit of the federal government. This means that Washington guarantees to make good on the bond, whatever it takes.

➤ *Savings bonds are purchased mainly through banks and thrifts.* They don't charge any fees or commissions for purchasing the bonds.

To learn more about savings bonds, you can get information by calling the Federal Reserve at 800-234-2931 or from the U.S. Treasury at www.savings-bonds.gov and www.ustreas.gov/opc/opc0035.html.

Your child may be holding savings bonds that he received as gifts from relatives and friends (maybe even some from the time he was born). He can see how much interest has been earned on them by checking www.savingsbond.com/chart.html.

EE Bonds

Double-E isn't just a shoe size; it's the name of a savings bond. EE bonds are *discount bonds* issued at one-half their face amount. If your child buys a $100 savings bond, it costs him only $50. Face amounts for savings bonds are $50, $75, $100, $200, $500, $1,000, $5,000, and $10,000. Each year, the value of the bond increases, and that increase is called interest. After a certain number of years, the value of the bond equals its face amount. The bond continues to earn interest, however, until its final maturity date 30 years from the date it was purchased.

The rate of interest varies depending on several factors, including when the bond was purchased and the prevailing interest rates. For bonds bought today, interest is 90 percent of the average yield for five-year Treasury bonds for the prior six months. A new rate is fixed each May 1 and November 1. As a rule of thumb, if you buy a $100 bond (at a cost of $50), it will be worth $100 in about 15 years.

Piggybank on It

Your child can become an automatic bond buyer through the EasySaver program set up by the Treasury Department. If he enrolls, his savings account will be tapped on a regular basis (that you determine) to buy a savings bond (in the amount you specify). For information, call 877-881-7283.

Watch Your Step

Some parents may be tempted to cash in all their children's bonds and put the money into higher-yielding investments, such as the stock market. While *all* of a child's money shouldn't be in savings bonds, there's still a place for them in your child's investment portfolio.

Savings bonds may be cashed in at just about any bank, but they can't be cashed in within six months of the date of purchase. If they're cashed in before five years, your child will lose the last three months of interest.

I Bonds

The government is always looking for ways to raise money. Recently, officials came up with a new marketing idea, called I bonds. These bonds, which first went on sale in September 1998, are sold at their face amount. A $50 bond costs $50. I bonds are sold in the same denominations as EE bonds. Pictured on the face of the bonds are famous Americans such as Helen Keller, Dr. Martin Luther King, Jr., and Albert Einstein (depending upon the denomination). There are even proposals to expand the current denominations.

I bonds pay two types of interest:

Watch Your Step

While your child is years away from having to be concerned, make sure that she knows when her bonds will mature after 30 years. They don't pay interest after the final maturity date. Today, more than $5.5 billion savings bonds have passed their final maturity and no longer pay additional interest but have yet to be cashed in.

➤ *Fixed rate.* This rate is set when the bond is sold. For bonds sold from September 1998 through April 30, 1999, the fixed rate is 3.3 percent.

➤ *Adjustable rate.* This rate changes every six months and fluctuates with the rate of inflation. The rate of inflation is determined by the Consumer Price Index-Urban, a figure determined by the Bureau of Labor Statistics. Bonds sold from September 1998 through April 30, 1999, have an adjustable rate of 5.05 percent. A new rate will be figured every six months.

As with EE bonds, I bonds can be cashed in for higher education expenses, with the interest treated as tax-free (see Chapter 16).

The Least You Need to Know

➤ As kids grow older, they should start to save where there money will earn interest.

➤ Savings accounts are completely safe and liquid but pay only modest interest.

➤ Once a child is older and has more money, CDs or other interest-bearing investments should be explored.

➤ Interest and principal can be lost if CDs are cashed in before maturity.

➤ Savings bonds, which are now sold as EE bonds and I bonds, are completely safe investments.

➤ Children of any age can buy savings bonds from a bank or thrift.

Chapter 18

Beyond the Corner Bank

In This Chapter

➤ Spreading the risk of investing

➤ Going for (more) income

➤ Investing for growth

Putting your child's money in a piggybank or the corner bank is a safe way to save, but it's not always the best way to save. Just as kids grow in size, they need to grow their savings by making the kinds of investments that produce growth. There must be a balance between income-oriented investments such as CDs and growth-oriented investments such as stock mutual funds.

While your child is a minor, you'll have to help with the investment process. Not only will you try to guide investments, but you'll actually be making them because your child's money must be held in a custodial account until he reaches legal age.

In this chapter, you'll learn about the importance of spreading savings among different types of investments. You'll see some more sophisticated income-oriented investments, and you'll also find out about growth investments and how suitable they are for kids. In the next part of the book, you'll learn all about making stock market-based investments.

Risk Reduction Without Return Reduction

When your child is saving her pennies in a jar, it's probably a good idea to keep everything in one place. This way, she'll see how her savings grow by looking at how high the coins rise in the jar. As your child's savings grow into the thousands of

Money ABCs

Diversification means that your child isn't putting all his eggs in one basket. He's spreading his risk of loss by using different investments because some may do well and others may not do so well.

Money ABCs

Asset allocation is a process of deciding how much of one's money to put into stocks, bonds, and savings accounts. The allocation is just a proportion selected for this purpose.

dollars, however, keeping things in one place—especially a jar—isn't the best idea. At this point, your child needs to *diversify* her investments.

Diversification means putting money into different investments. Maybe your child wants to own stock in Disney, McDonalds, and Apple Computer. Even if Disney goes down in value, this may be offset by increases in McDonalds and Apple. Overall, she's still in good shape financially. In effect, it's hoped that by spreading money around, your child won't suffer too great a loss if one or two investments do poorly.

You and your child must know two key things about diversification: how to allocate assets once her savings account reaches a critical mass, and at what point to change this allocation.

Allocating Assets

If your child has only a few dollars, he's probably going to put it all in one place, such as a bank account. But as his savings grow, he should be thinking about allocating his assets.

As you've seen, diversification is the idea of going into a variety of investments. Putting that idea into action requires some decisions on what's called *asset allocation*. There are no magic formulas to use in allocating assets for your child, but experts suggest many different formulas for asset allocation. Here are a couple to consider just to give you an idea of how the allocation process works:

➤ *80 percent rule.* Multiply your child's age by 80 percent to find the percentage of his investments that should be in bonds and other fixed-income investments. Subtract this from 100 to find the percentage that should be in stocks and stock mutual funds. For example, using this rule, your 15-year-old should have 12 percent of his total investments in fixed-income (15×80 percent) and 88 percent in growth stocks and stock mutual funds.

➤ *110 minus your child's age.* Here, just subtract his age from 110 to find the part that should be in stocks; the balance goes into fixed-income investments. So, your 15-year-old should have 95 percent of his investments in stocks ($110 - 15$) and only 5 percent in fixed income. Of course, this formula means that any child 10 or under should be *entirely* invested for growth, which may not be the best course of action.

The problem with formulas is that they fail to take into account your child's personal situation. If he has only a few thousand dollars or less to invest, then these formulas don't make much sense; they're intended for more sizable holdings. Also, if there's only a little money involved, your child is in less of a position to risk any losses.

Formulas also don't take into account other factors:

➤ *How necessary the money is to him.* If you can afford to pay for his college, then he's in a different investment seat than someone who's investing to get his tuition together.

➤ *How much risk he can stand.* Some people are more inclined to gamble with their money and don't lose any sleep over the ups and downs of the stock market. Others like to play it safe And are only happy knowing that their money is FDIC-insured. It's important to know what kind of risk-taker your child is so that he'll make the investment decisions he's more comfortable with. Of course, you'll want to encourage *some* risk taking, but how far you push things depends on your child's personality.

Money ABCs

Interest is a fixed rate of return on your money. It's expressed as a percentage. If your child puts in $100 and earns 5 percent interest for the year, she'll have $105 at the end of that year; the $5 is interest.

Income Versus Growth

Two main categories of investments exist: those that produce a fixed income, and those that go for growth. Fixed income mainly means interest income earned on savings accounts, bonds, and similar investments.

Other types of income relate to non-fixed income investments, such as stocks and stock mutual funds. These two types of income include dividends and capital gain distributions from mutual funds. This income is paid when companies make money and share their good fortune with their shareholders.

Fixed-income investments offer your child certainty. She knows when she buys a fixed-income investment exactly what she'll have when she's through. For example, if she buys a CD paying 5 percent interest for five years, she can figure today to the penny what she'll be paid five years from now.

Money ABCs

Dividends are payments by companies to people who own stock in them. Dividends usually are paid in cash, but they can also be made in stock or other property. For example, if your child owns one share of McDonalds, he'll earn a 36¢ cash dividend on that share for the year.

Capital gain distributions are paid by stock mutual fund companies. This represents capital gains the funds have received on selling the stock they've held. It's paid to fund holders like a dividend, but it gets more favorable tax treatment.

Fixed-income investments, however, don't offer any possibility that they'll be worth more than expected later on. There's no possibility for growth.

Financial Building Blocks

Let's take a history quiz. Over the past 60 years, long-term government bonds, a type of fixed investment, have given investors an average annual rate of return of just over 5 percent. In comparison, stocks, a type of growth investment, have yielded more than 11 percent annually. In the past four years, stocks have averaged more than 20 percent each year. So, in the long run, your child will probably have more money by investing in which of the following?

    a.   Fixed investments

    b.   Growth investments

Answer: b

Growth investments, which include stocks and stock mutual funds, are so named because they're held primarily for the chance to have the investment grow in value over time. This growth in value is translated into more money when the stock or fund shares are sold and result in capital gains.

Adults are always talking about capital gains, and this topic is important for two reasons.

Money ABCs

Capital gain is the appreciation in the value of assets since they've been bought. If your child paid $25 for a share of stock and sells it when the price has risen to $100, the $75 appreciation is capital gains; it's another word for **profit**.

➤ *Capital gains are taxed only when something is sold.* So, if your child buys Microsoft and the value of the stock rises by 200 percent, there's no immediate tax to him. The size of his savings has grown because of increases in the price of the stock he owns.

➤ *Capital gains receive special tax treatment.* Unlike ordinary income, such as salary, interest, or dividends (which is taxed according to graduated tax rates running from a low of 15 percent to a high of 39.6 percent), capital gains on assets held more than one year have a lower fixed rate of tax. Generally, they're taxed at 20 percent, but people in the lowest tax bracket on their other income pay only a 10 percent capital gains tax. For example, if your 16-year-old's only income for the year is a $3,000 salary, $1,000 in interest and dividends, and $5,000 in capital gains, the portion of his ordinary income that's taxable is subject to a 15 percent tax rate; the capital gains is taxed only at 10 percent. (For kids under 14, the kiddie tax can make them pay the 20 percent adult rate on their capital gains.)

Even without selling growth investments, your child can receive income from them. As explained earlier, growth investments may throw off income in the form of dividends or capital gain distributions by mutual funds.

Changing Allocations

As you've seen, kids have long time horizons for investments and so can wait out the ups and downs of the stock market. They can expect that over the long haul, as has been historically true, stocks will perform better than fixed-income investments. But your child may need money for something that's coming up—buying a car, going to college, starting a business. If the money is targeted for certain special uses, you may have to adjust allocations over time.

➤ *Very young children.* Here, allocations may be weighted more heavily toward growth investments. It's still many years away until college or other needs for the money.

➤ *Mid-teens.* If money is intended for college, then most experts agree that when your child is about three or four years away from starting, some or all of the money in growth investments should be shifted into fixed income. This will assure that the money needed for tuition will be there even if the stock market dips at the time your child enters college.

Income Investments: Step 2

In the last chapter, you learned how savings accounts, CDs, and savings bonds can be used to get safe, certain income for a child. These are no–brainers: You put some money in and you know immediately how much will be there at a certain point.

But you sacrifice something for all this certainty: the potential for more income. Here's where it pays to look at slightly more grown-up fixed-income investments—and you might not even have to give up any safety or certainty.

Piggybank on It

State and local governments issue bonds called municipal bonds. Interest on the bonds isn't subject to federal income tax (and may be tax-free for state income taxes as well). These bonds are primarily for individuals in high tax brackets: In these cases, the lower interest rate paid is essentially higher than the rate they could get on taxable bonds, after the tax-free aspect is factored in.

➤ Zero coupon bonds

➤ Treasury bonds

➤ Corporate bonds

➤ Money market mutual funds

➤ Bond mutual funds

Watch Your Step

There's a tax catch to zeros: Even though the interest isn't paid until the end, a portion of it is still taxable each year. If your child has little or no other income, however, the interest won't result in any tax.

Your child won't necessarily be putting his piggybank pennies into these investments today because these usually require more cash to get started. Still, it's helpful to know now the alternatives and whether they're even worth considering as investments for your child's custodial account. As a parent, you also might consider these investments for yourself as a way to help pay for your child's education or even for your own retirement.

Zeros Aren't Nothing

Zero coupon bonds—called zeros—work like CDs in that you know from the day you go in how much you'll earn. But there's one important difference: You don't get the interest until the end. In effect, they pay zero interest until the maturity date, which depends on what interest rate is being paid. The higher the interest, the shorter the maturity. Usually, you pick the maturity date and then see what the interest rate is for that period.

Piggybank on It

Zeros are a great investment vehicle for kids close to college age who are depending on the money to pay their tuition. Money from riskier sources, such as stock mutual funds, can be put into zeros scheduled to mature when the money will be needed. For example, your child should buy zeros that mature in August and January for each of the four years of college so that the cash will be there to pay the school's bill.

The difference between what is put in and what is collected is the interest earned. For example, if your child puts in $4,000, he'll collect $5,000 when the bond matures. Just like U.S. savings bonds, these are discount bonds because you buy them at less than their face amount.

Zeroes are completely safe because they're really U.S. Treasury securities. A bank or brokerage firm has stripped the interest coupon from the bond to create these investments, and they give them names like TIGRS, LIONS, CATS, and COUGARS. The U.S. Treasury has its own zero as well, called STRIPS. You don't have to understand the technicalities of how zeros are created, though. All you need to know is that you can count on the money to be there when you need it.

If your child needs the money before the set maturity date, he can sell the zeros. He might get more or less than his principal plus interest accrued to date, depending on where interest rates are compared with the rate the zero is paying. If interest rates are now higher, he'll get less. If interest rates have fallen since the zero was purchased, he'll get more.

Zeros make good investments for parents or grandparents to consider when kids are very young. Buy them when a child is born, and forget about them. Then when they mature 18 years later, the money put in will have more than doubled, even at today's modest interest rates.

Treasury Bonds Are Treasures

Besides taxes, the federal government raises money to pay its bills by borrowing from the public. This borrowing is done by selling government bills, notes, and bonds—collectively called Treasuries, for short.

Different types of Treasuries exist:

➤ *T-bills* are short-term bonds (with maturities of three months, six months, and one year). As with zeros, your child collects the interest when the bond matures. For example, if your child has already amassed a small fortune and buys a six-month $10,000 T-bill, she pays $9,750 for it. She'll collect $10,000 at the end of six months.

➤ *Treasury notes* are mid-term bonds with maturities between 2 years and 10 years. These pay interest twice a year. Minimum investments range from $1,000 to $5,000.

➤ *Treasury bonds* are long-term investments, with maturities as long as 30 years. These pay interest twice a year. They're sold in denominations of $1,000, but it really costs $10,000 to buy one bond.

Savings bonds also are available that serve the same function of raising money for the government but that don't have the same large investment requirements. Savings bonds are discussed in Chapter 16, "Setting Savings Goals That Work."

Treasuries are completely safe. Like savings bonds, they're backed by the full faith and credit of the U.S. government. Because they're also issued by the federal government, interest isn't subject to any state income tax.

When Treasuries are purchased, you don't get to hold an actual bond certificate. Today, all Treasuries are book entries, which means that they're entered on a computer under your Social Security number. Treasuries are noted on the statement from your child's bank or brokerage from which she bought the bond. Or, she'll get a receipt from the Federal Reserve Bank showing her purchase.

Piggybank on It

Treasuries can be purchased through commercial banks and brokerage firms for a small fee. They can also be bought directly through a Federal Reserve Bank with no fee involved (202-874-4000, or 800-943-6864 for those who have set up accounts) or online through the Treasury's Buy Direct Program (www.publicdebt.ustreas.gov).

Lending Money to IBM

Your child doesn't have to be J.P. Morgan to lend his money to a big corporation. He can do it by buying their bonds, called corporate bonds. In effect, the corporation gives an I.O.U. to your child in the form of a bond, and he becomes a creditor of the corporation.

Corporate bonds pay interest twice a year. The bonds mature at a set date, usually 20 or 30 years in the future. (Union Pacific even has issued 100-year bonds.)

Corporate bonds are only as good as the promise to pay by the company that issues them, so they pay a little higher interest than Treasuries. Most public companies, including Disney and IBM, sell bonds.

Bonds are sold in units of $10,000. Bonds purchased in the secondary market (after the initial offering), however, may be sold at a higher or lower cost, depending on the interest rates compared with those when the bonds were issued.

Piggybank on It

Money market mutual funds generally pay a higher return that bank mutual funds. There are some costs involved in fund ownership, however, that aren't charged for bank accounts.

Watch Your Step

The price of shares in a bond fund fluctuates with the rise and fall of interest rates. There's no assurance that what has been invested will retain its value or grow.

Money Market Mutual Funds

Banks offer money market accounts that pay interest on account balances, and mutual fund companies also have money market funds. These funds offer income that varies with the type of fund and prevailing interest rates. These funds also offer liquidity—investors can usually write checks to tap into their funds. While there's no absolute guarantee, if $1,000 is invested, $1,000 can be withdrawn.

Money market mutual funds are good for parking money between investment decisions or making other commitments for the money.

Not all money market funds are created equal, though. There's a great variety to choose from:

➤ *Treasury money market funds* invest only in U.S. government obligations. Because these are backed by the full faith and credit of the federal government, this is the safest investment that can be made—as safe as buying the Treasuries individually.

➤ *U.S. government money market funds* hold securities issued by the U.S. government *and* its agencies. Agency obligations don't necessarily have the full faith and credit backing, but they're pretty safe nonetheless.

➤ *General money market funds* hold short-term debt of corporations and banks. While not guaranteed in any way, the fact that they hold obligations of quality companies and that the debt is short-term makes these safe investments as well.

Some tax-free funds also hold debt from state and local governments.

The topic of mutual funds is quite extensive. Mutual funds for stocks are discussed in Chapter 21, "Mutual Funds Just for Kids," and many of the concepts apply as well to bond funds. The same companies offering stock funds may have corresponding bond funds. Use the information in that chapter (including Web sites of particular funds) to find a bond fund for your child.

Mutual Funds for Bonds

Your child doesn't have to own an individual bond: She can own a piece of many bonds by buying shares in a bond mutual fund. The advantages of using a mutual fund for bonds are listed here:

➤ Minimum investments may cost substantially less than the cost of individual bonds.

➤ Your child can diversify his investment portfolio because the fund holds many different bonds.

As with the variety to be found in money market funds, there's a great number of different types of bond funds. Just to give you some idea, bond mutual funds vary according to the type of bonds they hold, the quality of those bonds, and the average maturity of the bonds.

Money ABCs

Bond fund maturities are classified into three groups: short-term (1–3 years); intermediate-term (3–10 years); and long-term (more than 10 years). Bond funds don't mature on a set date, though: There's a rolling maturity. For instance, in a fund with long-term maturity, as one bond matures it's replaced with another long-term bond.

Money ABCs

Equity doesn't just mean being fair and just. It's another word for ownership in a company or a stock mutual fund.

Growth Investments Your Child Can Live With

Going for growth doesn't mean taking steroids or growth hormones. It means making investments that will increase in value over time. This means equity investments, and two types of equity let you try for growth: stocks and stock mutual funds.

With stocks, your child becomes an owner in a company. His ownership interest is represented by a stock certificate indicating the amount of the company he owns. For example, your child may buy shares in America Online. The more shares he buys, the greater his ownership percentage. (Of course, when he buys stock in publicly traded companies listed on national exchanges such as the New York Stock Exchange or NASDAQ, his percentage of ownership is miniscule.)

Stocks offer the opportunity to grow the value of your child's investment through appreciation. In other words, if he buys stock at $10 a share and sells it when the price of the stock increases to $15 a share, he has made 50 percent on his investment.

There's no ceiling on how high the price of stock can go. The stock may also pay a cash dividend, which is similar to interest in that it is a fixed amount based on the number of shares you own.

Instead of buying individual stocks, your child can buy shares in a fund that owns a variety of stocks. For example, a fund may own shares in 10 or more companies. This enables your child to enjoy the same benefits of stock ownership in each of these companies—appreciation potential and dividend earnings—and he also gains diversification.

Stocks and mutual funds are explained more fully in the next part of this book.

Watch Your Step

The downside to stock ownership is that there's no guarantee that your child will earn anything or, if she does earn anything, what amount it will be. She can even lose her entire investment if the company she owns goes under.

The Least You Need to Know

➤ Diversification means spreading the risk of loss among different investments.

➤ Allocating assets among savings accounts, stock, and bonds, is a process that depends on many different factors.

➤ Over time, equity investments have outperformed fixed-income investments.

➤ Zero coupon bonds are purchased at a discount and pay interest when they mature.

➤ Bond funds can be used to diversify bond holdings and may require smaller investments than the cost of individual bonds.

➤ Equity investments don't guaranty any income or appreciation, but they may wind up paying more than fixed-income investments with all the guarantees in the world.

Chapter 19

IRAs for Kids

In This Chapter

➤ Turning pennies into millions

➤ Picking the right IRA

➤ Investing IRA money

Retirement is something that comes toward the end of a person's life. Your child is just at the beginning of hers, but if she's working, she's already old enough to start doing something about her retirement.

The tax laws make it easy to save for retirement. The earlier your child starts, the more she'll have when she hangs up her coat at the end of her career.

In this chapter, you'll see how a child can wind up with millions at retirement, with just a few dollars to start. You'll learn about IRA options open to her—the same ones available to you as well—and how to decide which one is best for her. You'll also find out how to put those IRA dollars to work so that there will be a pot of gold waiting for her at the end of her working career.

A Millionaire in the Making

Unless your child becomes an Internet mogul or hits the lottery, he probably won't earn a million dollars in one lump sum. Still, he can amass this kind of fortune with very little effort. The keys to becoming a millionaire are starting young and enjoying the magic of compounding.

Getting your child to start thinking about retirement before he's even out of school can produce several benefits.

➤ He'll start to appreciate the need to think about the subject, something that many grown-ups put off until retirement is already upon them. He'll be able to learn about different ways to save for retirement, using tax-advantaged savings vehicles and other methods to build up a retirement fund.

➤ He'll start to learn about tax-favored ways to save for retirement. My teenagers started their IRAs the year they received their first W-2 form. The process of opening the account—they had to sign the papers—led to an explanation of what IRAs are all about and how they'll benefit from their contributions.

➤ He'll have less pressure to save for retirement if he starts doing it early. For example, if he wants to have $1 million by age 65 and he starts saving at 15, he has to put in only $56.33 each month (assuming an annual return of 10 percent). If he doesn't start saving for this fund until he's 30, he'll have to save $258.49 each month. If he delays until he's 50, the monthly savings amount climbs to $2,383.83.

Watch Your Step

Check out the treatment of IRAs under your state income tax law (if you have one). Most states allow for the same treatment as on the federal tax return, but some have different rules.

As long as your child is working—even part-time—he's in a position to start his retirement fund. The best way to do this on a tax-advantaged basis is by contributing to an IRA. An IRA, which is short for individual retirement arrangement or account, is a creature of federal tax law.

By starting young, your child has a longer time to save for retirement. This can mean that your child must save less to reach the same savings goal than someone who starts later in life. This also can mean a greater savings fund by retirement age.

Watch Your Step

Before you get carried away with the size of the fortune your child can have in retirement, don't forget to factor in how much it will really be worth at that time. Inflation will eat into the buying power of his retirement dollars.

If your child starts contributing to an IRA at the age of 18 and puts in the full $2,000 limit each year until he's 27, he'll have a $1 million by the time he's 67 without adding another penny. This example assumes an annual return of just 9 percent. Think what can be accumulated by retirement if he can get 15 percent or even 20 percent on his money each year (the S&P 500 has returned more than 20 percent for the past four years).

Choosing the Best IRA

IRAs have been around longer than your child has been alive. These special retirement savings plans offer a number of benefits, but they also contain a number of restrictions.

Three different kinds of IRAs exist—two traditional types and one relative newcomer:

➤ Traditional deductible IRAs

➤ Traditional nondeductible IRAs

➤ New nondeductible Roth IRAs

Kids who work should consider saving some money in either a traditional deductible IRA or a new nondeductible Roth IRA. (The traditional nondeductible IRA doesn't make much sense for kids because the other options are probably available.) All IRAs have certain things in common:.

➤ *There are no minimum age requirements for starting an IRA.* As long as your child is working, even an 8-year-old is eligible to make contributions.

➤ *Contributions can be made only if your child has earned income.* Your child doesn't actually have to use that money to open up the IRA; she can spend or save her earnings in a separate account. Then you can give her the money to put into the IRA as a gift. The contribution limit is all of her earnings, but no more than $2,000. So, if she makes $1,000 as a counselor at summer camp, she can put $1,000 into an IRA. If she makes $3,000 working part-time at a local book store during the school year, she can put in only $2,000 into her IRA.

Your child doesn't have to contribute the full $2,000, even if she's eligible to do so. She can put in any part of it she wants, and she doesn't have to contribute every year. Even if she puts money in this year, she's not obligated to so do next year, despite having earned income. The contribution can be split in as many IRA accounts as she wants, as long as the total contribution each year does not exceed the $2,000 limit. For example, if she earns at least $2,000, she can put $1,000 in a deductible IRA in a bank CD and $1,000 in a Roth IRA invested in a stock mutual fund.

➤ *Contributions can be made at any time during the year to which they relate, or as late as April 15 of the following year.* For example, 1999 IRA contributions can be made starting January 1, 1999, through April 15, 2000. Your child can make a contribution at the start of the year in anticipation of earning income, as long as

Watch Your Step

Don't confuse IRAs for retirement with the education IRA used to save for college expenses. These savings plans, discussed in Chapter 16, "Setting Savings Goals That Work," are completely different.

Money ABCs

Earned income is the kind you get from working. This can be a salary from being an employee or the profits from a business your child runs as a self-employed individual.

she'll really earn that amount. In other words, she doesn't have to wait until she's earned the money before making a contribution. If it turns out that she was overly optimistic about her earnings and she put too much in the IRA, she can withdraw it before she files her income tax return for the year and avoid any penalties. However, she can't carry over any unused contribution amount to a future year. So, if she contributes only $1,500 in 1999 even though she was eligible to contribute $2,000, she can't put in $2,500 in 2000.

You can find out more about IRA rules by getting IRS Publication 590, Individual Retirement Arrangements, from the IRS. You can download it from their Web site at www.irs.ustreas.gov or call them at 800-TAX-FORMS.

Deductible IRAs

As you may know, contributions to a traditional IRA can be deducted. (There are income limits imposed on people who participate in company retirement plans, but this probably won't apply to your child working part-time or for a modest income.) The deductibility feature is important in two respects. One benefit of the deduction is that it lowers the amount of income that will be taxable. In 1999, for instance, your child can earn up to $6,350 without paying any federal income tax if he puts $2,000 into a deductible IRA.

Another benefit from the deduction is that the government is, in effect, paying for part of your child's contribution, which becomes important if he earns more income in the year than is covered by his standard deduction. Instead of paying the money to the government as taxes, the money goes into the IRA. For example, assuming that your child is in the 15 percent income tax bracket (in 1999, this bracket covers taxable income of a single person up to $25,750), it's really costing him only $1,700 to put $2,000 in his IRA. He would have paid $300 in federal income tax on his $2,000 contribution if he had not funded his IRA.

During the time when money is left in the IRA, all income earned on it is tax-deferred. This allows the income to build up because it's not reduced by taxes.

Certainly, there are tax benefits to having money go into and stay in the account. Now consider the drawbacks to taking money out of an IRA.

➤ *Withdrawals are ordinary income.* When money is taken out of the IRA, it's all income to your child. It doesn't matter whether the money has been invested in stocks or mutual funds that produced capital gains to grow the IRA—it's all ordinary income. In your child's case, money would probably go in when he's in the lowest tax bracket but might be taxed at withdrawal when he's in a higher bracket. Of course, no one knows today what tax rates will be in the future, but you can pretty much bet there's going to be a tax rate higher than the current lowest rate of 15 percent.

➤ *Withdrawals before age 59$^1/_2$ may be subject to penalty.* Because the purpose of the IRA is to save for retirement, the law discourages withdrawals before a person reaches retirement age. Early withdrawals are subject to a 10 percent penalty, which is in addition to the regular amount that applies to the withdrawals. However, withdrawals before this age to pay for higher education aren't subject to a penalty.

Roth IRAs

Roth IRAs are sort of the flip-side to deductible IRAs. The tax benefits come at the tail end rather than when contributing to them. Contributions aren't deductible, but earnings on the contributions can be taken out tax-free as long as the funds have been in the account for at least five years and generally aren't withdrawn before age 59$^1/_2$. And the money your child has put in can be taken out without any tax consequences regardless of her age or how long it was in the account.

Roth IRAs require your child to take a long view of things, but there can be a great payoff for her and her children later. There's no requirement that money be withdrawn from the Roth IRA during her lifetime, so the fund can continue to grow, tax-free, for as long as she lives. She can decide to use the

Watch Your Step

While withdrawals to pay higher education costs are penalty-free, they're still subject to income tax.

Piggybank on It

If your child is young enough when she starts, she'll still be ahead of the game by putting money into an IRA, even though she'll owe tax when she takes it out. The reason is simply tax-deferral: The money can grow untouched by taxes until it's withdrawn.

Piggybank on It

If your child doesn't have an IRA but you do, you can use it to pay for his college costs without penalty. This is so even though you're under 59$^1/_2$. But tapping your IRA means paying current tax on the withdrawal and ending the opportunity to continue building up your retirement fund on a tax-deferred basis.

money in retirement or can leave it to her children and grandchildren as an impressive inheritance. Depending on how much goes in and what it earns over your child's lifetime, the account can be worth millions! In view of the potential benefits to making Roth IRA contributions if eligible to do so, you might consider making a gift to your child of the money needed to make her contribution, especially if she uses her earnings to pay her expenses or to save for college.

Is a traditional IRA or a Roth IRA better for your child? As a general rule, the Roth IRA should pay off more in the long run. While there's no current tax deduction, that write-off doesn't mean much to a child with only a little income. Think of what it means to be able to have tax-free income from the Roth IRA in retirement!

Piggybank on It

There's no tax on the withdrawal of earnings from a Roth IRA before age $59^1/_2$ if the money is used to pay first-time home-buying expenses. The cap on such penalty-free withdrawals is $10,000 in a lifetime. So, while your child can't take the money penalty-free for his education, it will be there for him when he buys a home.

Watch Your Step

Before your child gets started with a particular mutual fund, check for minimum investment requirements. For example, some have minimums of $1,000; others require as little as $50. Some waive minimums for IRA investments altogether. Also check for annual account fees—some have them, some don't.

If your child started a traditional IRA before 1998, she can convert it to a Roth IRA so that she'll enjoy all the benefits listed previously. The cost of conversion is picking up all the income that would result if she had simply withdrawn the funds and put them in her pocket. For example, if she's got $5,000 already in a traditional deductible IRA, then she'll have to report that $5,000 as income in the year she converts it to a Roth IRA. Still, picking up $5,000 in income today may be well worth it in the long run. The federal income tax cost for making the conversion is only $750 today if she's in the 15 percent federal income tax bracket (15 percent × $5,000). Every penny earned on the Roth IRA thereafter is tax-free.

Investing IRA Money

IRAs must be set up with a bank, brokerage firm, insurance company, or mutual fund that offers IRAs. These institutions supply the paperwork that your child will have to complete to set up the IRA and invest the contributions.

While there are no minimum age requirements for IRAs, not every place offering IRAs to adults also offers them to minors. After all, minors can't legally make a binding contract. Usually, accounts for minors are set up as custodial or trust accounts, with a grown-up acting as account manager until they reach legal age (when the custodianship can be removed). But IRAs aren't geared for this type of arrangement, and because not many kids take advantage of IRAs (even though they should), these companies don't publicize the availability of IRAs for minors.

Still, it's not too hard to find a place to put your child's IRA money. Your local bank may allow your child to open an IRA (although bank personnel may not know whether the bank offers IRAs to minors). Here are some other options to consider:

Mutual funds that don't bar kids include these:

➤ American (800-421-9900)

➤ American Express IDS (800-437-4332)

➤ Invesco (800-525-8025)

➤ Janus (800-525-8983)

➤ Neuberger & Berman (800-877-9700)

➤ Oppenheimer (800-225-2755)

➤ SteinRoe (800-338-2550)

➤ Strong (800-368-1030)

➤ T. Rowe Price (800-638-5660)

➤ Vanguard (800-635-1511)

Brokerage firms that offer IRAs to kids are listed here. You can find a local office by checking the listings in your Yellow Pages.

➤ Dean Witter

➤ Merrill Lynch

➤ Salomon Smith Barney

Types of Investments to Consider

Most types of investments are open to IRAs (there are limits only on holding collectibles, such as art and stamps). Here's a rundown of the different types to consider:

➤ *CDs.* Certificates of deposit offer safety of investment because your child can know going into the investment exactly what he'll have at the end. Bank CDs are protected by FDIC insurance up to $100,000. Most banks don't charge any fees for their IRAs.

➤ *Zero coupon bonds.* These are bonds based on U.S. Treasuries. They're issued at less than their face amount, and the discount depends on the maturity of the bond. For example, a bond maturing in 10 years may have a discount of 40 percent off its face. Put another way, it would cost only $600 to buy a $1,000 bond. At maturity, that bond pays $1,000. No current income is paid out—but because your child isn't taking any money from the IRA, this isn't important. As with CDs, he'll know what he'll have when the bond matures. Each zero coupon bond has a fixed maturity date.

Watch Your Step

Your child shouldn't think about buying tax-exempt bonds or annuities in an IRA. This is redundant because the IRA doesn't produce current income regardless of the type of investment selected. For example, why own a tax-deferred annuity under the umbrella of a tax-deferred IRA?

Money ABCs

Equities include stock and stock mutual funds. They're called equities because your child becomes an owner in the company in which she's buying shares.

➤ *Annuities.* Individual retirement annuities are sold by banks and insurance companies. They offer a guaranteed death benefit, which means that if your child should die before collecting on the annuity, his beneficiaries are guaranteed to get at least as much as he has put into it. For IRAs, however, annuities don't make much sense. There are usually steep commissions and fees for the purchase of IRA annuities.

➤ *Individual stocks.* If an IRA is opened with a brokerage firm, the account can hold individual stocks, such as Disney, Microsoft and AOL. This type of IRA is called a self-directed IRA because your child, as owner of the account, decides what stocks to buy and hold.

➤ *Mutual funds.* Your child can buy a stock mutual fund directly from a mutual fund company. This type of investment has no guarantees; the intent is to get appreciation. You're hoping that the value of the fund will increase over time.

Because your child has a long investment horizon—he won't be touching the money for many years—he should think in terms of *growth*. This means equity investments, generally made through mutual funds. Equity investments are discussed in greater detail in Part 6 of this book. CDs may sound good because they're safe, but given the long time before your child will touch the money, such low-yielding investment may prove unsound in the long run.

For example, if a child has 50 years until he plans to start tapping into the IRA and contributes $2,000 annually to his IRA (a total investment over those years of $100,000), here's how his investment strategy would pay off if he used conservative (CD-type) investments versus equities (returns that assume daily compounding). Remember that historic returns for large company stocks from 1926 to 1997 ran at 13 percent annually, while short-term government bonds (such as T-bills) produced an annual return of only 3.8 percent.

Annual Return on Investment	Fund After 50 Years
5 percent	$458,520.48
8 percent	$1,393,790.80
10 percent	$3,096,400.77
12 percent	$7,111,689.52
15 percent	$25,911,068.18

Of course, it's highly unlikely that your child can expect to maintain a return of say 15 percent year in and year out for 50 years. It's also unlikely that she'll contribute $2,000 consistently for that period of time. But if this were possible, then spectacular retirement funds would be there when she retired.

Changing Investments over Time

Don't feel that making a particular type of IRA investment is a lifetime commitment. Investments can be changed, and money can be moved around from one investment to another. For example, stock in a self-directed IRA can be bought and sold.

Money can even be moved from one IRA account to another. There are two ways to do it without having the change treated as a distribution that's taxable.

➤ *Rollover.* Funds can be distributed to your child and then re-invested in another IRA. As long as this change is completed within 60 days of the distribution, it's ignored for federal income tax purposes. However, only one tax-free rollover is allowed each year.

➤ *Direct trustee-to-trustee transfer.* Instead of taking the money and re-investing it, your child can tell the current custodian of the IRA (for example, Fidelity Mutual Funds) to send the money directly to the custodian of his new IRA (for example, Vanguard Mutual Funds). All he needs to do is complete a new IRA account form and authorize the transfer. There are no limits on the number of direct transfers that can be made each year.

Watch Your Step

While there may be no federal tax consequences to changing IRA investments, there may be commissions, fees, or even penalties charged by the company with which your child has his IRA. For example, there may be surrender charges for selling shares of a mutual fund before they've been held for a certain number of years.

The Least You Need to Know

➤ No child is too young to start saving for retirement.

➤ IRAs started by children can grow into the millions by the time of their retirement because of tax deferral.

➤ Your child must have earned income to start an IRA.

➤ IRA money can be put into deductible or Roth IRAs, or can be split between them.

➤ Traditional IRAs can be tapped to pay college expenses penalty-free.

➤ Because a child has many years until his retirement, it's generally better to invest for long-term growth.

Part 6
Investing Made Easy

The spectacular returns in the stock market over the past four years have made everyone sit up and take notice. Even kids can't help but hear the daily market quotes on the TV and radio news or see them when they go online.

For kids, learning about the stock market now is easier and more fun than ever. Kids can use many Web sites and materials to learn the Wall Street lingo and get started on making their own killing in the market.

In this part of the book, you'll learn what concepts and terms your child should know before he starts to invest. You'll find out what he needs to know about mutual funds and special funds just for kids, and you'll see what's online for your child to explore. You'll also find out about a stock market alternative that can be a great investment or just a lot of fun: collectibles.

Chapter 20

Wall Street Tycoons Aren't Just Born...They're (Self) Made

In This Chapter

➤ Getting a taste for playing the market

➤ Jumping in with eyes open

➤ Learning the lingo

➤ Making the move to investing

It wasn't too long ago that owning stock was only for the wealthy. But with the proliferation of 401(k) plans and IRAs for workers throughout the country—as well as discount brokerages and online trading—stock market investing has become part of mainstream America. What's even more fascinating is that a number of kids are also getting into the act. They're learning about stocks and building their own portfolios. Your child can become one of them, if you offer assistance.

Obviously, very young kids aren't typically going to be interested in stocks or have the money to get into the market. You may have a budding Alex Keaton (the yuppie-in-training from *Family Ties*), but most kids are more interested in following baseball scores than the stock market. As kids get older, receive larger cash gifts, start to earn their own money, and get out into the world, however, the stock market becomes an investment alternative to consider.

In this chapter, you'll find out what it means to invest in the stock market. You'll see what the risks can be and the protections that are available. You'll also learn what terms your child (and you) should know to develop some understanding of equity investments. Finally, you'll find out how to go about opening a stock account to start investing. You may be doing the investing for your child, with your child, or with your own money for the benefit of your child. In the next chapter, you'll find out all about mutual funds.

Rewards of Being a Stock Market Investor

In the past four years, we've seen record returns of more than 20 percent annually in the stock market, as measured by the S&P 500 (explained later in this chapter). You know that today you can't get 20 percent interest on your savings account. So, buoyed by the opportunity to make more in the market than with other types of investments, many people have put their money into stocks. They're also putting their kids' money into the market, and now kids are putting their own money in. Essentially, they're becoming stockholders.

Money ABCs

Someone who owns a part of a company is called a **shareholder** (or **stockholder**). The name comes from the fact that ownership in a company is evidenced by a piece of paper called a **stock** certificate. Each unit of ownership is called a **share**.

Money ABCs

A **bull market** means that stock prices have been rising over time. The opposite of a bull market is a **bear market**. Here, stock prices fall over time.

Two basic types of shares exist: common stock and preferred stock. Common stock is the most common, and it's what we're talking about in this chapter. Preferred stock offers certain special rights, such as preferential dividends.

If you're in the stock market, how do you put 20 percent into your pocket? It's not like a savings account that pays out interest each year. With stocks, the returns primarily come in the form of appreciation. This is really just a fancy way of saying that the price of the stock increases from the price you or your child paid for it.

The stock market as a whole may rise or fall. Today, we're in an unprecedented bull market where prices have been steadily rising for nearly a decade. But just because the market in general goes up is no guarantee that the price of an individual share will also increase. Market changes are measured by indexes, explained later. These indexes may not account for movement, up or down, in a particular stock.

Stocks offer another benefit: Not only can you enjoy a substantial return on your investment, but you also get a tax break. When stock is sold, you're not taxed on all the proceeds from the sale; you're taxed only on the profits (called *gain* for tax purposes). This is simply the difference between what you paid for the stock (including any commissions and fees)—your *basis* in the shares—and what you get for it on the sale. That gain may be taxed at special rates. While salary, interest, and most other income is called ordinary income and is taxed at rates ranging from 15 percent to 39.6 percent, capital gains on stock held for more than one year is subject to a 20 percent tax rate. For people in the lowest tax bracket of 15 percent, which includes most kids, the rate for capital gains is only 10 percent.

Of course, not at all stock picks may be winners, but even losses get special tax treatment. They can be used not only to offset gains, but up to $3,000 of losses are deductible against ordinary income.

It's important to keep these tax considerations in mind. After all, it's not what you make but what you keep after tax that's important. So, if your 16-year old child works a part-time job and pays 15 percent tax on her income, she's not doing as well as if she invests money in the market and pays only 10 percent on her gains.

For links to information about investing for kids, click on The Motley Fool Web site at www.fool.com/Money/InvestingForKids/ InvestingForKids08.htm.

Watch Your Step

If your child is under the age of 14 and has income of more than $1,400 in 1999, then capital gains are taxed to him at your capital gains rate. So, if you pay 20 percent on your capital gains, he will, too.

Cash Dividends

Appreciation isn't the only thing that stocks provide. Some, not all, may pay a set amount for each share owned. This payment is called a *dividend* and reflects the profits earned by the company and shared with its shareholders.

Even if the price of stock never goes up, a dividend-paying company is another way to earn income. You can figure what the dividend yield is by dividing the amount of the annual dividend by the price of the stock. For example, if the annual dividend is $4.00 per share and the current price of the stock is $50, the dividend yield is 8 percent ($4 ÷ $50). An 8 percent yield from a dividend certainly beats a 5 percent yield on the bank CD.

If paid at all, dividends are usually paid quarterly, although they can be paid semi-annually, annually, or just at one time. Dividends are quoted according to their annual amount, or four times the quarterly payment. So, a $4.00 per share dividend means that $1 per share will be paid each quarter.

Dividends are paid to shareholders "of record." Record shareholders are those who own the shares on that date. It's important to know who the record shareholders are because the stock can change hands by the time the dividend is actually paid out. Investors who buy stock that has gone ex-dividend (without dividend) don't get the shares. Ex-dividend is three trading days after the day the dividend is declared.

When you were in school and someone called you a drip, you were insulted. Today, however, DRIPs (*dividend reinvestment plans*) are great. Under a DRIP, cash dividends paid by companies are automatically used to buy additional shares (or fractions of shares) in the same company. More than 1,000 companies today, including AT&T, Ford Motor Co., Heinz, and Intel, have DRIPs. For some of them, one share of stock is necessary to get started. Brokerage firms also allow for automatic dividend reinvestment for shares held in "street name" (a shorthand way of saving the name of the brokerage firm).

To check on whether a company offers a DRIP, ask your broker or check out *Standard & Poor's Directory of Dividend Reinvestment Plans* at your local library.

Dividends are reported annually to shareholders (and to the IRS) on Form 1099-DIV. Taxes are paid on dividends even if they're reinvested in additional shares.

Stock Splits

Some companies may believe the price of their stock is too high to attract new investors, and they may decide to split the shares. For example, in a two-for-one stock split, an investor receives two shares in place of each one share he owns. If he starts with 100 shares, he'll have 200 after the split. Other examples of stock splits include a three-for-one split (three shares in place of each one) and a three-for-two split (three shares for each two shares owned). My daughter bought 10 shares of Gap with gifts she received for her bat mitzvah. Today, eight years later, she owns 45 shares without having put in another penny.

A split doesn't immediately affect the total value of what an investor owns. The value before the split is spread among the new shares. So, if 100 shares were worth $50 each, or $5,000, the new 200 shares are worth $25 each, for the same $5,000 total value.

As a practical matter, stock splits may result in eventual appreciation in an investor's holdings. The price of stock after a stock split tends to go up, and it takes only half as much of a price rise to boost the value following a two-for-one split.

Shopping the Stock Market

Markets aren't only for buying food—they're also a place where companies go to raise money they need to expand, carry on research, or build new facilities instead of going into debt by borrowing the money. This place is called the stock market. A number of different exchanges are part of the stock market: The New York Stock Exchange (sometimes called the Big Board), the American Exchange, and NASDAQ (over the counter).

Your child can shop the market for companies she's interested in owning and can start to build up a stock portfolio. While her ownership interest won't be significant, she'll still have all the legal rights of an owner (although they'll have to be exercised through you, as custodian, until she reaches legal age).

Financial Building Blocks

The New York Stock Exchange was formed in 1792 by two dozen brokers who agreed to trade with each other and charge commissions. Today, more than 51 million individual investors (and 2,000 institutional investors, such as pension funds) trade stock in more than 2,500 companies.

Even if she's not yet interested in or able to buy stocks, she can still "play" the market by following stocks of her choice. This can allow her to test the waters and see the ups and downs of investing. This dry run can translate into valuable experience she'll be able to use later to pick stocks and follow their performance. And this time around, her mistakes won't cost her a penny!

Understanding the Risks

When you as an adult go into a casino, there's no guarantee that you'll win—or that you'll even come out with the money you went in with. Unlike bank accounts, Treasury bills, and other fixed-income investments, there's no guarantee that your child will make money by owning stocks. In fact, some people have likened the stock market to casinos: You're really betting that the price of a stock will go up so that you can make money.

Financial Building Blocks

There have been two black days on Wall Street: Black Tuesday—October 29, 1929 ("the Crash")—and Black Monday—October 19, 1987. But, on average, investors who have weathered the storms and held shares for 15 years or more (including these black days) have come out ahead. Of course, some individual stocks may not meet this expectation.

Some investors may claim to have lost their shirts in the market. What they really lost was the money they put in. For example, if an investor puts in $5,000 to buy 100 shares of Z Inc. and the company goes out of business, the investor has lost his entire $5,000 investment (and not his investment plus his shirt).

However, there's no actual loss if the stock price falls: It's only a loss on paper. The real loss occurs only when the stock is sold at a lower price. So, day-to-day swings in the price of stock don't really affect what's in your child's pocketbook. If the money is needed for something and he's forced to sell when the price is down from what he paid, though, he'll have a real loss.

Watch Your Step

Selling short, which is like betting that the price of a stock will go down, can expose an investor to unlimited risk. Here's how: If an investor sells X Corp. short at 100 and closes her position when the price rises to 105, she has lost $5 (she must deliver shares that cost her $105 when she borrowed only $100). There's no cap on the risk of loss.

Given the possible risk, is stock market investing for kids? The answer depends. Can she afford to risk losing her investment? If she absolutely, positively needs the money a year from now to pay tuition, then it's better to keep the money in a bank, where she'll know for sure that it will be there.

But, if your child is 8 years old and is 10 years away from starting college, he can't afford *not* to become an investor if he has the money to do it. Over time, if he can wait out the ups and downs of the market, he'll probably have more money through market investing than through a savings account. There are also ways to minimize the risk so that if he needs the money sooner than expected, he won't be sorry he started investing.

Financial Building Blocks

The average annual return (without taking inflation into account) for the period from 1926 to 1997 shows the following:

Type of Investment	Annual Return
Short-term Treasury bills	3.8 percent
Long-term government bonds	5.6 percent
Large company stocks	13.0 percent

Source: Ibbotson Associates (1998)

Spreading the Risk

The best way to minimize risk, of course, is to do the homework. Your child should know what she's getting into and should do market research on a company she's interested in buying before she actually goes forward with the purchase. Of course, this information only helps her make an educated guess, but it's the least she should do before investing. Here are some basic suggestions for getting in the know about the market:

➤ *Learn what the market is about.* Read up on stocks and trends in financial newspapers, magazines, and newsletters. Listen to experts on financial networks. For example, find out about P/E ratios and profit margins. Check out the Young Investor Web site from Liberty Financial at www.younginvestor.com, as well as investment basics at www.thewhiz.com and the Motley Fool's "fool's school" at www.fool.com.

➤ *Read annual reports.* Companies that are public are required to provide annual reports. Many also have quarterly reports that track progress between annual reports. Public companies will provide this information upon request.

➤ *Follow the stock for a while.* There's no urgency in getting in today if your child plans to be a long-term investor and will stay around for some time. See how things are going with hypothetical dollars before putting in real dollars.

Once your child thinks she's ready to go, it's time to think again. The old adage of not putting all your eggs in one basket is a simple way of saying that it's better to diversify. Spread the money around with the understanding that even if one pick turns out to be a loser, the others will do better and offset the loss.

Even after a stock is purchased, there's still a way to keep risk to a minimum. An investor can put in a *stop order* to require that shares be sold if the price drops to the price specified. So, if stock has regularly been traded at around $90 a share and you don't want to risk losing all your money, you can put in a stop order to sell at $75. That stop order gets converted to a market order when the stock reaches the limit price. Then, when the stock drops to the

Money ABCs

The **P/E ratio** is the price of the stock divided by its annual earnings. When the ratio is too high, some experts say the price of the stock is overvalued; when the ratio is low, the stock may be a bargain.

Profit margin is what the company makes as its profit after paying taxes and other expenses. This is the after-tax profit divided by its revenues. Here, the higher the profit margin, the better.

Money ABCs

An **annual report** is one that comes out once a year describing the financial picture of the company to date.

221

Money ABCs

Diversification is the process of putting money into a number of different types of investments. For example, instead of buying just one stock, put the money into three or four different ones.

Watch Your Step

Stop orders can be tricky. A market drop might trigger your order when the overall movement of the stock continues to be up. The automatic sale costs you selling expenses (explained later) and buying expenses to get back into the same stock, if desired.

Watch Your Step

Generally, an investor is barred from taking his case to court. Papers that are signed to open up stock accounts with brokerage firms require investors to agree to binding arbitration on any disputes that may arise.

limit price, the stock will be sold at the price at which the stock is traded at that time—it may be $75, or it can be higher or even lower. There are also stop limit orders, a variation on the stop order.

A mutual fund is another way to spread the risk of loss. Instead of buying one stock, your child buys shares in the fund. In turn, the fund buys shares in a dozen or more different companies. So, in effect, she'll own a piece of each of these companies through her ownership in the fund. Some experts suggest that kids shouldn't own individual stocks but are better off with mutual funds. Mutual funds are discussed in greater detail in Chapter 21, "Mutual Funds Just for Kids."

Got It Covered!

While there's no protection for making bad investment choices, there are some protections to keep out phony companies, guard against unscrupulous brokers, and ensure investors against brokerage firm losses.

➤ *The Securities and Exchange Commission,* called the SEC for short, is an agency that oversees the stock market and tries to keep the playing field honest. It requires companies that want to sell shares to the public to meet certain requirements. For example, these companies must publish annually a report on how they're doing. Anyone interested can read the report.

➤ *Securities Industry Protection Corporation,* or SIPC, protects an investor's cash and securities held by brokerage firms in case they're liquidated. It works something like the FDIC for bank depositors, but protection is up to $500,000 ($100,000 of which is applied to cash). Many firms also carry additional insurance protection for investors of $2.5 million and up.

➤ *National Association of Securities Dealers,* or NASD, can help settle disputes with brokers and brokerage firms. For example, if an investor has been the victim of some unlawful practice by a broker, he may be able to recover damages through NASD's process of arbitration.

Speaking Like an Investor

To become a knowledgeable investor, your child must learn the terminology that's unique to the street—Wall Street, that is. As with learning any vocabulary list, it becomes easy only when the words are used over and over again. This section presents some things your child should know before he puts his money into the market.

Watch Your Step

A child who doesn't understand the risks might be willing to be too aggressive with his investments; he could lose it all on a speculative stock. A child should be encouraged to become a conservative investor who goes for long-term growth.

Your child can learn the lingo in many ways. Hearing you speak it is certainly the easiest way to go, but there are other ways to consider. For example, there's a self-study course called *Investing for Life* designed for kids under 18 by the National Association of Investors Corp. (NAIC) (click on www.better-investing.org). NAIC, an educational organization, also offers a youth membership that includes a newsletter and other benefits.

What Kind of Investor Will Your Child Be?

People are sometimes classified by their personality as Type A or Type B. The same goes for stock market investing. There are aggressive investors who are willing to take on a lot of risk and who hope to hit a home run and reap big profits. At the other extreme are conservative investors who don't want much risk and who are willing to settle for hitting singles on a consistent basis. Most people fall somewhere in between.

Money ABCs

Penny stocks don't necessarily sell for a penny a share—today they're usually priced at as much as $5 a share. These stocks got their name because such highly speculative, low-priced stock used to go for just a few pennies a share.

There's another category of investor: the speculator. He's more than just aggressive. He might, for example, invest in very risky investments, such as penny stocks.

Playing the Averages

We all hear it every day: The market is up. The market is down. What does this mean? The movements in the stock market are really only movements in certain indexes designed to present aspects of the market. These include the following:

➤ *Dow Jones Industrial Average* (DJIA). Started in 1896, the Dow is the oldest index and indexes 30 blue-chip (industry leader) stocks representing the industrial age. The Dow is quoted as the benchmark of market activity. If the Dow is up, then

223

people say the market is up. The stocks in the Dow (with the exception of General Electric) have changed over the years as industry evolved or companies have merged. The first day, the Dow closed at 40.94; today it's over 9,000.

➤ *Standard & Poor's 500* (S&P 500). As the name implies, this index represents 500 companies, mostly those listed on the New York Stock Exchange. These 500 are broken down as follows: 400 industrial companies, 40 utilities, 40 financial companies, and 20 transportation companies. Some investment advisers suggest that this index is more representative of the market as a whole because of the greater number of companies included in the index.

➤ *NASDAQ Composite Index* (NASDAQ) includes *all* companies traded on the NASDAQ Stock Market, a computerized market for many smaller companies. Today, it's over 5,000 strong and includes such giants as Intel and Microsoft.

➤ *Russell 2000* is an index that tracks 2,000 small capitalization stocks, those whose market value is below $500 million.

➤ *Wilshire 5000* is an index that tracks 5,000 stocks of all kinds.

Piggybank on It

The Wired Index, started in 1998 by *Wired* magazine, claims to represent the blue-chip stocks of the next millennium. It includes 40 companies, more than half of which are in computer-related technology, although it also includes some low-tech companies such as Walt Disney, Wal-Mart, and Marriott.

Buying from a Broker

If your child wants to own shares in McDonalds, she can't go to the golden arches on the corner and have the person at the register ring up her stock order. She can't even go down to the New York Stock Exchange on Wall Street in New York City. She has to buy shares through a broker. And, if she's under legal age, you—not she—deals with the broker.

Before your child can buy stock from a broker, though, she must open up a brokerage account. There are different kinds of brokerage firms, and it's helpful to know how to place an order.

Money ABCs

A **broker** is a person licensed to buy and sell shares to the public. Brokers operate from companies called **brokerage firms**.

Opening an Account

A brokerage account is a formal arrangement. For minors, this must be done in a custodial account. (Custodial accounts are explained in detail in Chapter 17, "Piggybanking It.")

Brokerage firms aren't all created equal. There are full-service firms, discount firms, and deep discount firms.

➤ *Full-service brokers* give advice, recommend different stocks, and execute orders. Because of the range of services they offer, these brokers charge the highest commissions for trading shares. Full-service brokers include Morgan Stanley Dean Witter (www.deanwitter.com), Merrill Lynch (www.merrilllynch.com), Paine Webber (www.painewebber.com), and Prudential Securities (www.prudential.com).

➤ *Discount brokers* also buy and sell shares but don't offer advice or recommend shares. As a result, these brokers charge lower commissions than full-service brokers. They do offer some services, like research reports on stock and free checking. Discount brokers include Charles Schwab & Co. (www.schwab-worldwide.com), Fidelity (www.fidelity.com), and Waterhouse Securities (www.waterhouse.com).

➤ *Deep discount brokers* are just like discount brokers, with one difference: Their fees are lower still they don't offer services such as stock research and free checking. Deep discount brokers include Arnold Securities (www.arnoldsecurities.com), National Discount Brokers (www.ndb.com), and Quick & Reilly (www.quick-reilly.com).

If your child uses a computer, he can buy and sell shares online. This kind of trading is the least costly. Online trading is explained in Chapter 21.

Placing Orders

When an adult goes to the betting window at a race track, he tells the cashier the amount of the bet, the horse's number, and the type of bet. For example, he might say, "$2 on number 6 to win." Just about the same procedure is followed to buy stock from a broker.

An investor tells the broker—usually over the phone—what he wants to buy: the name of the

Money ABCs

Commissions are fees charged for buying and selling shares. They're usually based on the number of shares traded, but there may be a flat fee.

Piggybank on It

Charles Schwab occasionally runs promotions for commission-free trading in custodial accounts. Ask if such promotions are available when you want to place an order.

Piggybank on It

Walt Disney has started a direct purchase plan that costs $10 to enroll (800-948-2222). The initial investment must be at least $1,000, or $100 by monthly debits to a bank account. No broker is involved in the purchase; the plan charges a small transaction charge plus 4¢ a share on new investments. Direct purchase plans are also available for more than 100 companies (www.netstockdirect.com).

company and the number of shares. He can put in an order at market price to buy the shares at whatever price they're currently trading at. For a custodial account, a broker will take an order only from the custodian, not from the child.

An investor can request that an order be executed at a certain price *if* the stock hits that price. That order can be good for the day (it will be executed by the end of the day, or all bets are off) or good until canceled, also called GTC (the order stands until it's executed or canceled). For example, if a stock is trading at 75, an order can be placed as GTC to buy at 73. If the stock price dips, the buy can be made; still, there are no guarantees that shares will be available to complete the order, and the price can even go back up before a buy has been made.

People who try to buy shares at a specific price are called *market timers* because they try to get the lowest price for the stock. However, statistics have shown that over time, being a market timer means very little. Your child is better off getting into a good stock whenever he can and holding it for the long term rather than waiting to buy at a bargain price.

Money ABCs

When a company first goes public (becomes publicly traded), it's called an **initial public offering (IPO)**. IPOs are offered mostly to special brokerage firm customers, such as pension funds and other large investors or favored customers.

Watch Your Step

Check confirmation statements (called *confirms*, for short) carefully. Make sure that the order it what it is supposed to be. Mistakes can be corrected easily if caught right away.

When shares are purchased, two different things can happen:.

➤ *You can request that a stock certificate be issued to you.* The certificate lists the number of shares owned by an investor. Some companies have great-looking certificates: Disney's is decorated with a picture of Walt Disney and many of the Disney characters.

➤ *Stock can be held in street name.* This means that the ownership gets registered in your brokerage account, and you don't actually receive a stock certificate. Instead, you receive a confirmation statement showing what was bought and how much it cost, including commissions. The number of shares and price per share also are reported on your monthly brokerage statement. It's better to keep stock in street name because it's easier to sell of you don't have to deliver a certificate.

Purchases must be paid by the close of the third business day following the day the order was executed. This is called the *settlement date.* So, if a stock was purchased on Monday morning, payment must be received by the close of business on Thursday. Payment can be made from cash within the brokerage account, by separate check, or by linking a brokerage account to a bank account.

Getting Out

Buying shares involves a lot of research and confidence, but selling shares involves even more. At a minimum, review the monthly brokerage statement to compare how stock is doing from month to month. Follow a stock's performance in the newspapers (such as *The Wall Street Journal, Investor's Business Daily, Barron's, The New York Times,* or *USA Today*) or on financial networks (such as CNBC). You'll need to know the stock's symbol (called a ticker symbol because it used to be reported over a ticker-tape machine). Some symbols are easy to figure: IBM is IBM, Pepsico is PEP, and McDonalds is MCD. The confirm received when stock is bought will show the symbol, or you can look it up on AOL at "Quotes" under the $ sign, at www.excite.com, and at many other Web sites of brokerage firms, mutual funds, and financial news. Just enter the name of the company to find its symbol.

Piggybank on It

An investor doesn't have to make it an all or nothing sale: He can sell some of his shares and keep the rest. For example, if your child invests $2,500 and the price of the stock doubles, he might sell half his holdings. In this way, he has recouped his entire investment and is still in a position to see his remaining shares appreciate even more. Keep in mind that commissions are charged for the number of shares that are sold.

Financial Building Blocks

Checking a stock in the newspapers? Here's what some of the letters following the stock symbol mean:

d is a new low for the stock's price in the past 52 weeks

s refers to a stock split or dividend

u is a new high for the stock's price in the past 52 weeks

x shows stock that has gone ex-dividend

When an investor wants out, she goes about it in the same way she did to get in: She tells the broker what to sell and when.

There's no absolute rule on when to sell, but here are some guidelines:

➤ *If you need the money for other things.* For example, if your child had invested all along and now needs cash for college, it may be time to sell some shares.

➤ *If you've held the stock for a long time and it just hasn't performed as you expected.* You may be better off selling now and putting the money into a stock that will be a better performer.

The Least You Need to Know

➤ Owning stock gives an investor the opportunity for appreciation.

➤ Gains from stock sales are subject to more favorable tax rates than those on salary, interest, and dividends.

➤ There are no guarantees of any profits from investing in stocks.

➤ Mutual funds are an alternative to owning individual stocks.

➤ Minors must use custodial accounts to buy and sell stocks.

➤ Knowing when to get out of a stock is just as important as knowing when to buy.

Mutual Funds Just for Kids

Mutual funds are becoming as common in households as cable TV. Today, in nearly 40 percent of households there's a mutual fund owner, and the numbers continue to grow. Total assets in the funds is more than $3 trillion, and there are more mutual funds than there are individual stocks.

There's good reason for this interest in mutual funds. Adults, who have learned to put their retirement money—401(k) plans and IRAs—into funds and have watched their money grow have begun to use funds for personal savings. They have also found the funds useful in saving money for their child's education. Now kids with a budding interest in the stock market through mutual fund investments can get into the act, with a little help from you.

The previous chapter explained the ins and outs of the stock market. In this chapter, you'll learn about mutual funds, an alternative to buying individual stocks. You'll see the benefits (and risks) of investing in funds and the different types of mutual funds to choose from. The choice can seem overwhelming, so you'll also learn how to choose the type of mutual fund that's best for you and for your child's situation. Finally, you'll find out how to go about taking the plunge and starting an investment program.

The Good and Bad of Mutual Funds

Mutual funds are becoming a very popular way for individuals to own a piece of corporate America. Instead of buying shares in individual stocks, an investor buys shares in a mutual fund that, in turn, buys shares in individual stocks.

A mutual fund offers three key benefits over buying individual stocks:

➤ *Diversification.* Unless an investor hits the lottery or inherits a fortune, she probably doesn't have the cash to buy stock from a large number of different companies. A mutual fund, however, has that much cash (from investments made by investors), and it uses the cash to buy large positions in a dozen or so companies. It's hoped that if one or two companies don't do too well, that will be more than offset by good performances by the others.

➤ *Professional management.* What's a good stock to pick? When should your buy? When should you sell? You might not know the answers, but a professional should. Fund managers are experienced in investing.

➤ *Liquidity.* Any time the money is needed for something, shares in the mutual fund can be sold. There's no guarantee that you'll get what you put into the fund (it may be more or it may be less), but you'll be able to cash out at your choosing.

Of course, for just about any benefit, there's a cost involved. For example, fees and costs are involved in owning mutual funds (explained later in this chapter), and there's no government insurance or other protection to help investors if the price of the fund drops. Investors can lose some or all of their money in the funds, and they must bear this market risk all by themselves.

Making Money in Mutual Funds

As we've said, there are no guarantees. But with some savvy selections and a little patience, investors can reap big rewards from investing in stock mutual funds. Returns from these types of funds come about in several ways:

➤ *Dividends.* When the fund collects dividends on stock it owns, it passes these on to investors.

➤ *Capital gain distributions.* Funds may get capital gains when they sell a stock. They can pass these gains on to investors in the form of capital gain distributions.

Money ABCs

A **mutual fund** is a pool of money from many investors that's invested in securities and managed by professionals.

Piggybank on It

Capital gain distributions are given long-term capital gain treatment for income tax purposes. They're eligible for the special capital gains tax rate of 20 percent (or 10 percent for those in the 15 percent tax bracket on their other income).

➤ *Capital gains from selling mutual fund shares.* An investor who sells his shares in the fund at a profit can pocket capital gains.

When you add up these sources of income from a fund, you get a picture of a *total return.* This is really the increase in the value of the shares in the fund, taking into account a reinvestment of dividends and capital gain distributions, plus rises (or declines) in the price of the shares (in effect, paper gains or losses).

Income paid by a fund is reported to investors (and the IRS) on Form 1099-DIV. Use this information return for guidance on what to report for income tax purposes.

Fund Fees

You don't get something for nothing, even with so-called no-load funds. Costs are involved in owning all types of mutual funds, including these:

➤ *Load charges to buy shares.* These are called front-end loads and can run between 4 percent and 8.5 percent of the funds being invested. (Low-load funds charge between 1 percent and 3 percent.) Shares with front-end loads are called A shares.

➤ *Back-end loads to sell shares.* Also called exit or redemption fees or contingent deferred sales charges (CDSCs), these are the opposite of front-end loads. These fees are charged to get out of the fund and are levied only on the amount invested, not on any reinvestments of dividends or capital gains or any appreciation in the value of the shares. However, they're usually based on a sliding scale that disappears over time. For example, there may be a 5 percent back-end fee to sell the fund in the first year of ownership, but the fee may be reduced by 1 percent each year. Thus, if the shares are held more than five years, there's no fee to sell. Shares with back-end loads are called B shares. Usually after B shares have been held beyond the specified time that the fees can be charged, they're automatically converted to A shares.

➤ *Expenses that the fund incurs in its operations.* Operating fees to cover amounts paid to fund managers and expenses of buying and selling

Money ABCs

No-load funds don't charge any fees to buy or sell their shares, but no-load funds aren't free. They have operating expenses that reduce returns to investors.

Piggybank on It

Just because a fund charges a load doesn't make it a bad choice. It's important to consider the fund's overall performance. If a load fund does better than a no-load, an investor may be better off paying the fee to get that edge.

231

shares can range from 0.25 percent to more than 2 percent of a fund's net assets. Some funds may waive some or all of their fees on a temporary basis for various reasons (for example, new funds may do this to improve the fund's yield). There are also 12b-1 fees that relate to the cost of distributing fund shares. They're called 12b-1 fees because of the section in the Securities and Exchange Commission rules that allow these fees to be charged back to investors. These 12b-1 fees are higher in B shares than in A shares.

Some funds also have C shares, D shares, and even T shares. The fees and charges on each class of shares differs, as explained in the prospectus. Which way does an investor come out better in the alphabet? Different funds are designed for different investment needs. Generally, long-term investors prefer B shares because all their money goes to work for them immediately. But there's also the school of thought that A shares will result in lower costs over the long run. If your child's investments in mutual funds are intended to pay for college expenses, keep in mind the time frame for when shares will have to be sold. For example, if you child is older than 12, it might not make sense to buy B shares because he'd have to pay surrender charges on a sale at college time.

The Feeling's Mutual

The numbers are overwhelming: Today there are over 8,000 different mutual funds, and all funds aren't the same. Funds have different holdings, different investment philosophies, and different fees. On the good side, there's probably a fund to suit just about every person's investing objectives.

Piggybank on It

Index funds have much to recommend them. They have low management fees (because there's not much to manage as the investment decisions are dictated by the index they're mirroring). These funds also don't create tax problems for investors (because they don't buy and sell shares too often, they make little or no capital gain distributions) and so are deemed tax-efficient. On average, index funds also have performed better than most stock funds.

Mutual funds that hold stocks fall into these general categories:

➤ *Index funds.* These funds hold stock that mirror the indexes they invest in. For example, an S&P 500 index fund holds shares in the 500 companies that make up the S&P 500 index. There's even a new index, created by *Wired* magazine called the *Wired* Index, that's comprised of 40 stocks it believes represents the next century (mostly tech stocks, as well as Disney, Charles Schwab, Wal-Mart, and other companies expected to do well in the next millennium).

➤ *Growth and income.* These funds aim for both appreciation and dividend income. Because dividends are one of these funds' goals, the funds invest in large, dividend-paying companies. In general, these types of funds are more conservative than funds that aim primarily for growth.

➤ *Growth.* These funds try to return to investors appreciation in the value of the stock they hold. Dividends are a lesser concern.

➤ *Aggressive growth.* These funds have the same investment goal as growth funds, only more so because they try to maximize long-term gains. Of all the different types of funds, these are the most volatile and therefore the riskiest.

Within these broad categories, there are some subspecialties you should know about. For example, a growth and income fund may be a large cap or it a small cap. *Large cap* refers to stocks with large capitalizations (their market value is more than $5 million). Large caps generally are companies that have been around a long time and have proven track records. Large caps also are known to pay dividends, for the most part. In contrast, *small caps* are companies with market values less than $500 million. These may be newer companies and usually plow earnings back into the company and don't pay out dividends.

International stock funds invest in companies overseas. Some are limited by country, continent, or region. In addition to the risks with any fund, international funds also have other risks. A *currency risk* can make fund shares worth more or less, depending on how foreign currencies fluctuate in comparison with the dollar. *Political risks* of foreign governments and economies can also affect fund performance.

Money ABCs

Sector funds concentrate in a particular niche of the market, such as technology, health, or energy. Because of this concentration, they're considered as risky as aggressive growth funds.

To learn about mutual funds in general, check out the Young Investor Web site from Liberty Financial at www.younginvestor.com as well as Investment Basics at www.thewhiz.com and Motley Fool's "fool school" at www.fool.com.

Selecting Funds

What's the goal for investing in mutual funds? Don't just say "to make money." Everyone wants to do this. But this desire must be balanced against concerns for safety, the need to liquidate holdings at a certain time to pay for college or other costs, and other considerations.

Money ABCs

A **prospectus** is a brief sketch of what a company is all about—what it does, who runs it, what the company owns, and its plans for the future.

Read a prospectus and annual reports to learn about the fund. Each fund must provide this information upon request and must provide a prospectus before an investment is actually made.

A prospectus will provide certain important information:

➤ *Fund philosophy.* The fund will identify whether it aims for growth, growth and income, or aggressive growth. For kids who can afford to wait around to see results, it's generally a good idea to go for growth (or growth and income).

➤ *Fund holdings.* The prospectus lists the stocks held by the fund at the time the prospectus was issued. This will show the number of shares as well as what percentage it represents of the fund's total holdings. Of course, the holdings aren't static, and shares may be bought or sold after the prospectus is printed.

➤ *Fees.* The prospectus must disclose all fees and charges. Look closely at load charges.

➤ *Management.* The prospectus tells who's managing the fund. Unfortunately, to most investors this information doesn't mean much because the names aren't familiar. Of course, managers can come and go.

Watch Your Step

Selling a fund to buy a different fund within the same fund family is still a taxable event. Any gains (or losses) on the sale of those shares must be reported. The only thing that's free on this type of exchange is the fees that would otherwise be charged to buy or sell.

Piggybank on It

The Web sites of many of the mutual fund families offer a lot of information on investing in general. Check out some sites for trends, definitions, and more.

It's important to understand what the company does. Peter Lynch, the mutual fund guru for Fidelity Funds, suggests buying stock in companies that produce things you know and like. For instance, if your kid is sold on his Compaq computer or loves his Nike sneakers, you might look for funds that hold these stocks.

Past Is Prelude

There's an old saying on Wall Street that past performance is no guarantee of future performance. With this said, funds all display their prior performance records as a sales device to attract new investors. If a fund has returns of 15 percent annually for the past 10 years, then an investor may think that's what he'll continue to receive in the future. It's helpful to compare how a fund has performed in comparison with other funds of similar investment philosophies; just don't rely too heavily on the numbers.

Typically, past performance will be quoted at one year, three years, five years, or 10 years. Of course, not all funds have been around long enough to have well-aged performance records.

Independent rating services evaluate a fund's performance using a number of factors. For example, Morningstar rates funds from one to five stars, with five stars being the best performance. Morningstar may be found in your local library (or click on www.morningstar.net).

Keeping It All in the Family

Mutual fund companies are fondly referred to as fund families. For example, Fidelity Mutual Funds offers dozens of different funds that are all in the Fidelity family. The good thing about buying a fund within a large family is the opportunity to switch without extra sales charges.

Of course, funds within a family may vary by quality. Just because one particular fund has done well doesn't mean others within the family will perform equally well.

Here's a listing of some of the large fund families:

Fund Family	Web Site
AIM	www.aimfunds.com
Alliance	www.alliancefunds.com
American Express-IDS	www.americanexpress.com/direct/mfunds/docs.mfund.html
Dreyfus	www.dreyfus.com
Fidelity	www.fidelity.com
Franklin Templeton	www.franklin-templeton.com
Kemper	www.kemper.com
MFS	www.mfs.com
Oppenheimer	www.oppenheimerfunds.com
Putnam	www.putnam.com
T. Rowe Price	www.troweprice.com
Vanguard	www.vanguard.com

Making Investments

Mutual fund investments for minors must be made in custodial accounts, which are explained in Chapter 17. So, if your 15-year-old wants to suggest investing in a particular fund, you'll have to sign the papers to complete the transaction.

Some funds today target young investors. They hope to capture not only their money today but also their loyalty (and money) tomorrow. These funds send special newsletters and other materials designed for children to understand, including these:

➤ *Stein Roe Young Investor Fund* is a stock fund packaged especially for kids, though there are no age restrictions on who can invest. The companies owned by the fund are those easily recognized by most children today, including Disney, Mattel, Coca Cola, and Wrigley. The fund also gives out educational material to all young investors. The minimum investment is $1,000 for an UGMA or UTMA account (non-UGMA/UTMA accounts have a $2,500 minimum), with additional investments of at least $50. Alternatively, accounts can be started with just $100 if you agree to a regular investment program that debits $50 each month from a bank account to invest in the fund. Click on www.steinroe.com.

➤ *FirstStart* from USAA (www.usaa.com/beta) is another long-term growth stock fund. Here, you must put in $250 to start a custodial account, and then you must add $20 a month through automatic transfers from your bank account.

You don't have to limit yourself to a child-focused fund to follow the same investment philosophy of buying a fund that invests in quality companies for long-term growth.

Money ABCs

Net asset value (NAV) is simply the total holdings of the fund at the end of a particular day (the value of all the shares it owns plus any cash it holds, minus any liabilities) divided by the number of shares that investors have in the fund.

Watch Your Step

Even though the money is reinvested, it's still taxable income to your child. Be sure to keep track of these reinvestments added to the basis of the fund holdings. Otherwise, the money is taxed twice (once when it's paid as income and again when shares are sold and gain is increased, because the basis hasn't accounted for the reinvestments).

Some other mutual fund families offering similar long-term growth funds allow you to make monthly investments of as little as $50, with no minimum initial investment if investments are made by automatic payments from your bank account. These include T. Rowe Price (www.troweprice.com), Strong (www.strong-funds.com), and Invesco (www.invesco.com). A number of other fund families have initial minimum investment requirements of only $200 or $500.

Putting Your Money Down

To buy a mutual fund, you'll have to complete an application form. Because the account is for a minor, the account must be a custodial account. You'll sign all the paperwork and place the order.

Orders can be made by mail by enclosing a check payable to the fund along with the application form. When buying an individual stock, the cost of the purchase is the number of shares times the price (plus commissions). This usually works out to an uneven number. For example, if you buy 10 shares at 38.25 per share and there's a $35 commission, the cost of the purchase is $956.25. But with mutual funds, a flat amount is usually submitted with directions to purchase as much as that investment will allow. For example, if you send the fund $950, you might wind up buying 104.9673 shares in the fund.

The price of stock fluctuates during the day, and the price you pay for an individual stock depends on when the order is placed. With mutual funds, however, the intraday activities don't affect an investor. The price that's paid to buy new shares is always based on the fund's closing net asset value the day you place the order.

When a fund pays dividends or capital gain distributions, there are two options:

➤ *The money can be distributed.* The fund will send a check payable to you as custodian of your child's account.

➤ *The money can be reinvested.* It will be used to purchase additional shares (or fractions of shares). In a way, reinvestment of fund income acts in much the same way as compounding of interest.

How many different kinds of funds should a child own? So many variables go into an answer to this question. Of course, the amount of money to be invested is important. If the money is modest, then only one fund may be owned. When holdings start to swell, it may make sense to have different funds with different investment philosophies. For example, it may pay to own an index fund and a large cap growth and income fund.

Keeping Tabs

Some people buy a fund and forget about it. They may be lucky enough to have bought a great fund, and there's nothing they'd want to do to change things. But it's always a good idea to follow how a fund is doing. As with individual stocks, you can check on fund performances in several ways:

➤ *Monthly or quarterly reports are sent by funds to investors.* Compare how the fund has done from the prior statement. Also compare it to how the market has been doing during the same period.

Financial Building Blocks

Checking a fund's activities in the newspaper? Here's some of the clues to look for:

NL means it's a no-load fund.

f means that the NAV is simply reprinted from the previous day.

r shows that there's a redemption fee.

p shows that there are 12b-1 fees.

t indicates both 12b-1 and redemption fees.

z mean that NAV wasn't available when the newspaper went to press.

➤ *Newspapers and magazines.* Look at mutual funds standings in the financial section of your newspaper. They're also reported in financial newspapers such as *The Wall Street Journal* and *Barron's.* You'll see two prices listed for most funds: a *sell price* (what you'd get if you sold the shares) and a *buy price* (what you'd have to pay to buy the shares). The sell price is quoted as NAV, or net asset value. On no-loads, the two prices are the same.

The Least You Need to Know

➤ Mutual funds offer certain investment advantages, including diversity and professional management.

➤ Mutual funds may pay out income in the form of dividends or capital gain distributions.

➤ Fees charged by funds can eat into returns.

➤ A prospectus lists a fund's philosophy, holdings, fees, and other important information.

➤ Fund families offer different types of funds and allow no-fee switching between funds within the family.

➤ Mutual funds investments by minors must be made through a custodial account.

Chapter 22

Online Options for Kids

In This Chapter

➤ Learning the rules of the game

➤ Getting online with Wall Street

➤ Playing games for fun and profits

You've heard of the baby boomers and Generation Xers. Well, now a local newspaper has dubbed the young who invest (and sometimes make a killing) online as "Generation$." These people are computer whizzes who are learning fast about the stock market, investing online, and becoming what's now known as a "cybervestor."

In this chapter, you'll explore what your child can do to learn about the stock market on line. The idea here is to provide you and your child with the resources that are out there for this purpose. You'll also find out about how kids can trade online, and you'll see what online stock market-related games and contests are available for kids individually and through their schools.

Surfing the Net to Ride the Wall Street Wave

Learning about any new subject isn't easy, but when a kid is motivated to do it, things get easier. Today, more kids are using computers regularly—in schools, libraries, and at home. Logging on is as routine for them as turning on a TV or a light switch. One of the newest things the computer can be used for is learning about investing.

For kids, there's a growing number of Web sites and activities designed to increase their understanding of investments and other money matters. Most kid sites and activities are geared to junior high- and high-schoolers, but precocious elementary school kids can take advantage of them as well. Here are some sites that can be used to learn the basics about the stock market and investing:

➤ *Stock Learning Center* offers a thorough explanation of the basics of investing, including picking a broker, buying stock, doing stock analysis, and even looking at stocks in cyberspace. This Web site was designed by kids at Palos Verdes Peninsula High School near Los Angeles and provides information from the very simple to the most sophisticated (such as investing in commodities). Click on tqd.advanced.org/3096/4learn.htm.

➤ *Young Investor Website,* from Liberty Financial, has information and games galore. Click on younginvestor.com.

➤ *Savelab,* part of Merrill Lynch's home page, provides kid-oriented advice and activities related to investing and saving. Click on www.plan.ml.com/family/kids.

➤ *Making $ense Online* provides kids with money ideas. Click on www.makingsense.com.

➤ *KidzBiz America Online* has general financial information for kids (click on AOL at kidzbiz).

Piggybank on It

How much does your child know about investing? Is he a beginner or an advanced investor? Let him test his knowledge of investing by clicking on these sites: tqd.advanced.org/3096/beginner.htm; tqd.advanced.org/3096/intermed.htm; and tqd.-advanced.org/3096/advanced.htm

Trading for Kids

Kids with an interest in computers and computer games probably read *PC, Wired, EM2,* and similar magazines. They see people in their 20s who were formerly called geeks but now are creating the fastest-growing Internet companies. Kids also see how these companies have gone public and have made these young owners instant millionaires. So, the idea of the stock market isn't an unfamiliar one to many kids. In fact, *Wired* has started tracking its own stock index made up of many so-called tech stocks, such as Dell Computer and AOL, but also stocks for the next century as well, including Walt Disney, Sony, and Wal-Mart. Ask a young subscriber, and he's probably familiar with these companies—he may even follow the ups and downs of the index in the magazine each month.

Kids today are now using computers for two key investment activities:

➤ *Making trades.* The process is quick and direct, and the commissions for online trading are less than those charged for making conventional trades. For example, Charles Schwab charges less for its online trades than it does for its conventional discount brokerage trades. Some online firms, such as Ameritrade, charge a flat, modest fee no matter how many shares are purchased or at what price. Online trading isn't limited to stocks, either: It's also possible to buy mutual funds, bonds, and other types of securities online.

➤ *Tracking investments*. Dozens of resources out there make things easily accessible and cheap. For example, instead of paying a subscription to a financial news-paper, much of the _____ be found on the Web for free.

___g Blocks

___ry people (non-professionals) trade ___ and Exchange Commission anticipates ___999. Given the reduced commissions ___ that this activity will increase as people ___ions for online trading.

___ ___nvestment activities is a smart way to ___ ___gh school child who's used to looking ___rack his portfolio when he goes off to

Me___

E___ ___ay as adults can. They can use
E___ ___companies offering online trading.
T___ ___t must be set up as a custodial
a___ ___counts generally can't be opened
o___ ___n (which you can do online) and
tl___

C___ ___y the custodian (typically that's you,
th___ ___an account holder of legal age will
tr___ ___the online account is in place,
th___ ___n doing their own trading. (A broker
ta___ ___ninor, but the computer doesn't
kr___ ___formation.) It remains to be seen
w___ ___e to prevent direct trading by
m___ ___-old puts in an order to buy 10,000
sh___ ___his custodial account for $1 million and then the price of the stock
tumbles to half of what it was when the order was executed? Who's left holding the bag?

Without industry controls in place to prevent online trading by minors, it's up to you as a parent to monitor your child's activities. You can't help but see articles from time to time in your local newspaper about how a 15-year-old has made millions by trading online. But that's the exception (that's why it's newsworthy). Your job is to provide necessary controls on what's otherwise a very easy investing process. Here are some of the strategies you can use to avoid online trading catastrophes:

➤ Discuss all proposed trades that your child wants to make. You wouldn't do otherwise if you were dealing directly with a broker, so why should it be any different with online trading?

➤ Set up procedures in your home for making trades. For example, you may insist that only you submit orders to buy or sell (while allowing your child to monitor investments online). Or, you may have a set time each evening that you sit down with your child in front of the computer to make any trades.

Watch Your Step

If you don't want your child to do online trading without your permission, don't give him your account password. Unlimited access may cause problems if a child puts in an order to buy something that costs more than he has the funds to pay for.

Piggybank on It

If you and your child want to do online trading, make sure that you understand the technology. Read up on all the information that the online brokerage firm provides.

Once the account is in place, a child can decide what to buy or sell. There's no broker making specific investment suggestions, so it's up to you and your child to make the stock picks. However, the same fundamentals used in investing in the conventional way (explained in Chapter 20, "Wall Street Tycoons Aren't Just Born...They're [Self] Made") apply with equal force to online trading.

➤ *Know what you're buying.* Understand the risks and potential rewards of your choices.

➤ *Take a long-term view.* Don't let the ease of the online investment method spur you to make foolish decisions.

The advent of online trading is still relatively new, and all the kinks haven't been worked out yet. There are still problems to be aware of:

➤ *The price of the stock that you see on the screen may not be the price you actually pay for stock.* For example, you might put in a market order for 100 shares when you see the price at $25. By the time your order is executed, the stock has jumped to $60. You expect to pay $2,500 (besides commissions), but the bill is $6,000—more than double what you anticipated. One online company waives the commission if it doesn't execute your order within 60 seconds, but there's no price guarantee for the stock.

➤ *You put in a market order to buy 100 shares but don't receive an electronic confirmation, so you enter the information again.* Now you've actually purchased 200 shares. The same thing can happen in reverse. You might try to sell the 100 shares held in your child's custodial account, don't receive confirmation, and you try to sell them again. Now you've actually sold 100 shares you've never even owned.

➤ *You put in an order to sell or buy but try to cancel immediately.* You think you've acted before the order has been executed, or you may even have received an acknowledgment of the cancellation. The sale can still go through, though, and now you have to buy the stock you never intended to.

Some brokerage firms are trying to accommodate inadvertent slip-ups; they'll cancel these errors and make you whole again. But policies differ from company to company, so make sure you know who you're dealing with.

Here are some companies specializing in online trading:

➤ Charles Schwab Online (www.schwab.com)

➤ Lombard Institutional, a division of Discover Broker Direct of Morgan Stanley Dean Witter (www.lombard.com)

➤ National Discount Brokers (www.pawws.com)

➤ E*TRADE (www.etrade.com)

➤ Ameritrade (www.ebroker.com)

➤ Datek Online (www.datek.com)

More than 100 brokerage firms now have online trading. Many of the full-service firms, such as Merrill Lynch and Paine Webber, also offer online trading at reduced commissions. A list of the Web sites of some of the major brokerage firms can be found in Chapter 20.

Watch Your Step

High volume trading can delay the execution of your order and cause the price that you ultimately pay to be radically different from what you expected. Instead of a *market order*, which means you'll pay whatever price the stock is trading at when your order is executed, consider using a *limit order*, which means you'll buy at a price you specify or one that's even lower.

Watch Your Step

Just because it's easy and cheap to trade online, don't start *day trading* (the practice of jumping in and out of a stock before the close of trading). Stick to long-term investing. Arthur Levitt, chairman of the Securities and Exchange Commission, warns that day trading, which is highly risky for professionals, can be disastrous for amateurs.

Keeping Track of Things

How is your kid doing with his stock picks? To know this answer, your child should keep track of things. Use personal finance programs, such as Quicken, to keep records of stock holdings. Here's the type of information he'll want to enter:

➤ When he bought the stock

➤ How many shares he owns

➤ What he paid per share

➤ What he paid in commissions or other charges

➤ Any dividends or other distributions that are paid on the stock

➤ Any dividends that were reinvested (and at what price per share)

This information will let him see whether the stock is increasing in value or lagging behind what he had expected. It's also necessary to have this information for tax purposes so that he'll be able to figure his taxable gain when he sells shares.

In addition to keeping good records, your child can also use the computer to research possible new stock picks and to keep tabs on how things are doing. This is so easy that it can be done every day.

Here are just some of the ways to do research with the help of a computer:

➤ *Newspapers online.* Each day, most local newspapers and all financial newspapers publish closing stock and mutual fund prices from the day before. Many papers now have online versions designed to let investors check the same information contained in the newsprint. Some information is free; other information requires the payment of a subscription fee. Here are some online Web sites to use: *The Wall Street Journal Online* (www.wsj.com) and *USA Today* Money section (www.usatoday.com/money/mfront.htm).

➤ *Magazines online.* Many financial magazines may not seem timely because they're published only once a month (or at some other interval). But magazines online are updated daily. For example,

Piggybank on It

Make is a practice to update these records on a regular basis. For example, enter information as soon as a confirmation is received on a buy or sell order. Also enter dividend information when it's sent to you, or update your records once a week or once a month.

Watch Your Step

Most quotes online are delayed—for example, they may be 15 minutes behind the actual trading quotes. If you look at a quote at noon, you're really seeing what happened at 11:45 A.M. For *real-time* quotes, you may need to pay a fee for this service. For most investors, however, a delayed quote will do.

Money Magazine Online gives a daily summary of important stories on investing (www.pathfinder.com/money/plus/index.oft).

➤ *Television programming online.* Financial news can be found on many cable stations. Now it can also be found on these stations' Web sites: CNBC (www.cnbc.com), CNN Financial Network (www.cnnfn.com); MSNBC Commerce (www.msnbc.com/news/COM_Front.asp), and Bloomberg (www.bloomberg.com). In addition to news stores, these sites contain stock quotes, market reports, and other information that changes constantly. There's also weekly programs such as Louis Rukeyser's Wall Street Week on PBS (www.pbs.org/mpt/rukeyser).

➤ *Other Internet locations.* Find daily or even up-to-the-minute market quotes on dozens of sites. Examples of stock quote sites include Data Broadcasting Corporation (www.dbc.com), PC Quote (www.pcquote.com), and Quote.com (www.quote.com).

Many search engines (such as Excite at www.excite.com) have market quotes available. Most brokerage firm Web sites also provide market quotes. Yahoo! News (in association with Reuters) presents business news items of interest to investors (dailynews.yahoo.com/tx/bs/summary.html).

Piggybank on It

If you're a subscriber, AOL lets you track your own stock portfolio. Enter your stocks and, at any time of the day, click on AOL (under "$ Quote") to see where they're at. The portfolio can be easily adjusted as dividends are reinvested or as stocks are bought or sold.

Watch Your Step

Games for investing are not the real thing. Strategies for winning the game, such as day trading, aren't appropriate for personal investment accounts. Be sure to teach your child the difference between playing with play money, where there are no consequences to losing (other than not winning the game), and using one's own money that you don't want to risk losing.

Games Kids Can Play

As a parent it's not news to you that games can be educational as well as fun. So it goes with games related to investing. These games teach some of the fundamentals while kids enjoy playing.

Some games have been packaged as contests and can even result in prizes and awards for your child. Schools also are now using some contests and games to teach kids all about investing.

Contests

A little competition and the lure of prizes can help drive some kids into the stock market, if only in a game. They can play with fake money (called *virtual dollars* in online contests) and hope to win real prizes.

➤ *The Stock Market Game.* Kids in grades 4–12 can vie for prizes and plaques by playing The Stock Market Game (informally called SMG 2000), an electronic game in which teams try to make money on a $100,000 investment of virtual dollars during a 10-week period. So far, more than 650,000 students nationwide already participate. To find out more about this game sponsored by the Securities Industry Foundation for Economic Education, click on www.smg2000.com.

➤ *Student Stock Tournament.* CNBC runs a stock market contest for student investment clubs in grades 4–12 (with between 3 and 25 students). The Student Stock Tournament runs for about a quarter. Teams get $100,000 in virtual money to invest. The winning team receives 200 shares of General Electric stock for its school, and the team gets to appear on CNBC. About 4,000 kids have competed in this tournament run twice a year. Click on the student stock market contest button at www.cnbc.com.

➤ *MainXchange.* The individual game MainXchange is designed for teens. Again, players try to make money with 100,000 virtual dollars in publicly traded companies. Games run weekly, monthly, and annually. For information, click on www.mainXchange.com.

➤ *E*TRADE's Stock Market Game* is open only to those age 18 and older. Games run in two categories: stock game, and stock and options game. Again, virtual dollars for playing start at $100,000. The game runs for three periods of one month each. First prize is $1,000 of real money. Click on the Contests button at www.etrade.com.

Watch Your Step

Pay close attention to starting deadlines for contests. Get all required consents (from school and parents), and then read the rules and follow them carefully.

Even if your child doesn't participate in a contest (for example, the deadline has passed or he doesn't meet the age requirements), he might just "play" along anyway. You can even set up your own rules. For example, consider starting him off with a set amount of virtual dollars, and see how well he can do with that money in the course of one month. By playing this contest, he'll get valuable practice for trading the real thing.

Games

Most computer games appear to be of the violent action type aimed at boys, but there's a growing number of games designed for kids of both sexes to learn about money. Here are some Web sites offering games that relate to investing and finances:

➤ *ThinkQuest Stock Game* can be played by someone of just about any age. There's no need to have any investing expertise; all your child needs to do to play is to set up a password and get started. Click on tqd.advanced.org/3096/61game.htm.

➤ *Liberty Financial's Young Investors Web site* provides a game room filled with games for kids of all ages. For example, a Young Investor Trivia Game tests a child's knowledge of investing and Wall Street. Other games at that site include Money-Tration (a memory game), Brain Teasers, Rebus Puzzles, and two crossword puzzles (one on currency; the other on money). Click on www.younginvestor.com/gameroom/shtml.

➤ *Lava Mind* provides three educational games suitable for kids from the age of 8 and up (including adults). The games range in complexity, starting with Gazillionaire, then Zapitalism, and finally Profitania. Click on www.lavamind.com/edu.html.

➤ *Cash University* (money management for kids) is starting up several arcade games related to investing and finances. Click on www.beseen.net/cashuniversity/home.htm.

In-school (and Out-of-school) Investment Clubs

Some schools also are getting into the investing act. Some teachers have set up investment clubs to teach not only math skills but also the fundamentals of investing through hands-on experience. These are called student investment clubs, or SICs for short. For example, eighth-graders in one school have an investment club called Wall Street Wiz Kids. The club meets for an hour each week and invests throughout the school year.

Just as computer games use virtual dollars, school investment clubs also use hypothetical money to fund their buying of individual stocks. The purpose of the clubs is to learn about buying and selling stock, which entails doing the research before making stock picks, and then using that research to decide when to sell. Some clubs work with a professional broker in much the same way as any other investor might do. Many clubs track their progress with school computers.

One teacher started an after-school investment club in 1990 called the Burnsville Investment Society. Like an adult investment club, this club uses real (though very modest) dollars to make investments. Now there are other investment clubs to be found in some locations.

Piggybank on It

If there's no investment club in your child's school, consider suggesting it. Several financial educational organizations will provide support and assistance. For example, teachers can use the Stock Game for Educators to demonstrate how to pick, buy, track, and sell stocks (tqd.advanced.org/3096/tutorial.htm).

The Least You Need to Know

➤ Computers can make learning about stock market investing both fun and easy.

➤ Computers can be used to make trades and track investments.

➤ Online trading accounts for kids under the age of 18 must be set up as custodial accounts.

➤ Online trading generally has lower commissions than purchases done in the conventional way.

➤ Kids can use games to learn how stock market investing really works.

➤ Check out school and after-school investment clubs in your area.

Chapter 23

Joys and Rewards of Collecting

In This Chapter

➤ Getting into collecting

➤ Finding ideas of collections to start

➤ Putting a collection together on a shoestring

Is your kid a pack rat? Does he seem to save every chewing gum wrapper and movie ticket stub he has ever had? You may have a collector in the making. A collector is someone who loves to amass objects that have a meaning or value to him. It's partly the joy of the hunt to put a collection of things together that inspires some people, but it's also the joy of having the collection completed.

In this chapter, you'll learn about collecting that's great for kids. You'll also find out about the benefits and rewards of collecting.

Collecting for Fun and Profit

Collecting has been around forever. People like to save things. The wealthy have been collecting antique paintings, porcelains, and furniture for generations. Today, however, collecting isn't limited to the rich. It seems that everyone—young and old, rich and poor—is getting into the act.

As with putting money into a bank or investing in the stock market, collecting has become another way for some people to increase their wealth. In this way, collecting is a form of investing. The idea is to buy an object today and hold onto it long enough until it appreciates in value.

Collecting is multifaceted. For kids, collecting can offer several benefits:

Money ABCs

Antiques, according to the definition of the U.S. Customs Service, are items more than 100 years old. In the real world, the term is used rather loosely to cover things dating back to the 1920s or so.

Collectibles don't have to be old—some are, but some aren't. Collectibles are objects that people want to save with the hopes that their value will increase over time.

Piggybank on It

Collecting is something a parent and child can do together. For example, mom and daughter may both like to collect miniature dollhouse items. They'll learn together, shop together, and share the fun together.

➤ *Fun.* There's the enjoyment of pursuing collecting as a hobby. Instead of sitting in front of the TV or playing video games, your child can be looking through pocket change to start a coin collection.

➤ *Educational.* Collecting can be a learning experience. Kids who collect stamps, for example, learn all about countries throughout the world. One boy who loved Godzilla toys got so into collecting Japanese toys of that ilk that he eventually pursued Japanese studies as his college major; he plans to work for an international company doing business in Japan when he graduates.

➤ *Low-cost.* Collecting can be an inexpensive way to start a high-priced collection. Kids can collect things they like for little or even no money and then can watch how the value of things changes over the years. For example, premiums from McDonalds and Burger King that cost a kid nothing can be worth a lot in the future (maybe even the near future). McDonalds gave away special Beanie Babies as part of their Happy Meals for kids; as you may know, Beanie Babies have become a division of collectibles unto themselves. Recently, the complete McDonalds Beanie Babies collection was valued at more than $100 (remember they cost nothing above the regular cost of the Happy Meals).

➤ *High-return potential.* While there's no guarantees with collecting, baby boomers who had saved their baseball cards or D.C. comics from the 1950s would be sitting with quite a valuable collection today. A 40-year-old Barbie in mint condition in the original box is worth about $10,000 today!

Getting Started on Collecting

You may not have to suggest collecting to your child: She may already be a collector of Barbie dolls, costume jewelry, or coins. Kids love to save things—no great news to a parent who has complained of piles of stuff in the child's room. But you may want to offer direction and support for your child. Here are just some of the things you should point out to your child *before* she becomes addicted to collecting:

➤ *Know what she's getting into.* As with the stock market, your child should know about what she's buying before she puts her money down. Learning about collecting is explained in greater detail later in this chapter.

➤ *Understand the responsibility that comes with collecting.* If she's investing her allowance or wages in her collection that she hopes will increase in value, she had better learn to take care of it properly. Most collectibles lose value very quickly if damaged in the slightest.

➤ *Put limits on how much money to put into a collection.* It's easy to get carried away, but collecting, like saving, should be an item that's budgeted for. Having only a set amount to spend at an antiques show will certainly mean that some things are beyond her grasp, but it's a bad financial habit to start spending beyond the budget for items and then falling short of cash to pay expenses.

Watch Your Step

There is no certainty that a collection will appreciate in value—what's desirable today may be out of favor tomorrow when a collector decides to sell. A child's primary reason for collecting should be for the love of the objects. Any financial gain is secondary.

Before your child decides to spend time and money pursuing a collecting passion, it's a good idea to know more than just a little about what she's collecting. This will help her define what she's looking for and avoid getting taken (for example, spending too much to buy something that, with a little research, would have been revealed as overpriced or a fake).

Also read a book on your child's area of interest. There's probably a book out there (or at least a chapter in one) for just about anything your child could conceive of collecting. As the old saying goes in collecting circles, "Buy the book"—and read it before starting. It's the only way to protect against getting ripped off by sellers who try to deceive or who don't know what they've got. Also check out general price guides, such as *Kovels Antiques and Collectibles Price List 1999* (it's revised every year), *Schroeder's Antique Guide*, or *Price Guide to Flea Market Treasures* by Harry L. Rinker. Page through specific books as well; for instance, *A Guidebook of U.S. Coins* by R. S. Yeoman is called "the redbook" and serves as a guide for coins collectors.

More Ways to Learn About Collecting

Learning about collecting coins or old lunch boxes isn't limited to books. You can get information in other ways about the items your child is interested in.

➤ *Join a club.* There are clubs for collectors of all kinds, and they're not hard to find. Ask a dealer, look in a book on the area of interest, or search the Web. Clubs are important to collectors of all ages for several reasons. Not only are they a social avenue to connect with people of similar interests, but they also offer valuable information about the collectibles. Most clubs have newsletters that detail what's happening, and schools may have stamp or coin clubs. Most schools also let kids start new clubs if they can show there's enough interest schoolwide.

➤ *Watch TV shows about collecting.* The premium show on collectibles is the *Antiques Roadshow* on PBS. People bring in old family heirlooms and other "treasures" for appraisals by the experts in their fields. Watching the show can demonstrate to your child how easily even a grown-up can fall for a fake.

➤ *Go to antique stores, antique shows, and flea markets.* Your child doesn't have to be a buyer to enjoy the viewing at these places. He'll get to see what's out there and will be able to talk with dealers and other collectors about his area of interest. There are usually shows and flea markets going on somewhere in the country every week.

➤ *Search the Web.* Today, the Internet is being used by collectors in a number of ways. Some collectibles clubs have Web sites that inform members of what's happening and help you connect with others of the same interest. For example, there's the Original Beanie Babies Club, with more than 6,900 members, at members.aol.com/BongoAmy/. Ralph and Terry Kovel, perhaps the best-known experts in the field of antiques and collectibles, offer online advice, information, and even a price check option at their Web site (www.kovels.com). Collectibles are now also being sold on the Internet through auctions and classified ads (explained later in this chapter).

Piggybank on It

Collecting isn't just for grown-ups. As proof, just watch the *Antiques Roadshow, Jr.,* a spin-off from the *Antiques Roadshow.* Here children bring in their valuables to get an idea of what they're worth. The show aired in November 1998 to a packed crowd in Richmond Centre in Richmond, Virginia.

Collecting Ideas

Kids can collect just about anything they want and can afford. It's not for you to suggest what your child should collect if she decides she's got the collecting bug. However, there are certainly things to which kids are more attuned than grown-ups, and your child may want to start a collection with one of the ideas listed here. These are items that kids may be interested in collecting in elementary school, and they don't necessarily require a lot of money to get started. Once kids reach high school, they may get interested in just about any collectible that appeals to adults.

➤ Action figures (such as G.I. Joe and Star Wars figures).

➤ Barbie dolls.

➤ Beanie Babies.

➤ Books or magazines.

➤ Buttons, badges, or pins.

➤ Cars (such as Matchbox cars).

➤ Coins.

➤ Comics.

➤ Disneyana (items related to Disney characters and Disney theme parks).

➤ Games (old board games and puzzles).

➤ Pez dispensers.

➤ Rocks or fossils.

➤ Scale models.

➤ Sports memorabilia. It's great if your child can get Mark McGwire to sign his St. Louis Cardinal's game program: It doesn't cost anything, and he'll know it's real. But be aware that about 70 percent of all "autographed" sports items are fakes.

➤ Model trains or planes.

Watch Your Step

Warn your child against paying big bucks for items that are only a passing fad. For example, during the past Christmas season, Furbys were selling online for upwards of $200 when they retailed for about $30. Some grown-ups believed that Furbys might replace Beanie Babies as the new hot collectible. After the holidays, however, it was easy to find them for the low retail price in most stores.

Miningco.com, a search engine for the Web, has a kids' collectibles site at kidscollecting.miningco.com. There you'll find a chat room for kids on collecting and links to sites related to your child's area of interest.

Building a Collection Without Going Broke

Unless your child has unlimited money and unlimited time, it's impossible to start with a great collection. It may take years to even get up to "good." But he has to start someplace, and getting there is half the fun. In putting a collection together, there are certain rules for anyone—young or old—to follow.

➤ *Buy what you like.* The most important thing is to enjoy what you're buying. Whether the thing goes up in value or not, your child will like having it around. Some people buy an object with the expectation that it will someday be worth a lot of money, but this doesn't usually turn out to be the case. In fact, it's often true that if the money had been put into a stock mutual fund instead of the collectible object, the collector would have had more money in the long run. If you buy what you enjoy, though, you'll get pleasure from it throughout the years—something that can't be measured in dollars. And there's always the possibility that your item will be the one that does, in fact, appreciate.

➤ *Buy the best you can afford.* Quality always counts, and collecting is no different. Most seasoned collectors will tell you that it's better to buy one quality item than several inferior pieces. That quality item has a chance of appreciating, or at least

Piggybank on It

It's best to deal with reputable dealers who offer protections. They'll guarantee authenticity, and they'll take things back if they're not what you expected. Ask if you can buy on spec if you have any reservations about a piece and want to check it out further.

holding its value, while the inferior pieces probably do not.

➤ *Trade up.* As your child's collection grows, she can weed out the things she doesn't treasure anymore. Sell those things and use the money to buy better-quality items for which she may have acquired a taste. One child who showed his collection of antique racing cars on the *Antiques Roadshow* explained that he could afford to buy a car for $1,500 by using the profits he'd made from buying and selling other cars in his collection. As with the stock market, however, it generally doesn't pay to be a day trader. If your child wants his collection to be an investment, then he should be prepared to buy and hold for the long term.

A-Hunting We Will Go

There's no telling where your child can find his next treasure—it may already be in your home or around the corner. The great thing about hunting for collectibles with your child is that it's a way to spend time together. A junior high school child may be loathe to be seen with a parent at a Saturday movie matinee, but she may gladly go garage sale shopping.

Here are some places to search for things to add to a collection. Where to look may depend on what your child is looking for:

➤ *Antique stores.* The sign says "antiques," but don't let that term keep you out. The merchandise (and the price) may be well below the standards for Sotheby's and Christie's, the two largest auction houses for fine antiques.

➤ *Antique and collectible shows.* Shows are run on a regular basis at various locations throughout the country. On just about any weekend, it's easy to find one well within driving distance if you live near a city. Local shows are usually well-advertised in newspapers and with signs in the neighborhood.

➤ *Flea markets.* Less pricey than antique and collectibles shows, flea markets may carry the kinds of things your child is looking for. Flea markets usually are held at regular times at a set location (for example, every weekend, or the first Sunday of every month).

➤ *Garage sales.* Someone else's unwanted discards may be your child's treasure: Garage and yard sales may contain things well within your child's price range. Of course, there's no going back if you find there's been some mistake, so make sure your child knows what he's buying before he puts his money down.

➤ *Thrift shops.* Like garage sales, thrift shops may yield real finds if your child has the patience to weed through the piles of items on the shelves and knows what to look for. Look carefully at the condition of wanted items: Poor condition may mean a low price, but there's little chance that the value of the item will ever increase.

Of course, there now are online ways as well to find and buy collectibles to suit just about anyone's interests.

Buying Online

Growing in popularity are the online auctions for collectibles, where people can bid for items they see at online sites. For kids, there's nothing to keep them from participating in this buying venue other than controls you may place. Setting controls is a good idea, something that one mother had wished she'd used when she learned that her son, thinking it was only a game, had bid almost $3 million and had won bids of over a $1 million at online auction sites. Of course, your child also will need your help to pay for items he's bought (usually a check, but increasingly a credit card).

Be extremely cautious about any online purchases. It's virtually impossible to be sure of an item's quality or authenticity just by viewing it online. Keep these other warnings in mind as well:

➤ *Buy from a dealer who's reputable to avoid rip-offs.* Don't know a dealer's reputation? Start with inexpensive purchases until a level of trust has been established.

➤ *Before buying, ask about the return policy if your child isn't satisfied.* Most online dealers are very amendable to returns, although you'll probably have to pay the cost of shipping and insurance. The dealers also may be willing to adjust the price (for example, if something sold as "mint" turns out to be slightly damaged and you decide to keep it in that condition).

➤ *Pay by credit card if the seller will accept it.* If the item is not as represented and the seller won't take it back, you can refuse to pay the credit card charge.

Auction sites to check out include these:

➤ *eBay* is by far the largest auction site, with nearly a million items listed in more than 1,000 categories. Click on www.ebay.com, or jump to ebay from AOL.

Watch Your Step

Before buying online, buyer beware—and then some. While most online sellers are reputable and stand behind what they sell, some don't. Things represented as "perfect" may be damaged. Things represented as "real" may be fakes. And after payment is sent, the objects may never be delivered. The online auction sites make no guarantees about the honesty of the sellers.

➤ *Auction Universe* is much smaller but may have things of interest for your child's collection. Click on www.auctionuniverse.com.

➤ *Yahoo!Auction* has a growing auction market. Click on auctions.yahoo.com.

➤ *Excite* has both an auction and a classified market for collectibles online at www.classifieds.2000.com.

Trading Up

One of the benchmarks of certain types of collecting—particularly of small or inexpensive items typically collected by children—is trading. One of the lines from the movie *Big*, in reference to the character's baseball collection, was "got it, need it, need it, got it." This is how it goes, and it's not limited to baseball cards. All it takes to trade is two willing parties.

Money ABCs

Trading is a means of commerce in which people exchange goods with one another.

Trading, or bartering, is one of the oldest ways by which people acquired something they wanted or needed. It typically didn't require any cash; it took only two parts: the willingness to give up something else of value, and someone else to want that thing. Trading is a way for your child to cull unwanted items from his collection and replace them with more desired ones. Trading is particularly useful to kids because they don't need to pay money to get what they want; they use what they already have.

Trading teaches kids some important money lessons as well. The skills acquired in trading carry over well beyond their experience in collecting:

➤ *Learning to fix value.* Until your child gets a good idea about value, he may give up more than he gets. Much to the chagrin of their parents, many elementary school children have traded an expensive toy for a cheap one because they've wanted the cheap one. But it doesn't take long for kids to learn about the value of items they're collecting. Most 11-year-olds who collect baseball cards know what it takes in trade to acquire a Mark McGwire rookie card.

➤ *Learning to negotiate.* Generally, trading involves compromise by both parties to arrive at a final deal. Each side wants to get the most for what's being traded; your child can't always get the exact deal she's hoping for.

The Least You Need to Know

➤ Collecting can be fun and educational—plus, there's a chance of making money.

➤ Don't start a collection before learning about the items to be amassed.

➤ Find information about collectibles in books, collectible clubs, on TV, in antique stores and shows, and on the Web.

➤ Start collecting things that are loved and that are free or that don't cost an arm and a leg.

➤ Buy quality, and continually improve collections by trading up.

➤ Use caution with online buying.

Part 7

To Be or Not to Be a Borrower

Borrowing money is just a basic fact of financial life. Grown-ups routinely do it to buy a car or a house; kids do it to pay for college.

Borrowing isn't inherently bad, but irresponsible people have borrowed their way into crushing debt. Some take years to get out from under it. Others have to take the drastic step of declaring bankruptcy and ruining their credit for years.

In this part of the book, you'll learn how to teach your child about the basics of debt. You'll find out about the dangers they face in borrowing from family and friends. You'll see when it's prudent for them to use credit. You'll also get some tips on getting and paying for student loans. Finally, you'll get ideas for helping your child go off into the world.

To CHARGE OR NOT TO CHARGE...

Chapter 24

All About Debt

In This Chapter

➤ Beginning with credit

➤ Getting credit

➤ Using plastic

➤ Living with loans

Buying on credit has become the American way. Some types of borrowing can't be helped—it's impossible for most adults to pay cash for a home or a car. It's also tough for most kids to pay for college entirely out of savings.

Borrowing isn't bad by itself; it's the abuse of the practice that leads people into trouble. Getting credit has become almost too easy, and some people get in over their heads. If your child can learn about debt and understand what problems can result if she doesn't handle things well, she's probably a step ahead of a lot of grown-ups.

In this chapter, you'll learn the key ideas that kids should know when it comes to debt. You'll find out about credit cards for your kids, and you'll learn when it's appropriate for them to use credit and how to help them stay out of trouble. You'll also get some ideas on repaying debt.

Borrowing Basics

In *Hamlet*, Polonius warned, "Neither a borrower nor a lender be." His cautionary words still ring true today. Using credit has become a quick way to instant gratification: You can see it, want it, and buy it now (pay for it later). Borrowing certainly has a place in money management: It's a way of being able to buy something today that would otherwise be out of reach. Borrowing also is a way to build up a credit history to ensure continued borrowing ability in the future. But easy borrowing can lead to overextending oneself, which means that unwise money-managers might be unable to repay debt and might ruin their credit history.

Money ABCs

Credit has two meanings when it comes to money. First, it's the amount remaining in a person's bank account. Second, with respect to borrowing, credit is the extent to which a person is trusted to make repayment of a loan.

Before your child becomes a credit card junkie and gets into serious debt, make sure he understands the uses and abuses of credit, starting with these issues:

➤ What borrowing is all about

➤ When credit should (and should not) be used

➤ What can happen if he gets into too much debt

➤ Why it's important to get—and keep—a good credit record

➤ How to get credit

Credit Fundamentals

When your child is young, she may want an advance on her allowance to buy something that her savings won't cover. Let's say that she sees a game for $25 and only has $20 saved up. She could wait, continue to save, and buy it later when she has saved another $5. Or, she could get an advance on her allowance of $5, buy it now, and repay the money (or forgo the allowance until the $5 has been made up). Is one way right or wrong? The answer depends on whether your child understands the consequences of borrowing and acts responsibly about it. (Advances on allowances are discussed in Chapter 25, "Borrowing from Family and Friends.")

Borrowing money doesn't mean that your child has more money *overall*—she only has the *use* of more money. Of course, she also has the obligation of repaying what she has borrowed.

It's helpful for your child to get the names of the players in the credit game right:

➤ The *borrower* is the person who needs to do the borrowing. He's also called a debtor.

➤ The *lender* is the person with the money who makes the loan to the borrower. He's also called the creditor.

Borrowing can be helpful to pay for big-ticket items that are needed now but for which savings falls short. The cost of these things usually is high, and repayment of loans to afford them now can stretch for years. It's not unusual to borrow for these purposes:

➤ To buy a car

➤ To go to college

➤ To start a business

➤ To buy a home

Unless you, or a rich aunt or uncle, are the lender, borrowing usually isn't free. The cost of borrowing is the interest that's charged on the loan.

Let's look at an example to see what the real cost of borrowing is. Suppose your child needs to borrow $3,000 to buy a car (and a bank is willing to lend it to him based on his job or your agreement to make good on the loan if he doesn't). If the loan is for 36 months and the interest is 9 percent annually, his monthly payments are $95.40. After 36 months, he'll have repaid $3,434.40, which is $434.40 more than he borrowed. This additional amount represents interest.

Borrowing isn't limited to big-ticket items. Credit cards are often used to borrow money for smaller things, such as books at college, new jeans, or gas for a car. Credit cards are (or should be viewed as) a convenience. Instead of carrying cash that can be lost or stolen, many people use plastic to pay for things. The idea is to have on hand the money needed to pay the credit card bill when it comes due.

Unfortunately, many people find plastic *too* convenient and start to turn them into instant loans. Instead of paying the balance of the bill in full each month, they repay only a portion. The other portion becomes a loan, and these "loans" are generally at very high interest rates. Even though interest rates in general now stand at record lows, many credit cards still have annual rates of 18 percent or more.

Money ABCs

Interest is an amount of money that's owed in addition to the amount borrowed. Interest is calculated on a percentage of the amount borrowed.

The Importance of Having Good Credit

It's important to have good credit, and this is something your child should aim for. The reason is simple: Without good credit, a person can't borrow money—or if she can, she'll pay more than someone with good credit. For example, a person with bad credit may not even be able to get a credit card.

Bad credit not only affects a person's ability to borrow and what it costs her to so do, but it also can boost the car insurance premiums she'll have to pay. Bad credit can even keep a person from getting the job she want because some employers do credit checks on people they're thinking of hiring.

Your child will get good credit by building up a credit history of paying bills on time from the time she's 18 and onward. That's the time when she's old enough to make legally enforceable contracts under the law, so that's also the time when credit companies start keeping track of things. If she has never paid a telephone company bill or had a credit card, she probably doesn't have any credit history.

After she's 18, she'll start to be flooded with offers from credit card companies. Some kids think that because the credit card companies make the cards available, they can use them without regard to their ability to repay. They keeping using the cards until the credit card companies turn off the flow of money. As a result, they're in debt over their heads and have ruined their credit history.

Bad News of Borrowing

The concept that borrowing costs money isn't hard to grasp, but some people don't take this seriously and don't handle credit well. They borrow too much and can't repay in a timely fashion, which can get them into a lot of financial trouble:

➤ *They wind up paying a lot of their income each month toward interest.* At this point, they're unable to use their money on other things because they're using their money just to pay back what they owe. They can't save, and they can't get ahead.

➤ *They may not be able to pay what's required.* As a result, they might go into default on their obligation. At this point, they can lose the collateral for the loan (for example, a car can be repossessed on an unpaid car loan). They can be *dunned* for payment with phone calls and letter demanding immediate payment or else. Make sure that your child knows he has rights, though, even if things come to this. Under the Fair Credit Collection law, a person usually can be called only during business hours and can't be harassed.

➤ *They may be sued by the credit card company or other lenders.* Make sure that your child understands that she shouldn't ignore any official papers that may come her way to inform her of this legal step in the collection process. If she doesn't respond when she's supposed to, she loses her right to contest the claim later.

➤ *They may be forced into bankruptcy.* Bankruptcy is a court-supervised process of settling up debts with existing assets, maybe only for pennies on the dollar, and wiping a person's financial slate clean. Most debts are extinguished in bankruptcy so that the debtor can start anew. But bankruptcy stays on a person's credit history for 10 years, negatively affecting his ability to buy on credit during that time.

Money ABCs

Dunning is the practice of bill collectors trying to get money that is owed by writing or calling. It's hoped that by if the practice is annoying enough, the debtor will pay up.

As a practical matter, if the debt is $50, no creditor is going to spend the time and effort to go this extra mile for collection. But if the debt runs in the thousands and many creditors are owed money, there may be no choice but to seek protection in bankruptcy—or be forced into it by creditors.

Financial Building Blocks

The current law makes it rather easy to gain bankruptcy protection. However, Congress is seriously looking at ways to make it more difficult to ring up large debts and then seek shelter under the umbrella of bankruptcy protection.

Getting Credit

You may be willing to give your child credit by making a loan. Loans to children from people they know are discussed in the next chapter.

Once your child reaches legal age, however, he can go out into the real world and get credit from strangers, including credit card companies and other lenders. Good credit means that these strangers believe in your child's ability and promise to repay what's borrowed. It's a question of trustworthiness.

Loans are not based only on a promise; they're also based on past performance. Borrow a little, repay it, and voilà, you now a pattern of good repayment performance. This marks the start of a good credit history.

When your child applies for a credit card or a loan, the decision to give him what he asks for depends on his credit history. He won't find credit history in a civics text book—his credit history is maintained by credit bureaus that lenders and others can access (with your permission by applying for a loan) to find out about him.

Financial Building Blocks

The three main credit reporting companies (called credit bureaus) are: Equifax (800-685-1111; www.equifax.com); Experian (800-687-7654; www.experian.com), and TransUnion (800-916-8800; www.transunion.com). For a small fee (about $8, depending on your state), your child can request a copy of her credit report from any of these companies to check the facts and take steps to clear up any problems. She can request her report online, by phone, or by mail, although all reports are sent by mail for security purposes. If she applies for a loan and is turned down because of her credit history, she's entitled to ask for a copy of the credit report for free. She has 60 days to act.

Because your child is young, his credit history may be a blank page in creditors' files. He doesn't have *any* credit history because he hasn't borrowed before or paid a telephone bill.

Two ways exist by which to start up a credit history. The first is to apply for credit by filling in a credit card application. Your child may need to show a little initiative to convince the first credit card company to ante up. For example, when applying for a credit card, your child should attach a note to the application and be up front about the fact that he doesn't have any credit history (something it'll find out soon enough). Your child should explain that he can afford to pay his bills and should encourage the company to give him a chance. This approach has worked for everyone I know who's tried it. Or, your child can apply for credit at a department store near him, pay for purchases by store card, and pay his bill on time. Once he has some history under his belt, he can then apply for a bank credit card.

If he's denied credit, it may not be because of a bad credit history or even no credit history. It may be because he has lived at a certain address or held a job for only a short time. Or, he may have been confused with another person with the same name. Again, he can usually overcome these deficiencies with a brief explanation of the situation.

Money ABCs

A **guarantor** is someone who promises to pay a loan if the borrower fails to do so. The guarantor is putting his credit history on the line.

For some loans, such as a bank loan for a car, your child's good word or even good credit history may not be enough. The lender may not think that his income is enough to repay the loan. However, the lender may be willing to give him the loan anyway if there is a guarantor, like you, who is able to stand behind him.

Keeping a Good Credit History

As your teenager probably knows, keeping a good driving record means lower insurance rates. The same holds true for borrowing: Keeping a good credit record can mean lower interest rates when borrowing.

Financial Building Blocks

How long do bill-paying mistakes haunt a person? That depends on how serious the error is. Most negative information in credit reports remains on file for seven years. Bankruptcy, just about the most serious financial mess possible, stays on a record for 10 years.

Once your child starts paying her own way, she won't want to mess up her credit. To maintain that good credit, she should follow these simple rules:

➤ *Pay bills on time.* Keep bills in a place where they won't be lost. Your child's best bet is to set up a place on a desk for incoming bills so that she won't forget to pay them. Bills should be mailed about five days before they're due so that they'll be *received* on time—and don't forget the stamp.

➤ *Don't take on more than what's manageable.* Your child should cut expenses to reduce monthly outlays. Of course, this is easier said than done, but doing so will save headaches in the future (this situation is explained later in this chapter.)

Paying with Plastic

The most memorable word in the movie *The Graduate* was "plastics." But the man who said it wasn't referring to a form of credit. Still, to most people, plastic is more than just a man-made building material; it's a way to pay for things instead of using cash.

Two types of plastic cards can be used to pay for things:

➤ Credit cards

➤ Debit cards

While your child is living at home, using plastic as a form of payment may not be essential because you're there to help out by paying for things or lending him your own credit card on occasion. However, if he goes away to college or moves out, he'll probably need to have credit cards or other forms of plastic to pay for things. It's vital that your child understands what credit cards are all about even before he has any.

How many credit cards should your child have? Even if he's given the cards by the credit card company without any effort on his part, it's generally not a good idea to have more than one or two cards. First, the cumulative credit lines can lull

Money ABCs

Credit cards allow your child to pay for things up to a certain credit limit (a fixed dollar amount set by the credit card company). For example, your child may have a $1,000 credit limit, allowing him to buy up to $1,000. Once he pays this back, he can again spend up to this limit.

Debit cards are tied to a bank account and allow a person to spend up to the amount in the bank account. The spending limit is determined solely by the amount in the bank account.

Watch Your Step

Some financial experts believe strongly that college kids shouldn't have *any* credit cards. However, there's also the school of thought to which I subscribe: Starting with credit cards while youths are still under some parental control is better than waiting until they're entirely on their own.

him into buying over his head and getting into debt. Second, he'll have too many bills to keep track of. Third, credit cards can cost money just for owning them. Many (but not all) charge an annual fee ranging from $20 and up. Fourth, just having the cards can adversely affect his ability to borrow. When a potential lender assesses a borrower's ability to repay and looks at his current debt, the credit limits on all his credit cards are treated as having been borrowed, even if not one penny is outstanding.

Some general information written by college students about credit and debit cards is available at www.cohums.ohio-state.edu/english/People/Hogsette1.eng.htm.

Credit Cards

You probably don't have to tell your child what credit cards are used for; he's seen you use plastic to pay for clothing, groceries, and many other things. What you do have to tell him is *how* to use credit cards so that he stays out of financial trouble.

Financial Building Blocks

According to statistics reported in *USA Weekend*, college students graduate with an average of $14,200 in debt ($12,000 from student loans and $2,200 in credit card debt). This is higher than the debt of any previous generation.

Three types of credit cards exist: bank cards (which are general credit cards—MasterCard, VISA, Discover), general credit cards issued by companies (American Express, Carte Blanche, Diners Club) and proprietary cards (used by stores for use only at such stores—Staples, The Limited, or Sears, or gas companies such as Texaco and Exxon).

Two types of bank credit cards exist: unsecured and secured. Unsecured cards are issued on the basis of a person's good credit. Secured cards require the holder to deposit a set amount, such as $300, with the bank issuing the card. The holder then receives a credit line equal to the amount on deposit. Using a secured credit line is costly because the holder may earn little or no interest on the deposit. However, it's a good way to build up a good credit history. Once such history is in place, a person can get an unsecured credit card.

Your child also can use his credit card to get cash. He can use the credit card like an ATM (automated teller machine) card and can receive cash if he has arranged with the credit card company to get a PIN (personal identification number) number. Of course, the amount of cash he can withdraw cannot exceed his credit limit. Often there's a cost to ATM withdrawals as well: the transaction fee (a percentage of the withdrawal, such as 2 percent or 3 percent), plus interest to repay the withdrawal (and this interest rate may be higher than the usual credit card rate).

Rebate cards are credit cards that entitle the holder to certain paybacks if he spends certain amounts (www.cardlearn.com/rebate.html). For example, Discover card gives a cash rebate of 1 percent of annual purchases. Other cards may give frequent flyer miles, long-distance calling time, or other benefits, although there may be a higher annual fee for these cards.

Repaying Credit Card Borrowing

When your child charges a sweater on a credit card, it's a form of borrowing that must be repaid. Each billing cycle, which is typically every 28 or 30 days, she'll receive a bill. She should check it carefully against receipts she has saved from her purchases because mistakes can be made—for example, she may be charged for something she didn't buy.

The bill contains a lot of information that your child should know about.

➤ Purchases for the month are listed with the price, the store, and the date of purchase. Sometimes store or catalog charges appear under a name or location different from the actual store patronized or the catalog ordered from. For any questions, call the 800-number for the credit card company and ask about the discrepancy.

➤ The minimum required payment amount that must be sent on time to avoid a negative mark on your child's credit history.

➤ Space for the payment your child decides to make.

➤ If your child didn't pay her bill from the prior month in full, it will also show the interest that has been charged. It may surprise you to learn that a study by Visa shows 56 percent of college students paid their balances in full each month compared with just 40 percent of other cardholders.

Watch Your Step

If your child doesn't pay his bill in full each month, he'll rack up interest charges. Over time, he can wind up paying more in interest than he charged on the card in the first place. The lesson: He shouldn't charge more than he'll be able to pay off when the bill arrives.

Debit Cards

A debit card may look and feel like a credit card and can be used to pay for things in much the same way, but it's a different piece of plastic. A debit card is only a way to access the money that's in a bank account or the funds that have been paid for the card. Phone cards and student campus cards are forms of debit card because they let your child spend the money that was put into the card.

Like a credit card, a debit card also can act as an ATM card. There's no need to use a separate card to withdraw money from a checking account.

Debit cards are explained in more detail in Chapter 5, "What's Money."

Buying on Credit

Using a credit card to pay for things is more common in many places than using cash. So it's important as teens become more independent to be able to get their own credit cards and handle them well.

It's not too hard for most college kids to get; the credit card companies inundate them with offers. What is hard is knowing how to resist the ease in which they can be used to their maximum credit limits, the ease in which multiple cards can be obtained, and the ease in which debt can mount up and overwhelm them.

How to Get a Credit Card

In deciding among various general credit cards, the choices aren't limited simply between MasterCard and VISA, or Discover or American Express. Your child can choose from different banks and other companies offering such cards. Before he signs on for any "free" card or applies for one on his own, though, make sure he gets the best deal.

> ➤ *Annual fees.* Some cards are no- or low-fee cards; others charge a significant annual fee just for the privilege of holding the card. The fee doesn't change whether or not the card is used. In some cases, the fee is tied to the interest rates charged on outstanding balances. For example, some no-fee cards may charge a higher rate than a fee card. Why pay the fee when there's no need to? But your child shouldn't overlook a fee card that may prove to be a bargain in the long run if he uses the card and carries a monthly balance.

Watch Your Step

Don't let your child send in any credit card application without reading the fine print. Check for annual fees, interest rates, grace periods, and cash advance terms. What may appear to be a good deal because of "no annual fee" may turn out to be a bad deal because of other terms.

> ➤ *Grace periods.* Most credit cards give 25 days or so to pay the bill before any interest will be charged on purchases. But some cards don't advertise the fact that they charge interest from day one—there's no grace period. Look for the fine print that spells out the grace period before taking on the card.

> ➤ *Interest rates.* Rates are expressed in annual terms even though the bill comes monthly. A 12 percent annual rate means that your child is paying 1 percent each month. But some cards have an initially low rate as an incentive to get a person to take the cards and use them. The initial rate may be 6 percent a year, but this may be in effect for only the first six months you have the card. The

rate may jump to 18 percent after the introductory rate expires, which means that in the long run the card is not as good a deal as one charging just 12 percent annually, year in and year out.

➤ *Other items.* While annual fees, introductory rates, and interest rates are the main features to check out, also look for any penalty interest rates (interest plus an additional amount) that may be imposed for violating the terms of the credit agreement (for example, exceeding the credit limit or failing to pay on time). Don't take on any card that uses a two-cycle average daily balance to figure interest rates (about 15 percent of credit cards do this), which results in higher interest charges. Also look for cash advance terms that may be unfavorable (for example, a higher interest rate on advances than the rate charged on purchases).

Money ABCs

The **annual percentage rate (APR)** is simply the interest rate charged for the full year. On credit card bills, this rate is broken down to a monthly rate of one-twelfth of the APR.

Teenagers may be flooded with offers from credit cards. Before accepting one, shop around to find the best deal possible. Check out Web sites that provide information on credit cards, such as these:

➤ *Bankrate.com,* an online publication, rates the best credit card deals, depending on the borrower's profile (for example, pays in full each month or is looking for the lowest interest rate)(www.bankrate.com/brm/ccard.asp).

➤ *Credit Card Network, USA* maintains a consumer information library with good links (www.creditnet.com).

➤ *Credit Card Rate Guides* compares more than 165 cards (asque.com/credcard.htm).

➤ *CreditChoice* provide information and a comparison of credit cards (www.creditchoice.com).

➤ *National Institute for Consumer Education's Consumer Education Resources* page provides information about credit cards and other consumer topics (www. eimch.edu/public/coe/nice.htm).

➤ *United College Marketing Service* is a VISA site with good information about credit cards, but remember that it's mainly there to push cards on college kids (www. college-visa.com).

Keeping Out of Credit Card Trouble

It's so easy to whip out the plastic to pay for something that looks appealing on the store mannequin. However, such impulse buying and other irresponsible uses of credit cards can get a person into serious trouble. The first decision should be whether the item is needed. As with that slice of chocolate cake, if a person waits a few minutes before taking it he may decide to forgo the extra calories.

Once your child decides that she needs an item, the best policy to follow is never to charge any amount she knows she doesn't already have the cash to pay for. In this way, when the charge bill arrives, she simply pays off what she has bought (the balance) all at once.

Sometimes your child may not have the cash on hand but might anticipate that she'll have the money by the time the charge bill is due (for instance, she's expecting a pay check). Sometimes she needs to buy something that costs more than she'll have the money to pay for all at once (such as a computer). Here's where it's easy for the unwary to get into deep financial trouble.

Before charging anything that your child doesn't already have the money on hand to pay for, make sure that she has a plan to pay off the debt. It may take her months or even a year or more to do it, but she needs to take control so that her debt doesn't control her. In the meantime, put the card away where she won't be tempted to use it until the debt is paid off.

Don't just pay the *minimum payment* listed on the bill, either: It will take her a very long time to get out of debt by doing this (although it will keep her eligible to continue charging up more debt).

If your child is finding it hard to make more than the minimum payments and keeps charging up new debt, it may be time for help. Your child obviously didn't get all the information on debt that she should have, so review it with her. Check out Web sites that provide consumer information on debt, such as the National Institute for Consumer Education (www.emich.edu/public/coe/nice.htm).

Before she gets into trouble, advise that she only get one credit card so that she can't buy more than that single credit limit. But if she gets into credit card trouble, make sure that she knows she can turn to you for guidance—and perhaps financial assistance. You can then steer her in the direction of a debt counselor, who can help her work out a repayment plan. Or, you might be in a position to lend her money to pay off her high-interest loan to the credit card company—provided that she then pays off her loan to you. Making loans to your child is discussed in the next chapter.

Piggybank on It

If the charge bill is paid in full each month, this allows the holder to enjoy the use of his money for a longer period of time. This grace period gives him a float because he can keep his money sitting in an interest-bearing account from the time he buys the item until he pays the charge bill, earning interest that he would not have earned had he paid cash for the item. However, some cards may initiate an annual fee for holders who always pay in full.

Money ABCs

A **minimum payment** is the least amount that can be paid on a credit card bill without being in default. The minimum amount may be a percentage of the balance or, if the balance is low, a fixed amount.

The Least You Need to Know

➤ Borrowing doesn't increase what a person has overall—he just has it sooner.

➤ Borrowing usually costs money, called interest.

➤ Getting and keeping good credit is important to your child's financial well-being.

➤ Debit cards are safer than credit cards because a person can't spend more than he has.

➤ Paying only the minimum payment amount on a credit card bill will keep a person in debt for years.

➤ Your child should check out a credit card's fine print and comparison-shop before applying for it.

Chapter 25

Borrowing from Family and Friends

In This Chapter

➤ Getting an advance

➤ Borrowing from friends

➤ Borrowing big-time from Mom and Dad

If your child needs money to buy something now that he otherwise can't afford, what better place to turn than to you for help: You may be in a position to let him do what he wants now. However, borrowing money from family and friends doesn't come without problems. This kind of borrowing can lead your child into trouble—financial and otherwise.

In this chapter, you'll learn when it's okay to advance some allowance to your child. You'll learn about borrowing from friends and other strangers, and you'll discover some problems that your child can encounter when taking these loans. You'll also get some ideas about lending big money to your child to pay for college, buy a car, or move out on his own. Finally, you'll get some tips on providing financial assistance in other ways.

Making Advances

When a child gets $5 or $10 a week, it may not go as far as she likes. She may have to put some money into savings that you don't let her touch, and she may be required to pay for some things on her own. This doesn't leave too much extra for miscellaneous things.

If your middle-schooler is short a few dollars before the next scheduled payment of allowance and wants to buy the school yearbook that has just come out, she may ask for an advance on her allowance. In this case, you may want to give her the advance she needs.

Money ABCs

Advances aren't only discoveries in medicine and science. They also payments made before they're due.

Piggybank on It

Keep track of advances. Parents have a way of forgetting what they've already paid to their child when allowance day rolls around. Then, if they overpay, they're only teaching their kids about bad memories, not about financial responsibility. Mark the advance on a calendar, or post it on the refrigerator door.

Before you accommodate her, though, make sure that you have some ground rules straight.

➤ *What's the money going to be used for?* In other words, is the advance really necessary, or does your child just know you to be a softy? Maybe she can wait for another week's allowance to make the purchase. Maybe she can cut back on expenses for a time. Maybe she doesn't need to buy the thing at all.

➤ *Does she understand that an advance is like borrowing money?* She's using money that isn't hers yet to pay for things. If her allowance is tied to doing chores, then she's really getting paid today for work she'll do tomorrow. She'll still have to do the work even though she already has been paid for it.

➤ *How often does she ask for an advance?* If it's once and a while, you may be only too glad to oblige. But if it's becoming a habit and she's always a dollar short and a day late, you may want to just say no. If you grant her the advance, you're only encouraging her poor money management. She may have to re-examine her priorities: Does she need to buy everything she's spending her money on? Does she need to do all the activities she's using her money for? It may be a good idea to go back to earlier chapters on spending (and budgeting)—Chapter 13, "So Many Choices (So Little Money)," and Chapter 14, "Buying on a Budget."

Borrowing from Friends

Kids forget their lunch money, or they may be short for candy at the movies. Who do they turn to for help? Sometimes they'll ask their friends to borrow money.

Small loans in what they may view as emergency circumstances aren't necessarily bad. Their friends are showing compassion by helping them to pay for lunch or occasionally are lending money when they've left money at home or are just a little short for the time being. And the borrowers aren't looked upon as impoverished or objects to be pitied.

The key to borrowing from friends, however, is *repayment*. It's vital that your child understands that repayment should be made in full *and* done as quickly as possible. After all, the loan to him has been made solely on his promise to repay the money. "Loan me a dollar and I'll give it back to you tomorrow."

If your child fails to repay a loan made by a friend, severe problems can result.

➤ *It can ruin a friendship.* Kids might not say so, but they may be hurt or angry if a loan they've made isn't repaid. Your child could lose a friend over a few dollars. As Mark Twain noted in *Pudd'nhead Wilson*, "The holy passion of Friendship is of so sweet and steady and loyal and enduring a nature that it will last through a whole lifetime, if not asked to lend money."

➤ *It can give your child a bad reputation for not keeping his word.* That might not seem like a big deal today: Contracts a foot high aren't always worth the paper they're written on because the people signing them don't stand by their word. In the old days, though, a handshake was all that was needed to make a binding contract. There's something to be said for the old days—in my opinion, it's worth teaching the value of keeping one's word.

➤ *It can prevent your child from being able to borrow in the future.* If your child doesn't repay a loan to a friend, that person will be reluctant to make a new loan at another time. And, if word gets out, other kids will also hesitate to give even small loans to your child.

It's up to you as a parent to advise your child to be very careful about borrowing from friends. Make sure the borrowing is only once and a while. Frequent borrowing means that your child isn't handling her money well and needs to re-think her budget or look for ways to earn extra cash. Also advise her to pay up as quickly as possible. It may seem like a small amount, but it can cause a big rift in a friendship if repayment is late or overlooked entirely.

On the flip side, you should also caution your child about becoming the J.P. Morgan of the third grade. Just because he has a sympathetic soul doesn't mean that he should become an easy target for everyone in need. He'll run out of cash very soon and will lack funds for his own needs, and he'll be in the uncomfortable position of having to say no to friends who don't repay loans he's made in the past.

Borrowing Big Bucks from Parents

What if an advance on an allowance just isn't enough to help your child out? For example, what if your teenager wants the latest electronic game platform that costs a few hundred dollars and he doesn't want to wait until he gets his birthday money from Grandma? Should you become a banker and loan the money to your child?

You have three choices:

➤ You can say no and refuse to help. Maybe you're saying no because you don't want your child to have the money. Or, maybe you just can't afford to help. Either way, it's an important lesson for your child to learn that, as the Rolling Stones have said, "You can't always get what you want."

➤ You can give the money that's wanted without asking for any repayment. Here you're making a gift, not a loan. You might want to label the gift as a reward for something—making the honor roll or getting the lead in the school play.

➤ You can make the loan and set conditions. For example, you can insist on interest or make the loan interest-free.

When to Be (or Not to Be) a Banker

It's not easy to say no to your child. But when you're asked to lend her money, when is it okay to say yes? And when should you say no?

Say yes in these cases:

➤ *The money is needed for a good reason.* For example, your child needs help buying a car that she can afford to keep up. Or, her savings won't cover her college expenses and she prefers to borrow the money rather than get it as a gift from you.

➤ *You believe your child is responsible enough and able to repay the loan.* If she has an after-school job and has repaid a loan from you before, you can be pretty comfortable with the situation. But if she's always asking for more, there's something wrong with this picture. Again, go back to the chapters on spending (and budgeting) to see where the problems lie (Chapter 13, "So Many Choices [So Little Money]," and Chapter 14, "Buying on a Budget").

➤ *You can afford to make the loan.* Don't let guilt drive you to financial problems. Just because a child asks for a loan doesn't mean that a parent is required to make it. Doing so might force a parent into debt of her own, which doesn't make much sense.

Before lending any large amounts of money to your child, consider the impact that such a loan might have on your other kids. Are you depriving them of something to make the loan to one child? Are they going to want (and expect) the same treatment? Is the loan going to cause jealousy among your children? It's a good idea to address these questions before you agree to make a large loan.

Say no in these cases:

➤ *You disapprove of your child's use of the money.* If your 16-year-old wants to buy a motorcycle and you're horrified at the prospect, just say no. This is really more a question about the motorcycle than about making a loan, but you can quickly end the possibility that he'll get a motorcycle and then later discuss your feelings about his riding a motorcycle.

➤ *Your child is becoming a chronic borrower.* If he always seems to be in need of cash and constantly asks you for loans, it's time to say no and have him brush up on his budget-making or spending skills. Maybe his spending column adds up to more than his allowance or earnings for each period. Or, maybe he makes a great budget but just doesn't stick to it.

➤ *You can't afford to make the loan.* You may be on a strict budget that doesn't have room for loans to your child. Don't feel guilty. That's just a fact of life that your child will have to learn.

➤ *You'd create problems within the family.* Your other children may resent your constant financial underwriting for one child, especially if it comes at the expense of the others. In one family, the mother was always bailing out the baby from financial trouble. Over the years, his siblings grew to resent him for this favoritism.

Money ABCs

A **promissory note** is a written pledge to pay a set sum at a set time or on demand.

Make It Formal

When kids get a little older and want more than just an advance of $5 or $20, you may not want to keep things casual. A big advance on an allowance or a loan to buy a big-ticket item should be treated formally.

➤ *Put it in writing.* Make your child sign statement about what has been loaned to him. This statement is really a type of promissory note in which he agrees to repay the amount stated.

Piggybank on It

There's a very good reason to put a loan to your child in writing. Should your child default and you're unable to collect, you'll be able to write off the loan as a non–business bad debt on your income tax return. Without proof of the loan, your deduction may be lost.

PROMISSORY NOTE (FOR A TERM OF TWO YEARS)

IN CONSIDERATION OF VALUE RECEIVED, I promise to pay to [ADD NAME OF LENDER] the sum of [ADD AMOUNT BORROWED], payable with interest of [ADD INTEREST RATE]% per annum on any unpaid balance.

Payments of not less than 1/24th of the initial principal balance are due on the first of the month starting on [ADD MONTH AND YEAR], time being of the essence. The borrower may prepay this note, in whole or in part, without penalty.

Upon default, the borrower agrees to pay all costs of collection (including attorneys' fees) to the extent permitted by law.

Signed on [DATE]

In the presence of:

_____

Borrower

_____

Lender

➤ *Set a repayment schedule.* You can leave the time for repayment open-ended or can make the loan payable on demand when you say so. It's probably a better idea to set a timetable for repaying the loan, though, so your child doesn't overlook this obligation. Don't leave the debt to be repaid "when he has the money." Require him to make small repayments (or to forgo a portion of his allowance) on certain dates.

If your child is borrowing from you to pay college expenses, you might not want to start repayment until after graduation. By then, he'll be working full-time.

➤ *Charge interest.* If the loan is going to run for more than just a few weeks, it can be a good learning experience to charge interest. You won't get rich on the interest, but your child will see the real cost of borrowing. How much should you charge? You don't want to make the interest too low, because it's not realistic. Nor do you want to make it too high. It's probably a good idea to use the commercial rate being charged on a personal loan in your area. To find out the going rate, just call your neighborhood bank or look at ads in the local newspaper. Remember that the purpose of the interest isn't to create an income for you, but to teach a lesson to your child.

Keep in mind that the tax law may treat you as if you had charged interest even if you make the loan interest-free. Under so-called imputed interest rules, a lender is treated as receiving interest that he effectively waived by not charging.

If the lender makes a low-interest loan, he's treated as receiving the difference between the amount charged and what the government thinks should have been charged. The amount of interest is based on applicable federal interest rate (AFR) at the time the loan is made. That rate changes every month, and there are different rates for loans of three years or less (short-term), loans of three to nine years (mid-term), and loans over nine years or more (long-term). However, no interest is imputed to the lender in two situations:

Piggybank on It

Adults who take loans receive coupon books or get billed monthly to remind them of their obligation. If you're making a loan to your child, consider using some mechanism to track repayments. Notations on a calendar may be enough of a reminder.

Money ABCs

Imputed interest is interest income that the lender is treated as having received, and the lender can be taxed on this amount even though it's only a fiction created by the tax law.

➤ *$10,000 gift loan.* If the amount of loans between the lender and borrower—you and your child—isn't more than $10,000, there's no imputed interest as long as the money isn't used to buy income-producing assets (such as stocks or CDs).

➤ *$100,000 gift loan.* If the amount of loans between you and your child is no more than $100,000, there's no imputed interest as long as your child's net investment income isn't more than $1,000. For example, if you make an interest-free loan of $25,000 that your child uses for college, there's no imputed interest to you as long as your child's interest, dividends, and capital gains do not exceed $1,000.

Other Ways for You to Help

You don't have to become your child's banker to provide help. You also can provide counseling and advice to him. Maybe he needs to learn better money management skills. Review with him the material on budgeting and spending, and help him redo his budget and reconsider his future purchases.

Maybe he's already in money trouble and needs professional help. Teenagers with credit cards can too easily fall under the spell of easy buying. Suggest that he look at consumer credit information on the Web at www.creditnet.com and www.bankrate.com/brm/ccard.asp. Or call Consumer Credit Counseling Services, a non-profit organization, at 800-388-2227, to find a consumer counseling office near your child.

Money ABCs

A **guarantor** is someone who promises to pay a loan if the borrower fails to do so. The guarantor is putting his credit history on the line.

If your child needs money for a large purchase, such as a car, and can't borrow from a bank or other outside lender on the basis of his own credit history, you can still help out without lending the money yourself: You can become a guarantor for a loan he has applied for.

Before becoming a guarantor, be sure that you fully understand the consequences of what you're promising. If your child fails to repay the loan, you're legally obligated to do so. Are you in a financial position to add his monthly payments to your budget? In addition, if you need to borrow money during the term of your child's loan, you must include your guarantor obligation on your loan application. This can adversely affect your ability to get a loan.

The Least You Need to Know

➤ Advances on allowances are like loans because they must be repaid by forgoing future allowances.

➤ Parents should keep track of advances on allowances so that they don't pay their kids twice.

➤ Borrowing from friends can ruin friendships if loans are not repaid.

➤ When your child needs funds from you, decide if and whether you'll make a loan or a gift of the money.

➤ If a loan to a child is substantial, put it in writing and follow formalities.

➤ Instead of lending money to your child, find other ways to provide financial help.

Studying Up on Student Loans

If your name isn't Rockefeller and you can't pay your child's tuition and other costs with savings, scholarships, or earnings, then you're in good company. Most people have to borrow to meet college costs. Most aid comes from the federal government (nearly 70 percent), but there's also state aid, aid from schools, and even private sources that can to help pay for the cost of a higher education.

Saving for college was discussed in several earlier chapters (Chapter 16, "Setting Savings Goals That Work," Chapter 17, "Piggybanking It," and Chapter 18, "Beyond the Corner Bank"). In this chapter, you'll learn all about student loans. You'll learn how your child can qualify for student loans, and you'll learn about loans that parents can use to help out their children. You'll also get some idea about how repaying student loans works.

Borrowing to Pay for College

A college education is a good financial investment. On the whole, college graduates make more money throughout their working years than high school graduates. A college education also is the first step toward becoming a professional or getting an advanced degree.

But paying for all this education takes money—more money that most people have at their fingertips. The overwhelming number of college students receive a student aid package in the form of scholarships, loans, grants, or school-arranged part-time work. Of all these types of aid, by far the most common is the college loan.

The amount and type of aid your child can receive depends on two key factors: his financial picture and yours (including savings and income and the number of other children in the family attending college), and the costs for the school your child will be attending.

For a general guide on how much aid is available for the school your child will be attending (or is thinking of attending), consult the *College Money Handbook* (Peterson's Guides) or *The Scholarship Book* (Prentice-Hall). Both deal with all sources of college money, from scholarships to loans, and are updated each year. You can also get *The Student Guide to Financial Aid* (U.S. Department of Education), which is free by calling 800-433-3243.

Deciding How Much to Borrow

Before your child can figure how much she'll need in financial aid, she needs to get a clear idea of what the cost of college will be. Use the following chart to add up what it's expected to cost for *one year* at college. In filling in the information, use the college's current costs for this purpose. Then multiply your result by 10 percent to factor in some cost increases likely to occur.

Now look at what has been put aside for college. Add the savings in your child's name for college as well as what you've put into a college fund for your child. Don't forget to include money in a savings bank or in CDs, stocks, mutual funds, and U.S. savings bonds.

Piggybank on It

Don't think that because you make a good living, your child won't qualify for aid. Even with an income of more than $100,000, she may still get aid if you have more than one child in college at the same time.

Piggybank on It

In projecting college costs, be sure to factor in inflation. The cost of higher education has been increasing faster than the rate of inflation for most other things. In 1998, for example, college tuition increased between 5 percent and 10 percent, while the Consumer Price Index showed only a 1.6 percent increase.

Type of Expense	Estimated Cost
Tuition	$_____
Additional fees	$_____
Student activity fee	$_____
Computer fee	$_____
Library fee	$_____
Room and board	$_____

284

Type of Expense	Estimated Cost
Dormitory or off-campus housing	$_____
Meals (meal plan or food)	$_____
Laundry	$_____
Books and supplies	$_____
Textbooks	$_____
Lab supplies	$_____
Other supplies	$_____
Transportation	$_____
Travel between home and school	$_____
Travel while away at school	$_____
Other expenses	$_____
Health insurance	$_____
Cost of social activities	$_____
Clothing	$_____
Computer	$_____
Total	$_____
Total × 10 percent	$_____

This savings is supposed to supplement *four years* of college, not just the one year for which expenses have been projected. To get a rough idea of what your child or you will need to borrow, you might want to divide the savings by four (one-fourth for each year of college).

From the annual cost that has been projected, subtract the savings allocated to that year (one-fourth of the total). This is the shortfall that must be made up by scholarships, part-time work, and borrowing.

Piggybank on It

When figuring money available to pay for college, don't forget to add in any funds that have been put into an education IRA or a qualified state tuition plan for your child.

The Student Loan Process

If your child will need any kind of financial aid, he must complete a standard financial aid form. This form is called the Free Application for Federal Student Aid (FAFSA). There's no cost to your child to apply for federal aid, so he has nothing to lose by trying.

The following is the first page of FAFSA. As you can see, the form is lengthy and detailed; there are nearly 100 questions to answer. These questions cover the income and assets of both you and your child.

Free Application for Federal Student Aid

OMB 1840-0110

July 1, 1999 — June 30, 2000 school year

Step One: For questions 1-37, leave blank any questions that do not apply to you (the student).

1-3. Your name

1. LAST NAME

2. FIRST NAME

3. M.I.

4-7. Your permanent mailing address

4. NUMBER AND STREET (INCLUDE APARTMENT NUMBER)

5. CITY (AND COUNTRY, IF NOT U.S.)

6. STATE

7. ZIP CODE

8. Your Social Security Number

9. Your date of birth

MONTH / DAY / YEAR 1 9

10. Your permanent telephone number

AREA CODE

11. Do you have a driver's license?   Yes ○ 1   No ○ 2

12-13. Driver's license number and state

12. LICENSE NUMBER

13. STATE

14. Are you a U.S. citizen? Pick one. **See Page 2.**

a. Yes, I am a U.S. citizen. .... ○ 1

b. No, but I am an eligible noncitizen. **Fill in question 15.** ○ 2

c. No, I am not a citizen or eligible noncitizen. .... ○ 3

ALIEN REGISTRATION NUMBER

15. A

16. Marital status as of today

I am single, divorced, or widowed. ○ 1

I am married. ○ 2

I am separated. ○ 3

17. Month and year you were married, separated, divorced, or widowed

MONTH / YEAR

For each question (18 - 22), please mark whether you will be **full time**, **3/4 time**, **half time**, **less than half time**, or **not attending. Mark "Full time"** if you are not sure. See page 2.

18. Summer 1999   Full time ○ 1   3/4 time ○ 2   Half time ○ 3   Less than half time ○ 4   Not attending ○ 5

19. Fall semester or quarter 1999   Full time ○ 1   3/4 time ○ 2   Half time ○ 3   Less than half time ○ 4   Not attending ○ 5

20. Winter quarter 1999-2000   Full time ○ 1   3/4 time ○ 2   Half time ○ 3   Less than half time ○ 4   Not attending ○ 5

21. Spring semester or quarter 2000   Full time ○ 1   3/4 time ○ 2   Half time ○ 3   Less than half time ○ 4   Not attending ○ 5

22. Summer 2000   Full time ○ 1   3/4 time ○ 2   Half time ○ 3   Less than half time ○ 4   Not attending ○ 5

23. Highest school your father completed   Middle school/Jr. High ○ 1   High school ○ 2   College or beyond ○ 3   Other/unknown ○ 4

24. Highest school your mother completed   Middle school/Jr. High ○ 1   High school ○ 2   College or beyond ○ 3   Other/unknown ○ 4

25. What is your state of legal residence?   STATE

26. Did you become a legal resident of this state before January 1, 1994?   Yes ○ 1   No ○ 2

27. If the answer to question 26 is **"No,"** give month and year you became a legal resident.   MONTH / YEAR

28. Most male students must register with Selective Service to get federal aid. Are you male?   Yes ○ 1   No ○ 2

29. If you are male (age 18-25) and not registered, do you want Selective Service to register you?   Yes ○ 1   No ○ 2

30. What degree or certificate will you be working towards during 1999-2000? **See page 2** and enter the correct number in the box.

31. What will be your grade level when you begin the 1999-2000 school year? **See page 2** and enter the correct number in the box.

32. Will you have a high school diploma or GED before you enroll?   Yes ○ 1   No ○ 2

33. Will you have your first bachelor's degree before July 1, 1999?   Yes ○ 1   No ○ 2

34. In addition to grants, are you interested in student loans (which you must pay back)?   Yes ○ 1   No ○ 2

35. In addition to grants, are you interested in "work-study" (which you earn through work)?   Yes ○ 1   No ○ 2

36. If you receive veterans' education benefits, for **how many months** from July 1, 1999 through June 30, 2000 will you receive these benefits?

37. Amount per month? $

Page 3

There are several ways to obtain and submit the FAFSA:

➤ *FAFSA Express.* This Web site allows you to download filing software to your computer. You can print a version of the form from your computer, complete it, and then send it off by mail to the Department of Education. Click on www.ed.gov/offices/OPE/express.html.

➤ *From your child's high school guidance or college office.* After completing the form, you then mail it in.

➤ *From the Department of Education.* Call 800-433-3243 for the form, complete it, and then mail it in.

Your child completes the FAFSA, and then both you and he sign. As his custodial parent, you also complete a separate application, called a PLUS loan application.

Colleges use the FAFSA to determine how much they'll award in tuition reductions, loans, or other financial help. The law sets limits on qualifications for and the amounts that can be borrowed under the different types of loans. Get the form in on time—generally, you should get it in as soon as possible after January 1 of your child's senior year of high school.

It's helpful to understand how the federal government and other lenders evaluate the information to determine your eligibility. This is based on both your child's income and assets and your income and assets.

➤ *Your child's financial picture.* Generally, 35 percent of all assets in your child's name are taken into account in determining aid. Your child's earnings are also taken into account. According to a report in *USA Today,* nearly two-thirds of college students work outside the classroom to help pay for college. This money counts against them when it comes to determining financial aid.

➤ *Your financial picture.* About 6 percent (5.65 percent, to be exact) of assets in your name are taken into account in determining aid to

Watch Your Step

The FAFSA may not be the last step in the aid process. Some private colleges want additional information and may require your child to complete the College Board Financial Aid Profile (more detailed than the FAFSA).

Piggybank on It

Don't let your child fail to complete the FAFSA. Just because you have a good job or your child's grandparent has set up a bank account for her doesn't mean that she won't qualify for a loan. Your child may be eligible for some federal loan program.

your child. Amounts in your retirement accounts aren't counted for this purpose. If you're the custodial parent, it's you they're looking at—and if you're remarried, it includes your new spouse's income and assets. Some private colleges also include the noncustodial parent's financial picture in determining any financial aid. In addition to your assets, your income plays a role in what your child can qualify for. Your assets and income, as well as those of your child, make up your EFC (expected family contribution)—what you're expected to contribute toward college costs.

This rather complicated financial aid formula will result in a decision about what your child is eligible to receive and to borrow under special loan programs. He'll usually receive his Student Aid Report within a month of submitting the FAFSA.

Finding Student Loans

Before your child looks for loans, check out the availability of funds that don't have to be repaid: scholarships and grants. Scholarships are discussed in Chapter 11, "Getting Money Out of the Blue." The two major federal grants to undergraduates, called gift aid programs because they aren't repaid, are Federal Pell Grants and Federal Supplemental Educational Opportunity Grants (FSEOG). To find out more about these grants, check out the U.S. Department of Education at www.ed.gov or call 800-433-3243.

If your child must rely in part on loans, then under the federal government's Direct Loan program, the FAFSA is used to qualify for four types of direct loans:

➤ *Direct Stafford/Ford loans (subsidized loans)* are available to students with financial need. The size of the loan is limited, as listed in the following table. Interest is paid by the government while your child is in school.

➤ *Direct Stafford/Ford loans (unsubsidized loans)* are available without regard to your child's financial need, but your child pays all interest charges.

➤ *Direct PLUS loans* are available to parents whose children are still their dependents. Borrowing up to the cost of attendance (minus other financial aid received) is permitted.

Piggybank on It

If your child is a sophomore or junior in high school and you know he'll need aid for college, you might want to reduce the assets in his name. Do this by using *his* money, instead of yours, to buy him a computer or a car (or any other item that's not considered part of your legal obligation of support) if you were otherwise planning to do so. Then you can use the money you didn't spend yourself to help out at college time.

Watch Your Step

The raise you get when your child is finishing high school can cost you dearly in financial aid. Each dollar over the federal limit reduces aid by 47¢. It's your income from her senior year of high school to her senior year of college that will be used to determine her aid package.

➤ *Direct Consolidated loans* combine one or more federally sponsored education loans into one loan for a student. This is a repayment plan for the other loans.

Here's a listing of the Direct Stafford loan limits for students who are dependents:

Year of Higher Education	Loan Limit*
1st undergraduate year	$2,625
2nd undergraduate year	$3,500
3rd and 4th undergraduate years	$5,500

These limits may be increased by federal law changes.

Direct loans from the federal government aren't the only way to raise money for college. Here's a listing of the major other types of aid currently available:

➤ *Federal Perkins Loans* are low-interest loans to low-income students. Interest (which is lower than on most other student loans) accrues while the student is in school and for a nine-month grace period after graduation.

➤ *Federal work-study* provides on-campus or off-campus employment to students with a financial need. Work can be community service work or related to the student's field of study. Pay is at least the federal minimum wage, but can be more, depending on the job.

➤ *Bank loans.* Rates on private loans from banks generally run higher than federally sponsored loans. However, these loans can be useful in filling in the gaps of your child's student aid package. The following banks are the most aggressive in providing student loans: PNC Bank, First Bank, Signet Bank, Union Bank & Trust, Crestar, Norwest Bank, U.S. Bank, and Wells Fargo.

Piggybank on It

A new law makes federal borrowing easier. The interest rate on federal student loans has dropped to 6.46 percent, the lowest rate in 17 years. The ceiling on Pell Grants also has increased.

To find out more about federal rules on college loans, visit the following Web sites:

The College Board (some aid and scholarship information)	www.collegeboard.org
Department of Education (details on federal financial aid, including a FAFSA available for downloading)	www.ed.gov/
FastWEB (scholarship search program)	www.fastweb.com

| The Financial Aid Information Page (information on all aspects of the aid process) | www.finaid.org |
| The Ambitious Student's Guide to Financial Aid (overview of the aid process) | www.synet.com |

Parental Loans

You're not under any legal obligation to send your child to college (unless you have a divorce agreement requiring you to), but you probably want to help out as much as possible. If you don't have the cash to pay the tuition bills when they come in, you're in the same boat as your child: You'll have to borrow the money or take it from your own savings. (Loans you may be willing to make to your child to help him pay for college are discussed in Chapter 25, "Borrowing from Family and Friends.")

As an adult, you have many different sources of borrowing or sources of savings that probably aren't available to your child. Here are some places you might look to find money to help your child through college.

➤ *Home equity loans.* If you own your home and it's worth more than the mortgage that's still outstanding, you may be able to borrow money. Your home is security for the loan. If the home equity loan is no more than $100,000, the interest you pay is fully deductible on your income tax return.

Watch Your Step

Don't take out a home equity loan lightly. If you fail to repay the loan, you could lose your home.

➤ *IRAs.* You may have put away an impressive sum for your retirement into an IRA, and you can use that money to help put your child through school. But before you touch the money in this tax-deferred account, consider certain things. First, you're hurting your own retirement savings. Once the money is out, after 60 days you can't put it back into the IRA. Second, you lose the opportunity to build up your savings on a tax-deferred basis. Third, whatever you withdraw is fully taxable.

Piggybank on It

If you're under age $59^{1}/_{2}$, you aren't subject to a 10 percent early distribution penalty for funds used to pay higher education costs for your child.

➤ *Brokerage accounts.* You can take a loan from your brokerage account by going on margin. In effect, you're borrowing using your stocks and bonds as collateral. You can borrow up to 50 percent of the value of your securities (90 percent of Treasuries). Interest rates on margin loans are generally lower than rates charged by banks for personal loans, but this type of borrowing isn't advisable for long-term needs. If you find that your child is short of cash for a little while (for example, she has a CD coming due in two months, but tuition is due this month), it's worth considering.

➤ *Student loans for parents.* Direct PLUS loans are loans under the federal student loan program for parents whose child is still a dependent. The interest rate is the same as the rate for other federal loans.

Repaying Your Student Loan

Getting the loan is only one half of the equation. The loan also must be repaid at some time unless your child qualifies for some forgiveness or debt discharge (explained later).

Generally, a federal student loan is repaid in fixed monthly amounts of at least $50 per month over a fixed period of time (as long as 10 years). The time your child has to repay the loan depends on how much she has borrowed. Obviously, the shorter the repayment period, the lower her total interest payments will be. She always has the option of paying her loan more quickly, or paying it off in full, whenever she chooses. This will limit her total interest payments.

She may be eligible for an extended repayment plan that may give her up to 30 years to repay. While monthly payments will be smaller under this alternative, total interest will be greater.

She also may be able to opt for a graduated repayment plan, under which payments increase every two years. Presumably, because payments start out small, her increased earning ability over the years will make it easy to manage payment increases as they come along.

There's also an income contingent repayment plan that modifies required payments according to your income each year, for up to 25 years. If there's still principal unpaid at the end of 25 years, it's discharged (but this discharge is treated as income to the borrower, resulting in income taxes on the discharged amount).

Your child can change repayment plans if his circumstances warrant a change.

Instead of repaying her loan, your child may be eligible to have some or all of it discharged so that

Piggybank on It

Your child can consolidate your various loans so that they're treated as if he had only one loan outstanding. This means he'll make only one monthly payment instead of monthly payments on each loan he has taken.

Piggybank on It

Your child may be able to deduct interest she pays on the student loan on his income tax return. This tax deduction reduces his out-of-pocket cost for repaying the loan because the federal government is, in effect, subsidizing his interest to the extent of benefit from his tax deduction (he saves some taxes he'd otherwise have to pay by deducting his interest payment).

she doesn't have to repay it. If she undertakes certain work in certain locations, she may qualify for debt discharge. For example, if she agrees to teach on an Indian reservation for a certain length of time or provide nursing in an economically depressed area, she does not have to repay her student loans. What's more, unlike most other debt forgiveness, this debt forgiveness isn't treated as income that she'd otherwise have to pay tax on.

Financial Building Blocks

What can happen to your child if he fails to make timely student loan payments? After 180 days, he's considered in default. Then the boom is lowered and any of the following can happen:

➤ The Department of Education can demand full and immediate repayment of the balance due and can start collection activity (he'll pay the cost of collection).

➤ The default is reported to credit agencies and becomes part of his credit history, damaging his credit rating.

➤ He becomes ineligible for any further student aid or loan deferments.

➤ If he holds a job, his wages may be garnished (a portion is withheld to pay off the loans).

➤ Any federal income tax refund can be applied to defaulted loans.

There's a way for you to borrow money to help your child and cut your repayment costs. Look for a loan that will be sold to the Student Loan Marketing Association (Sallie Mae, for short). Sallie Mae rewards those who make prompt repayment. If you do so for the first 24 months, all but $250 of the loan origination fee is refunded. If you do so for 48 months, the interest rate charged for the remaining period is reduced by 2 percentage points. Also allow the credits to debit your bank account for repayment in this case, and you'll receive an immediate reduction of 0.25 percent off the interest rate. You can find a local bank offering loans sold to Sallie Mae by calling 800-891-1387.

The Least You Need to Know

➤ Investing in a college education makes good financial sense because college graduates earn more than high school graduates.

➤ The amount your child needs to borrow to pay for college depends on what has been saved (by both you and him) and how much his intended school costs.

➤ All kids applying for financial aid must complete FAFSA, a free financial loan application from the Department of Education.

➤ FAFSA takes into account the financial picture of both the parent and the child.

➤ Parents who borrow to help with their child's education have different sources of loans to consider.

➤ There are various loan repayment plans to pay back student loans.

Chapter 27

Leaving the Nest

> ## In This Chapter
>
> ➤ Testing your child's money IQ
>
> ➤ Preparing for a move
>
> ➤ Adding to your child's money vocabulary
>
> ➤ Giving new help to your independent child

The day has to come sometime when your child moves out on his own. Some parents look forward to it; others dread it. But once this happens, your ability to guide and influence your child's money decisions is greatly limited. While the emotional aspects to your child's independence are hard to prepare for, you can make sure that he starts out on a sound financial footing.

In this chapter, you'll see how to make sure you've done your job and to ensure that your child has mastered certain money management concepts needed for independent living. You'll help your child prepare for his move and will learn about some new things he should know about when he's on his own. You'll also find out how you can continue to provide help and guidance on money issues even when he's no longer living under your roof.

Checking Up on What Your Child Has Learned

Let's say your child is about to go off to college, join the Navy, or move into her own apartment. You probably want to offer some last-minute advice on how to stay safe, how not to get sick, and how to keep in touch. It's not the time to start quizzing her about her savings account or getting enough car insurance.

But before you wave goodbye at the front door, it's a good idea to see that your child has mastered some money management basics. This will give both you and your child confidence that she'll be able to manage things on her own. Here's a checklist of the money-related things your child should know before she tries to handle things entirely on her own:

Task or Concept	Yes	No
Make a budget?	_____	_____
Know how and why to open a savings account?	_____	_____
Write a check?	_____	_____
Balance a checkbook?	_____	_____
Apply for a credit card?	_____	_____
Read a credit card bill?	_____	_____
Know what a debit card is?	_____	_____
Be able to complete a Form W-4?	_____	_____
Have job information together?	_____	_____
Know her Social Security number?	_____	_____
Read a pay stub?	_____	_____
Know about filing an income tax return?	_____	_____
Know what stocks and bonds are?	_____	_____
Know what a mutual fund is?	_____	_____
Know about IRAs?	_____	_____
Know about financial advisers (accountant, stock broker, insurance agent)?	_____	_____

Watch Your Step

If your child doesn't know most of the basic money concepts, maybe he shouldn't be too quick to move out on his own. He might not like to hear this, but he may benefit from some additional time at home to learn the money skills he needs to survive in the outside world.

If your child knows the answers to most or all of these questions, you can pat yourself on the back because you've done a good job of explaining the important money topics to your child. If your child can't answer a large number of these questions correctly, you'd better go back to square one and start with money basics.

Preparing to Move Out

Living on one's own is a natural part of growing up. Some kids put off the day of reckoning as long as possible, and some don't leave until they get married. Others stay at home for years—well into their 30s—because they like the conveniences you provide and don't want to live in the accommodations their wages can pay for. Kids who have gone off to college and then returned home to live are called "boomerang kids."

Other kids are chomping at the bit to fly the coop. If your child has lived away at school, he already has had a taste of independence. He may be eager to move out on his own.

At some point, however, most kids clear out their closets for good. It's a big step, and an expensive one as well. Make sure that your child knows what it takes to live on his own and that he prepares accordingly.

He needs to know two things concerning what it costs to live on his own:

1. The initial outlays he'll probably have to make
2. The ongoing or monthly bills he'll have to pay

Knowing what it costs to move out will allow him to plan ahead so that he can start off on a sound financial footing.

First Things First

Moving out isn't as easy from a financial perspective as it may seem. It may take time and planning to be able to take the big step. Here's a listing of some initial costs that your child must have the cash to cover if she plans to move out on her own:

➤ *Lease security deposit.* When she rents an apartment, generally she's required to pay not only the first month's rent, but also another amount equaling one or two months' rent. This is called a security deposit. For example, if her monthly rent is $500 and she's required to make a two-month security deposit, she'll have to come up with $1,500 to sign the lease ($500 for the first month's rent, plus $1,000 for the security deposit).

➤ *Broker or rental agent's fee.* In some places, rentals are hard to come by. Currently, New York, Boston, and San Francisco are experiencing new zero vacancy rates, which means that there aren't many apartments for rent. Your child may have to use an agent to help her find a place. An agent may charge a fee equal to one to two months' rent, or a percentage of the annual rent (such as 15 percent). Obviously, if your child can find a home without using an agent, she's ahead of the game because she can save on this expense. But if she wants or needs to live in a tight rental market, she may have no choice.

➤ *Utility deposits.* Some utility companies, such as the telephone company or the electric

Piggybank on It

State law dictates how the landlord must treat a security deposit. In many states, the deposit must be held in a separate bank account and must earn interest. The tenant is entitled to this interest when the security deposit is refunded at the end of the lease.

company, may require a deposit before starting your service. This is especially true if your child has never used the utility before and so has no track record of making payments on time.

➤ *Moving costs.* If she has a lot of things to move from your home to her own place and she doesn't have a truck she can borrow, she'll probably have to incur some moving expenses. She may not need to pay a professional mover, but she may have to rent a truck or a van to carry her things. To rent a truck or van, she'll have to show a major credit card. In some locations, she must be over a certain age to rent a vehicle.

➤ *Fix-up costs.* Generally, a landlord paints an apartment before it is rented. In some places, however, fix-up is up to the tenant. (Some landlords may, in fact, reduce the rent if a tenant agrees to fix up the place.) Before your child invests any serious money into her place, though, make sure that she knows what she can and cannot do. Check the lease for restrictions on papering, putting up walls, or making any structural alterations. (She may be able to do it if she agrees to put the place back the way she found it when she moves.)

Making a Budget

The fact that your child has a job and wants to live independently is great, but he had better know how much he can afford to pay for rent and other expenses in light of his *current* income. It's not a good idea to plan on the basis of anticipated raises, job changes, or other unknowns.

Watch Your Step

It's important that your child pay her bills on time. Most bills will state the date when payment must be received. If she's late, this action becomes part of her credit history. (Special credit companies track this information.) Her lack of prompt action can come back to haunt her later when she applies for a loan to buy a car or when she wants to rent a new apartment.

By now, your child may have experience in making a budget: He may have done so as early as the day he first started getting an allowance. If he doesn't yet feel confident about this skill, he might consider taking an adult education class in his area (for example, the Learning Annex in New York City or the Boston Center for Adult Education in Boston). He can ask at his local library about such programs in the area.

Once he actually has made the transition into his new home, he should be prepared for ongoing costs of living on his own. He should make a budget that includes these items:

➤ *Monthly rent.* How much rent can he afford to pay? It's usually suggested that rent should be no more than one-quarter to one-third of monthly take-home pay. However, in high-rent cities, such as New York, most young people starting out may have to pay a greater portion of their income for housing. Generally, rent is due by the first of the month, but the schedule can have another due date. Make sure that he knows when he must pay the rent each month.

➤ *Utilities.* To keep the place running, your child will have to pay certain basic bills each month. These include bills from the electric company (he may also have to pay a gas company) and the telephone company. However, he may want to have other services if he can afford them, especially if he's used to having them in your home. For example, he may want cable TV or an online service for his computer (to receive e-mail and access the Internet). This, too, costs money each month. For instance, AOL's unlimited monthly use cost is $9.95.

➤ *Insurance.* While the law doesn't require him to have insurance, he should protect his property from theft or damage and should protect himself from claims in case someone is injured in his home. To cover these contingencies, he'll need to pay for tenant's insurance. Generally, this is an annual bill that runs only a few hundred dollars or less. A tenant's policy is a form of homeowner's insurance, and the size of the premiums depend in part on how much property—from his computer and stereo, to furniture and more—your child has in his home. He'll be glad he paid for coverage if a storm or fire ravages his apartment and destroys his belongings. (Other types of insurance he may want to carry are discussed later in this chapter.)

➤ *Living expenses.* In addition to the bills he must pay, he'll also have to budget for food, personal items, transportation (car payments, gas, car insurance, and bus, subway, and taxi fares), entertainment, and other costs of daily living.

Watch Your Step

If your child took out student loans to get through college, be sure that his budget includes loan payments. This can be a substantial monthly cost.

It's helpful if your child puts this information together, along with other expenses, by making a monthly budget. He can use the following chart for this purpose.

Projected Budget of Monthly Expenses for Living on Your Own

Type of Expense	Monthly Amount
Rent	$_____
Electrical use	$_____
Telephone	$_____
Cable company	$_____

continues

continued

Type of Expense	Monthly Amount
Online service	$_____
Tenant's insurance (divide annual bill by 12)	$_____
Food	$_____
Toiletries and other personal items	$_____
Transportation costs	$_____
Entertainment	$_____
Repayment of student loan	$_____
Miscellaneous	$_____
TOTAL	$_____

Advanced Money ABCs

Moving out isn't just about having the money to do it—it's also about handling the day-to-day things that grown-ups take for granted, such as arranging for a long-distance carrier for your telephone or buying car insurance.

Your child already knows about paying the bills, and that's great. But how do the bills start coming in? As a minimum, your child should know about dealing with utility companies and getting insurance.

Dealing with Utility Companies

When your child lives at home, he takes for granted the ability to flip on the light switch. When he moves into his own apartment, however, turning on the lights usually requires him to take some action first. He must establish an account with the utility company providing electricity (and perhaps gas as well). He may need to make a deposit to protect the utility company in case of nonpayment. This deposit is refunded when he moves or can even be refunded after he's lived there for some time and has built up a solid history of paying his utility bill on time.

Here's a listing of the various types of additional utility companies your child may have to contact to arrange service before or at the time he moves in:

➤ *Telephone company.* The telephone company providing local service may assign a long-distance carrier—such as AT&T, MCI, or Sprint. However, your child is free to select whichever long-distance carrier he wants. If he plans to make a number of long-distance calls each month, he should check out various calling plans to see which plan is best for his calling pattern. In many areas, he can also select his local telephone company.

➤ *Cable company.* Most areas today have cable TV companies to provide this service. Check out the monthly plans available. All cable companies offer a basic service plan, plus a number of premium channels for additional cost. Some housing may offer satellite TV (with or without the option of taking cable stations).

➤ *Internet services.* Depending on what your child needs and can afford, he may want to subscribe to an online service provider to receive e-mail and have access to the Internet. Alternatively, he may want to use an Internet service provider that features a local telephone number for making connections. Check out and compare costs of online service providers and ISPs in consumer magazines such as *PC World* (www.pcworld.com).

Getting Insurance

When your child is young, she's probably totally unaware of the existence of insurance and what it's all about. Her first encounter with it may be car insurance, when she goes to buy her first car, or it may be medical insurance to cover doctor's visits, prescription drugs, and dental care.

The need to pay for insurance is a grown-up thing to grasp because it may be costly and may never be needed. But it's a good idea to be as well protected as possible for all contingencies.

As your child becomes independent, it's helpful for her to know about the different types of insurance available and whether she needs to carry them:

➤ *Liability insurance* protects her if someone else is injured on her property. Property damage liability covers the costs of the other party's property if she caused the damage in an accident. Bodily insurance liability pays for medical costs for another party injured in an accident that was her fault. Your child buys this coverage as part of her car insurance or a homeowner's (or tenant's) insurance policy.

Money ABCs

Insurance is simply a way of shifting the risk of loss you may suffer to a deeper pocket—the insurance company. You, the insured, pay premiums to provide you with certain coverage in case some specified event such as an accident or illness occurs.

➤ *Property protection* covers the cost of repairing or replacing her property when it is damaged in an accident or is stolen. Collision coverage for a car gives her protection regardless of whether an accident was her fault or someone else's. Comprehensive coverage for her car covers the cost or repairing or replacing her car for damage resulting from something other than an accident (such as a tree falling on it or theft). Again, she buys this coverage as part of her car insurance or her homeowner's insurance policy.

➤ *Medical insurance* covers some or all of the costs of the bills from hospitals, doctors, and even pharmacies for prescription drugs. The extent of medical coverage varies widely. She may have coverage while at college under a college plan or under your family's plan. Medical payment and personal injury protection under a car insurance policy cover *her* medical costs that result from an

Money ABCs

COBRA is a federal law that gives your child the right to convert his coverage under a parent's company plan to individual coverage once he reaches age 21 or is otherwise no longer covered under that plan. COBRA coverage runs for up to 18 months thereafter.

Watch Your Step

A car owner (or leasee) *must* carry car insurance. The car can't be registered or re-registered without it. While your child is under the age of 25, she's going to pay dearly for the coverage.

Piggybank on It

If he buys more than one type of insurance from the same insurance company (for example, his car insurance and tenant's insurance), he may be entitled to a multiple policy discount.

accident. Generally, coverage under your medical plan ends when your child turns 21 or stops being a full-time student. However, she may be able to pick up the coverage herself if your insurance is subject to COBRA rules, or she might be able to get coverage from the company she works for. Don't go "bare" (without insurance), though, if at all possible. If she doesn't yet have coverage from an employer, she should compare the cost of COBRA coverage (which is individual coverage at group rates, plus a small administrative fee) with individual coverage she could obtain on her own. Compare apples to apples, contrasting benefits provided under different plans with the cost for each.

➤ *Car insurance* covers several things. For starters, it covers liability coverage if you cause the damage or injury to someone else's car or person. You also may carry collision to fix your car if it's damaged, whether or not it was your fault.

Your child will become acquainted with other types of insurance as she gets older, including life insurance to provide benefits after she dies and disability insurance to give her income if she becomes disabled and can't work. To find out more about the different types of insurance, visit www.fool.com/FamilyFool/1997/ FamilyCollection971029b.htm.

Knowing that she needs insurance is one thing, but buying it is another. There are two main ways to buy insurance:

➤ *Directly from an insurance company*, such as buying car insurance from Allstate Insurance Company. The person she'll deal with is called an insurance agent. Usually she can visit local offices of major companies to discuss her insurance needs.

➤ *Through an insurance broker*, who places her order with the insurance company that supposedly best fits the bill in terms of the extent of coverage and the cost for the coverage.

As with most other things, the key to buying insurance is shopping around. In comparing price, be sure to check whether each company is offering the same extent of coverage.

A Lifetime of Help

Your child is your child for the rest of his (and your) life. Just because he's on his own doesn't mean that you need to stop providing help and guidance. True, your abilities in this regard become limited in some cases by distance and your desire to encourage independence. But there are still ways that a parent can provide helpful and needed assistance.

Being a Guarantor

Your child may want to get an apartment, take out a car loan, or apply for a loan to start a business. Unless she's independently wealthy, the landlord in the case of an apartment, or the lender in the case of a loan, your child may find people who are reluctant to deal with a young person with limited or no credit history. This is so even if your child truly believes she'll be able to pay the rent or repay the loan. Here's where you come in.

You can act as a guarantor for your child. The landlord or lender will do business with a child if there's a responsible adult backing her up.

> **Money ABCs**
>
> A **guarantor** is a person who agrees to make payments if the person obligated to so do fails. In effect, you're assuring the landlord or lender that he'll get his money no matter what. A guarantor must be a financially responsible person with a good credit history who's willing to take on this job.

Lending a Hand

Even if your child has a good job and knows how to handle money well, there may be times that he can use a little extra financial help. For example, even though he's got a paycheck coming in regularly, he may need cash in certain situations:

➤ *To get an apartment.* He knows he can pay the rent each month, but he doesn't have the funds for the two-month security deposit or the 15 percent fee to an apartment broker to find an apartment. He could save up for these expenses, or he could take some cash out of his credit card (if he has one), although he'll probably be repaying that kind of loan at exorbitant rates. As another alternative, you could lend him the money with the understanding that you'll be repaid (with or without some reasonable rate of interest).

➤ *To cover expenses temporarily.* Maybe he's laid off and his unemployment insurance isn't enough to cover both his rent and his car payments. Here you may want to step in to provide temporary assistance until he's back on his feet.

➤ *To buy a house.* Maybe he's able to pay the mortgage but is a little short on the down payment needed to close the deal. A bank loan for the down payment may not be possible, but a loan from you might clinch it.

➤ *To go back to school.* Your child may be able to handle some of the cost by taking out student loans or getting a scholarship. But you may be able to help with any shortfall.

In deciding whether to lend money to your child, review the section in Chapter 26, "Studying Up on Student Loans," on when to be a banker. The same principles apply to lending money to your emancipated child as to one still living under your roof. You probably want to help in these cases:

Watch Your Step

Helping your child by lending her money once or twice or in very special circumstances won't undermine her financial independence. But don't always come to the rescue. Let her try to solve her financial difficulties on her own before turning to you for help.

➤ *The money is needed for a good reason.* If the need is temporary (only while he's between jobs), or the situation giving rise to the need was beyond his control (he got ill and couldn't work), you may be more sympathetic than if he was just a poor money manager who got into a financial fix by overusing his credit cards. You may also want to help out if your child decides to return to school, for example, to pursue a graduate degree.

➤ *You believe your child is responsible and able enough to repay the loan.* If he's working and his budget has room for debt repayment, then you can be reasonably assured that he'll make good on the loan.

➤ *You can afford to make the loan.* There's no point in creating financial problems of your own just to appear to be the good guy to your child. If you don't have the resources to make the loan, don't do it.

Lending an Ear

No matter how old your child gets or how far away she's living, she's still your child and you're still her parent. You can continue to provide help as she faces new financial questions.

She may need advice about having a roommate. Obviously, having a roommate is a great way to share expenses, but it's up to you to point out some of the financial questions your child should address.

➤ *Whose name is on the lease?* This is the person who's responsible for paying the rent. If your child is on the lease and her roommate doesn't ante up or is late, this doesn't relieve her of this responsibility. She'll have to either pay her roommate's amount or face eviction on account of her deadbeat roommate.

➤ *Whose name is on the electric company bill?* As with the rent, the person whose name is on the utility bills is responsible for the entire amount. The failure to pay the bill in full can hurt that person's credit history even though he's paying his fair share.

➤ *Will there be one phone line or two?* Having one phone line is less costly overall but can cause problems when roommates use the phone unequally (especially when long-distance calls are involved).

➤ *What happens when one person wants out?* Decide in advance who must move if the living arrangement doesn't work out. Also work out details about what happens when one person wants or needs to move (because of a job relocation, marriage, or otherwise).

Your child may want your help in deciding whether and how much to contribute to her company's 401(k) plan. You may have already explained about making IRA contributions, but company retirement plans are another thing.

Your child also may need your advice when trying to decide between a job with a small company that's offering a larger salary and no benefits, and a large company with less salary but medical insurance and other benefits. She'll know which company she'd rather work with according to the work she'd be doing, but your guidance on which may be the better financial deal can be very helpful.

It's probably best to offer advice only when asked or when you see a situation ripe with impending financial doom. Otherwise, let your child make her own decisions—and her own mistakes. These mistakes are part of a lifelong learning process.

The Least You Need to Know

➤ Your child should know about basic money concepts before attempting to live on her own.

➤ Before moving out, your child should have a handle on what it will cost—initially and on an ongoing basis.

➤ Part of growing up means dealing with utility companies and buying insurance.

➤ No matter how old your child gets, you can continue to provide help and guidance on money matters.

Glossary

adolescence   The period from puberty to maturity.

advances   Payments made before they're due, as in giving an allowance before it's supposed to be paid.

after-tax return   The income you get to keep after subtracting the taxes you owe on it.

allowance   An amount of money given to a child (usually weekly).

annual percentage rate (APR)   The interest rate charged for a full year, even though you may pay monthly amounts.

annual report   A report that a public company compiles once a year to describe its financial picture.

antiques   Defined by the U.S. Customs Service as items more than 100 years old, but used to refer to anything old.

asset allocation   An investment strategy that spreads your money around into different kinds of investments so that you reduce your risk of loss.

automated teller machines (ATMs)   Machines by which you withdraw cash from your bank account or credit card.

balancing a checkbook   A way to make sure that the bank and you agree on what's in your account.

bear market   A period of declining stock prices.

beneficiary   A person who enjoys certain benefits, such as receiving an income from a trust.

bonds   Investments in which you become a creditor and are owed money (interest) on what you've lent (invested).

boomerang kids   Kids who go off to college and return home after graduation to live with parents.

bouncing a check   Writing a check but not having the money in your account to pay it.

broker   A person licensed to buy and sell shares to the public.

brokerage firm   A company through which brokers operate.

budget   A plan you make to spend or use your money during a certain period (for example, each month).

bull market   A period of rising stock prices.

capital gain   The appreciation in the value of assets since you've bought them. Capital gain generally is taxed at lower rates than the same amount of income from wages, interest, or dividends.

capital gains distribution   A type of dividend that may be paid by a mutual fund.

certificates of deposit (CDs)   Investments that earn a fixed rate of interest for a set period of time (for example, 5 percent for a five-year CD).

certified check   A check drawn on your own bank account that is guaranteed by your bank to have the funds to back it up and that will be honored no matter what.

check ledger   The place where you enter the checks you write and the deposits you make in your checking account (also called a checkbook register).

checking account   A type of bank account in which you access your money by writing checks.

COBRA   A federal law that gives your child the right to convert his coverage under your company plan to individual coverage once he reaches age 21 or is otherwise no longer covered under that plan.

collectibles   Items worth saving, without regard to their age.

commissions   Fees charged for buying and selling shares of stock or other assets.

compound interest   See *compounding*.

compounding   Earning interest not only on the money you put into something, but also on the interest you're earning.

credit   A plus or addition of money, or an amount that's given on the promise to repay.

credit cards   Cards that allow you to pay for things at any location in which the cards are accepted, up to a set spending limit.

credit history   Your experience in paying your bills on time.

creditor   Another term for a lender.

currency   A country's money in circulation (coins and bills).

custodial accounts   The main way that people under the age of 18 can own investments. These accounts let a custodian (an adult) oversee investments in your name.

cybervestor   A person who invests using the Internet.

day trading   The highly risky practice of jumping in and out of a stock before the close of trading.

debit   A subtraction, or minus an amount of money.

debit cards   A way to withdraw from or use money in your bank account. You can spend up to the amount in your bank account at any location that will accept the cards.

deductions   See *tax deductions*.

deep discount brokers   Brokers who charge greatly reduced commissions for buying and selling stocks, bonds, and mutual fund shares and who do not provide any investment advice to customers.

delayed gratification   Postponing the time when you'll get to enjoy what you want, such as saving money so that it will be there for you in the future.

dependent   A tax term for a person under age 19, a full-time student under age 24, or someone who receives more than half of his or her support from someone else and who meets other requirements.

deposit   An addition to an account.

depreciating asset   Something that's going to be worth less and less as time goes on.

discount bonds   Bonds issued at less than their face amount; for example EE bonds, U.S. savings bonds, are issued at one-half their face value.

discount brokers   Brokers who charge reduced commissions for buying and selling stocks, bonds, and mutual fund shares and who do not provide any investment advice to customers.

diversification   Putting your money into different types of investments so that you spread your risk of loss.

dividend reinvestment plans (DRIPs)   Arrangements to allow for dividends to be used automatically to buy additional shares of the same stock.

dividends   Payments made by companies to people who own stock in them. Usually dividends are paid in cash, but they can also be made in stock or other property.

dollar cost averaging   A way to put your money into stocks and mutual funds in a systematic way so that you buy more shares when the stock market falls and fewer shares when it rises, averaging out the price of the shares over time.

Dow   The Dow Jones Industrial Average (DJIA), a composite of the prices of 30 stocks on the New York Stock Exchange.

down payment   A partial payment on the purchase price of an item made prior to or when you receive the item.

dunning   The practice of bill collectors trying to get their money by persistence.

earned income   Income from working, such as wages and salary.

education IRA   A tax-advantaged higher education savings plan for those under age 18.

EE bonds   See *savings bonds*.

entrepreneur   Someone who undertakes to start and run a business, assuming all the risks with the hope of turning a profit.

equity   An ownership interest in a company or a stock mutual fund.

FICA   Social Security and Medicare taxes withheld from a paycheck.

fiduciary   A person who holds a position of trust, such as a trustee.

fixed expenses   Expenses that are more or less stable in amount from month to month.

fixed-income investments   Investments that pay a set amount of income (the amount doesn't vary).

fringe benefits   Items that your employee pays or reimburses you for, such as medical insurance.

full-service brokers   Those who charge non-discounted commissions for buying and selling stocks, bonds, and mutual fund shares and who provide investment advice to customers.

grantor   A person who sets up a trust.

gratuity   See *tip*.

growth investments   Investments that offer the opportunity for appreciation in the value of the assets.

guarantor   A person who promises to make good on your obligation to make a payment if you fail to do so.

I bonds   See *savings bonds*.

imputed interest   Interest income that the tax law views a lender as receiving on a no- or low-interest loan.

inflation   An increase in the amount of money in circulation that reduces the value of money and thus makes the price of goods and services rise.

information returns   Reports made to the IRS about your income and certain expenses (you receive a copy of the returns).

insurance   A way of shifting the risk of loss you might have to your property or yourself.

interest   A fixed rate of return on your money, expressed as a percentage.

investing   Putting your money into things that will earn more money for you.

IRAs   Tax-advantaged retirement savings plans for workers in which contributions can be deducted.

kiddie tax   The way of figuring income tax on a child under the age of 14.

lender   See *creditor*.

liability   You owe something (for example, "tax liability" means that you owe the government taxes).

limited liability company   A way to organize a business under state law to obtain personal liability protection and partnership tax treatment.

liquidity   Being able to sell an investment at any time without penalty.

marketing   The process by which people get what they want through creating and exchanging products or services with each other for value (money, products, or services).

market timers   Investors who try to only buy stock at the low and sell at the high.

Medicare   A federal health care system primarily for those age 65 and older, with contributions to the system made by workers regardless of age.

miles per gallon (MPG)   An expression of how efficient a car is when it comes to using gas (how far a car can go on each gallon of gas).

minimum payment   The least you can pay on a credit card's monthly bill without going into default and falling subject to collection activities.

modified adjusted gross income (MAGI)   Adjusted gross income without regard to the foreign earned income exclusion for purposes of making contributions to education IRAs.

money   Any medium of exchange that can be used to pay for goods and services and to measure the value of things.

money market funds   Funds offered by banks and mutual funds that invest your money in interest-bearing instruments, such as certificates of deposit and treasury bills, and that pay you a variable rate of return.

money order   A check issued by the post office or a commercial business that you get by paying cash, plus a small fee. You can use a money order just like a personal check drawn on your own bank account.

311

municipal bonds   Bonds issued by state and local government. Interest on such bonds is free from federal income tax.

mutual funds   Investments that allow you to own a small piece of many different things by buying shares in the funds; for example, stock mutual funds own shares in a number of different companies, and you get an ownership interest by owning shares in the stock mutual funds.

net asset value (NAV)   The total holdings of a mutual fund at the end of a day divided by the number of shares in the fund.

partnership   A business formed by two or more people who work together with the goal of making a profit.

penny stocks   Highly speculative, low-priced stock (generally selling for under $5 a share).

p/e ratio   The price of the stock divided by its annual earnings.

personal identification number (PIN)   A three- to five-digit number code you select as your personal identifier and use to access money through an ATM.

philanthropist   Someone who gives to charity.

philanthropy   The act of giving to charity.

portfolio   The collection of investments you own.

preowned   Another term for "used" (such as a preowned car).

priorities   An ordering of things in terms of importance.

promissory note   A written pledge to pay a set sum at a set time or on demand.

profit margin   What the company makes as its profit after paying taxes and other expenses (after-tax return).

prospectus   A brief sketch of what a company is all about.

qualified state tuition program   A tax-advantaged savings plan for higher education for those under the age of 30.

reference   A person who can vouch for you—usually a teacher, former boss, or even a friend or neighbor.

résumé   A summary of your personal information, including your name, address, telephone number, jobs you've already held, and your education.

risk   The measurement of how likely it is that you'll lose on an investment that you've made.

Roth IRAs   Tax-advantaged retirement savings plans for workers in which contributions are not deductible but earnings can be taken tax-free if certain conditions are met.

sale   A reduction in the price of an item.

saving   Holding onto your money instead of spending it so that you'll have it for the future.

savings bonds   Bonds (series EE and I) offered by the federal government that pay interest on your investment.

scholarships   Money awarded to cover the cost of education that doesn't have to be repaid.

seed money   The cash needed to start a business.

self-employment tax   Social Security and Medicare taxes paid by a self-employed person on net earnings from self-employment.

settlor   See *grantor*.

shareholder   Someone who owns stock in a corporation.

Social Security   A federal system to pay benefits to retired or disabled workers, their spouses, and their dependents.

spending money   Cash given to a child for a specific purpose (for example, an afternoon at the movies).

stipend   A payment for your services that's typically made in one lump sum, usually at the conclusion of a job.

stockbroker   See *broker*.

stockholder   See *shareholder*.

stocks   Ownership interests in corporations.

substantiation   Proof required by the tax law to take certain deductions.

tax credit   A dollar for dollar reduction of taxes owed.

tax deductions   Expenses you're allowed to subtract from your income when figuring your income taxes.

tax-deferred   Postponing the time when income will be subject to tax.

taxes   Payments made to the government.

tax-free   Income that is never subject to tax.

tip   Money given as additional payment for services (also called a *gratuity*).

trust   A legal ownership in which property is held by a fiduciary for the benefit of someone else.

values   Acts, customs, and ways of dealing with things; or the worth of things in terms of money.

313

variable expenses   Costs that change from month to month.

variance   A change or alteration in a zoning rule in response to one homeowner's request.

withdrawal   Taking money out of an account.

withholding   A part of income due you that is sent to the government on your behalf as a prepayment of taxes you owe.

zero coupon bond   A type of investment that earns interest that is not paid until maturity.

Online Resources for Kids and Money

Information You Want	Where to Find It
Allowances	pages.prodigy.com/kidsmoney/allstats.htm
Awards (see *Contests*)	
Brokers (full-service)	www.deanwitter.com
	www.merrillynch.com
	www.painewebber.com
	www.prudential.com
Brokers (discount)	www.schwab-worldwide.com
	www.fidelity.com
	www.waterhouse.com
Brokers (deep discount)	www.arnoldsecurities.com
	www.nbd.com
	www.quick-reilly.com
Brokers (online)	www.schwab.com
	www.lombard.com
	www.pawws.com
	www.etrade.com
	www.ebroker.com
	www.datek.com
Budgeting	www.mastercard.com/cgi-bin/ budget_worksheet (making a budget)
	www.finitycorp.com/hazam.htm (keeping track of a budget)
Charitable giving	www.americanheart.org
	www.freshair.org

continues

continued

Information You Want	Where to Find It
	www.giveonline.org
	www.guidestar.org
	www.wish.org
	www.wishingstart.org
Clubs and organizations on businesses and working	www.4h-usa.org
	www.deca.org
	www.fbla-pbl.org
	www.ja.org
Collecting	www.kovels.com (collectibles guide)
	AOL: members.aol.com/ BongoAmy/ (Beanie Babies)
	www.ebay.com (auction online)
	www.aucionuniverse.com (auction online)
	www.classifieds.2000.com (buying online)
College costs (calculator)	www.troweprice.com/college/ trowecollegeFundHome.html
	http://personal1431.fidelity. com/planning/collect_toc.html
College loans	www.collegeboard.org
	www.ed.gov/
	www.fastweb.com
	www.finaid.org
	www.synet.com
Commercialism in school	www.commercialfree.org
	www.consunion.org/other/ captivekids.htm
	www.corpwatch.org
	www.rethinkingschools.org
	www.uwm.edu/Dept/CACE?
Consumer credit counselors	www.nfcc.org
Contests and awards for kids on money and investing	www.quicken.com (Kids Speak Out About Taxes Contest)
	www.nefe.org/hsfla/ default.htm (High School Financial Literacy Awards)

Information You Want	Where to Find It
	www.smg2000.com (SMG 2000)
	www.cnbc.com (stock market game)
	www.mainXchange.com (individual game)
	www.etrade.com (game for those age 18 and up)
Credit-reporting bureaus	www.equifax.com
	www.experian.com
	www.transunion.com
Credit cards and debit cards	ww.cardlearn.com/rebate.html
	www.cohmus.ohio-state.edu/ english/People/Hogsette1. eng.htm
Education IRAs	www.irs.ustreas.gov
Entrepreneurial skills	www.kidsway.com
	www.youngandsuccessful.com
Gambling problems	www.gamblersananoymous.org
Games on money and finance	www.BrainPlay.com
	www.moneyfactory.com/ index.htm
	www.younginvestor.com/ gameroom.shtml
	www.lavamind.com/edu.html
	www.beseen.net/ cashuniversity/home.htm
Income taxes	www.irs.ustreas.gov/taxi
Insurance	www.fool.com/FamilyFool/1997/ FamilyConnection971029b.htm
Investing (general investment information)	www.fool.com (key word on AOL: motleyfool)
	www.younginvestor.com
	www.plan.ml.com/family.kids
	www.makingsense.com
Investing (online quotes)	www.dbc.com
	www.quote.com
	www.excite.com
	www.pcquote.com

continues

317

continued

Information You Want	Where to Find It
Investing (magazines online)	www.pathfinder.com/money/plus/index.oft
Investing (newspapers online)	www.wsj.com
	www.usatoday.com/money/mfront
Investing (self-study course for kids under 18)	www.better-investing.org
Investing (television programming online)	www.cnbc.com
	www.msnbc.com/news/COM_Front
	www.bloomberg.com
	www.pbs.org/mpt/rukeyser
IRAs	www.irs.ustreas.gov
Money (coins)	www.ustreas.gov/opc/opc033.html
Mutual funds (information)	www.morningstar.com
Mutual funds (minimum investment requirements)	www.invesco.com
	www.seinroe.com
	www.strong-funds.com
	www.troweprice.com
	www.usaa.com/beta
Mutual funds (other mutual fund families)	www/aimfunds.com
	www.alliancefunds.com
	www.americnexpress.com/direct/mfunds/docx.mfunds.html
	www.dreyfus.com
	www.kemper.com
	www.mfs.com
	www.oppenheimerfunds.com
	www.putnam.com
	www.vanguard.com
Online trading (see *Brokers*)	
Parenting skills	www.ciccparenting.org
	www.kidscampaigns.org
	www.tnpc.com

Information You Want	Where to Find It
	www.positiveparenting.com
	www.familyeducation.com
	www.connectedfamily.com
	www.parentsoup.com
Savings bonds (see *U.S. savings bonds*)	
Savings calculator (for figuring your investment over time)	www.national-city.com/ natcity/personal/savings/ savcal
Scholarships for college	www.fidalgo.net/~clifford/ scholar1.html
	www.aol.com/ox13qu/webpages/ eyfswm1.html
	www.fie.com/molis.scholar.htm
Social Security	www.ssa.gov/kids
Stock market investment game	www.mainXchange.com
Student loans	www.ed.gov/
Taxes	www.irs.ustreas.gov
U.S. savings bonds	www.savingsbonds.com/ chart/html
	www.ustreas.gov/opc/ opc0035.html
Volunteering	www.impactonline.org

Bibliography

Barbanel, Linda, M.S.W., C.S.W. *Piggy Bank to Credit Card: Teach Your Kids the Financial Facts of Life.* Crown Publishers; New York, 1994.

Berg, Adriane B. and Arthur Berg Bochner. *The Totally Awesome Money Book for Kids and Their Parents.* Newmarket Press; New York, 1993.

Bernstein, Daryl. *Better Than a Lemonade Stand.* Beyond Words Publishing, Inc.; Hillsboro, Oregon, 1992.

Blue, Ron and Judy Blue. *Raising Money-Smart Kids.* Thomas Nelson Publishers; Nashville, 1992.

Bodnar, Janet. *Dr. Tightwad's Money-Smart Kids.* Kiplinger Books; Washington, D.C., 1997.

———. *Mom, Can I Have That? Dr. Tightwad Answers Your Kids' Questions About Money.* Kiplinger Books; Washington, D.C., 1996.

Estess, Patricia Schiff and Irving Barocas. *Kids, Money & Values.* Betterway Books; Cincinnati, Ohio, 1994.

Godfrey, Neale S. *Money Doesn't Grow on Trees: A Parent's Guide to Raising Financially Responsible Children.* Simon & Schuster; New York, 1994.

———. *A Penny Saved: Teaching Your Kids the Values and Life Skills They Will Need to Live in the Real World.* Fireside; New York, 1996.

———. *Ultimate Kids' Money Book.* Simon & Schuster, Inc.; New York, 1998.

Lewin, Elizabeth, C.F.P., and Bernard Ryan, Jr. *Simple Ways to Help Your Kids Become Dollar-Smart.* Walker and Company; New York, 1994.

Otfinoski, Steve. *The Kid's Guide to Money; Earning It, Saving It, Spending It, Growing It, Sharing It.* Scholastic Inc.; New York, 1996.

Pearl, Jayne A. *Kids and Money: Giving Them Savvy to Succeed Financially.* Bloomberg Press; Princeton, New Jersey, 1999.

Shalov, Jeannet, Irwin Sollinger, Jules Spotts, Phyllis S. Steinbrecher, and Douglas W. Thorpe. *You Can Say No to Your Teenager.* Addison-Welsey; Reading, Massachusetts, 1991.

Spock, Benjamin, Dr. and Dr. Michael B. Rothenberg. *Dr. Spock's Baby and Child Care.* Pocket Books; New York, 1992.

Weltman, Barbara. *The Complete Idiot's Guide to Starting a Home-Based Business.* Macmillan; New York, 1997.

Wood, Heather. *101 Marvelous Money-Making Ideas for Kids.* Tom Doherty Associates, Inc.; New York, 1995.

Wyatt, Elaine and Stan Hinden. *The Money Book.* Tambourine Books; New York 1991.

Index

K-L

J